UNTYING THE MOTHER TONGUE

Cultural Inquiry

EDITED BY CHRISTOPH F. E. HOLZHEY AND MANUELE GRAGNOLATI

The series 'Cultural Inquiry' is dedicated to exploring how diverse cultures can be brought into fruitful rather than pernicious confrontation. Taking culture in a deliberately broad sense that also includes different discourses and disciplines, it aims to open up spaces of inquiry, experimentation, and intervention. Its emphasis lies in critical reflection and in identifying and highlighting contemporary issues and concerns, even in publications with a historical orientation. Following a decidedly cross-disciplinary approach, it seeks to enact and provoke transfers among the humanities, the natural and social sciences, and the arts. The series includes a plurality of methodologies and approaches, binding them through the tension of mutual confrontation and negotiation rather than through homogenization or exclusion.

Christoph F. E. Holzhey is the Founding Director of the ICI Berlin Institute for Cultural Inquiry. Manuele Gragnolati is Professor of Italian Literature at the Sorbonne Université in Paris and Associate Director of the ICI Berlin.

UNTYING THE MOTHER TONGUE

EDITED BY
ANTONIO CASTORE
FEDERICO DAL BO

ISBN (Hardcover): 978-3-96558-048-0
ISBN (Paperback): 978-3-96558-049-7
ISBN (PDF): 978-3-96558-050-3
ISBN (EPUB): 978-3-96558-051-0

Cultural Inquiry, 26
ISSN (Print): 2627-728X
ISSN (Online): 2627-731X

Bibliographical Information of the German National Library
The German National Library lists this publication in the Deutsche Nationalbibliografie (German National Bibliography); detailed bibliographic information is available online at http://dnb.d-nb.de.

Cover design: Studio Bens. Based on a drawing by Patrick Vernon, Babel la tour, ink on paper, 43 x 33 cm, n.d.

In Europe, volumes are printed by Lightning Source UK Ltd., Milton Keynes, UK. See the final page for further details.

Digital editions can be viewed and downloaded freely at: https://doi.org/10.37050/ci-26.

ICI Berlin Press is an imprint of
ICI gemeinnütziges Institut für Cultural Inquiry Berlin GmbH
Christinenstr. 18/19, Haus 8
D-10119 Berlin
publishing@ici-berlin.org
www.ici-berlin.org

Contents

Introduction

ANTONIO CASTORE AND FEDERICO DAL BO

> Why do you talk 'Virginny' — that vile gibberish — whenever you are in high spirits?' 'It's my mother-tongue, sir; and when I'm very happy — very — I can't speak any other.
>
> John Neal, *Brother Jonathan* (1825)

The term 'mother tongue' is still used to designate a particular language to which one is attached, a primary language in which one is supposed to have a potentially flawless competence, or the 'place' at which thoughts may emerge in coherent form. Although the term is thought to be self-evident, its definition is somewhat vague, like other important cultural concepts. For instance, dictionaries frequently provide unsatisfactory pseudo-synonyms like 'first language' or 'native language' to explain it. People typically experience their mother tongue as natural and unproblematic, unless it is challenged by the presence of other languages and cultures or, more dramatically, endangered by socio-political circumstances.

Critical thought has extensively investigated the emergence and history of the — gendered, kinship-based — term 'mother tongue' and provided insightful elaborations on the cultural-political implications of the metaphors of maternality and nativity in relation to language.[1] A simple look at the instances of the term 'mother tongue' listed in the *OED* can help single out some assumptions that have been accompanying, charging, and connoting the concept since its first occurrences. Let us examine them briefly:

> A. 1. One's native language; a first language. Also in extended use; 2. language which gives rise to others; *esp.* one regarded as the source of a group or family of other languages, or (occasionally) as the source of all other language.[2]

First of all, there is the assumption that the mother language not only is 'someone's native language' but also can be the 'mother of other languages'. In this respect, the notion of 'mother tongue' also has a genetic function that, if extended to anthropological terms, can be addressed in connection with distinctive patterns in particular civilizations and ethnic groups. This assumption serves as the basis for the interesting sentence cited in the *OED* as an 'extended use' of the term. In his *History of the Decline and Fall of the Roman Empire*, Edward Gibbon notes of Shakespeare that 'he was ignorant of the Greek language — but his mother-tongue, the language of nature, is the same in Cappadocia and in Britain'.[3] Identifying the mother tongue with the language of nature, Gibbon envisions the possibility of a universal mother tongue. Indeed, his sentence seems to evoke the Renaissance image of the 'book of Nature', whereby nature lays open meanings through a system of signs and signatures that do not require any kind of cultural interpretation to be understood. In a nutshell, nature speaks a language, and this language is universal. So, to assert that Shakespeare's mother language is the language of nature is perhaps equivalent to saying that his poetry

---

1 See, for instance, Thomas Paul Bonfiglio, *Mother Tongues and Nations: The Invention of the Native Speaker* (New York: De Gruyter Mouton, 2010). The notion of 'maternality' does not simply designate the capacity to become a mother but also alludes to Kristeva's notion as a boundary at the threshold of meaning and being, as it problematizes the connection between the maternal body and motherhood. See Julia Kristeva, 'Stabat Mater', trans. by Arthur Goldhammer, *Poetics Today*, 6.1/2 (1985), pp. 133–52.

2 'Mother tongue, *n.* and *adj.*', in *OED Online* (Oxford: Oxford University Press, 2020) <https://www.oed.com/view/Entry/122678> [accessed 8 January 2023].

3 Edward Gibbon, *The History of the Decline and Fall of the Roman Empire*, 1st edn, 6 vols (London: Strahan and T. Cadell, 1776–88), III (1781), chapter 27, p. 15 n. 29.

is universal and transcends boundaries related to culture, history, ethnicity, and geography.

Studies in both linguistics and social sciences have emphasized the role of unique languages as cultural archives and markers of ethnicity.[4] Ethnic markers in speech — inflections that can sometimes be heard as an accent — are carried over from the mother tongue. Yet this assumption can be deconstructed when analysed in a multilingual context. When an individual speaks more than one mother tongue, the choice to use one rather than another is not simply practical but also functions as a powerful indicator both of the way one identifies one's self with an ethnic community and of the way others identify one's self with an ethnic community.[5] In multilingual contexts, therefore, the use of a specific mother tongue is negotiated in the midst of different options and deconstructs the supposedly clear-cut distinction between self-identification as an intentional act and belonging to a language 'naturally', without deliberate choice. In this respect, the choice of a specific mother tongue in a multilingual context shows that different forms of 'linguistic adaptation' are often at work to allow inter-generational and inter-ethnic communication, especially in contexts where one language is dominant over the languages of minorities. Besides, a change in the mother tongue is also linked to specific aspects of group integration and is a clear sign of acculturation. This phenomenon typically occurs in minority groups in a context of diglossia, for instance, in second or third generation Turkish-German speakers.[6] A genuine interest in, or 'love' for, one's mother language does, in fact, need the perception of the 'other' as well as self-reflection on one's own culture or education. This is what Heymann Steinthal, for instance, argued when stating in 1863 that the absence of the term 'mother tongue' in ancient Greek indicated that that civilization had little interest in learning foreign languages.[7]

4 Gillian Stevens, 'Nativity, Intermarriage, and Mother-Tongue Shift', *American Sociological Review*, 50.1 (February 1985), pp. 74–83 (p. 74).

5 Ibid.

6 Cf. Yasemin Yildiz, *Beyond the Mother Tongue: The Postmonolingual Condition* (New York: Fordham University Press, 2013).

7 Heymann Steinthal, 'Von der Liebe zur Muttersprache', in *Gesammelte kleine Schriften*, 2 vols (Berlin: Dümmlers, 1880), I, pp. 97–107.

One usually takes 'mother tongue' to be a natural condition of language acquisition, equally valid for every individual speaker. Yet throughout history, the use and connotations of the expression 'mother tongue' have undergone several changes. In the Middle Ages and Early Modern period, the Latin '*lingua materna*' referred to the vernacular languages in opposition to the learned Latin. In the eighteenth century, 'mother tongue' became an emotionally charged term: establishing a more intimate, supposedly natural and privileged relationship between the speaker and her primary language, it lent authority to the Romantic aesthetics of originality and authenticity.[8] The new emphasis on the 'maternal' element in the metaphor inscribed the speaker into broader networks of relationships, from kin to nation. Carrying gendered and political meanings, the term 'mother tongue' thus links its fortune to a 'monolingual paradigm' coeval with the historical constellation of the emerging nation states.

French post-structuralist thought has problematized the notion of a 'mother tongue' by dividing it into two discrete elements — the 'maternal' and the 'linguistic' — and by exposing their metaphysical and colonial presuppositions. Thus, Derrida has exposed the metaphysical implications of the dream of a 'mother tongue': a desire for origin, purity, and identity. In his *Monolingualism of the Other* — permeated with reflections about his affective relation to French —, Derrida has maintained that 'the language called maternal is never purely natural, nor proper, nor inhabitable'. Julia Kristeva, on the other hand, has addressed the relationship between 'maternal' and 'language' in her elaborations on Plato's concept of *chora* — a sort of pre-ontological condition of reality. While the Platonic *chora* is a formless matrix of space, in Kristeva it becomes 'a non-expressive totality': paradoxically, both a generative principle through which meaning constitutes itself and a force subverting any established linguistic or epistemological system.

This collective volume seeks to re-think the mother tongue as an affective and cognitive attachment to language while deconstructing the metaphysical, colonial, and nationalist presuppositions of the mother tongue as well as the opposition between monolingual nationalism

8 Yildiz, *Beyond the Mother Tongue*, p. 9.

and multilingual globalization. If traditional conceptions of the monolingual, pure 'mother tongue' reveal the ideology of the European nation state, then today's celebration of multilingual competencies simply reflects the rise of global capitalism and its demand for transnational labour markets.

The project of this book goes back to 2016 when we organized, as postdoctoral research fellows at the ICI Berlin, a conference with the aim of exploring the manifold entanglements of what many languages designate with the term 'mother tongue'.[9] The questions we sought to raise included: how does a deconstructed notion of a 'mother tongue' overcome the traditional opposition between monolingualism and multilingualism? Should revision of these terms take place individually or in their vexed constellation? How would such revision affect the notion of language as a medium for expressing emotions, particularly in relation to traumatic experiences? How would such revision affect the theory and practice of (literary) translation? How would it modify our perception of linguistic errors, slips of the tongue, and other mistakes? In this new conceptual constellation, what role would linguistic phenomena such as language mixing, hybridization, and incorporations of multiple vocabularies play?

The large response to our call for papers convinced us of the necessity to elaborate on some of the questions that had been discussed during the limited time of the conference. Therefore, we invited some of the speakers to explore further the questions that they had focused on in their work or that had been brought to the fore by the collective confrontation. These contributions are collected here, together with the essays by Teresa Prudente, Caroline Sauter, and Libera Pisano — three scholars who for different reasons could not attend the conference.

In her contribution, 'But You Don't Get Used to Anything: Derrida on the Preciousness of the Singular', Deborah Achtenberg puts Derrida's deconstruction to the test of accounting for the significance of loss with respect to language(s) in a 'plurilingual, multicultural era' such as ours. She summarizes some simplistic reconstructions of the

9 'Untying the Mother Tongue: On Language, Affect, and the Unconscious', conference programme, ICI Berlin, 11–12 May 2016 <https://doi.org/10.25620/e160511>.

French philosopher's thought that have read it as compliant — and complicit — with the instability, precarity, and rootlessness fostered by a globalized labour market and the economic power structure beneath it. In opposition to these readings, Achtenberg demonstrates that Derrida's work is in search of a paradigm that would combine two apparently contrasting sets of affirmations: on one hand, the affirmation of 'flexibility, plurality, and change'; on the other, the importance of understanding language loss as a real loss. Achtenberg's argument that Derrida offered such a paradigm proceeds by focusing on five examples in which his work expresses a sense of loss: circumcision, in which incision involves excision; hospitality, in which openness requires some closure; subjectivity, in which foreground requires background; language, which is mine but not mine (and subject to being taken away); and neighbourhood, which is constituted through the incorporation of others (who may overwhelm us).

Michael Eng addresses a quite intriguing question: 'Philosophy's Mother Envy: Has There Yet Been a Deconstruction of the Mother Tongue?'. He argues that it is difficult to find uncritical references to the mother tongue in modern cultural theory. There is little to persuade of the mother tongue's continuing conceptual validity, given the extensive critique of the will to origins, the wealth of scholarship that reconstructs the various ways women have been figured as mothers in the conception and reproduction of the nation, and the convincing arguments that the very concept of the mother tongue is a relatively recent invention, one that appeared within the intertwined machinery of modernity and coloniality. Using Philippe Lacoue-Labarthe's critique of onto-typology, along with the concept of the *outre-mère* (the 'beyond-mother'), Eng argues that it is impossible to deconstruct the mother tongue if our affective tie to theory is left untouched.

The enigmatic literary universe of Edmond Jabès is introduced by Federico Dal Bo in his contribution, '"My Mother Tongue Is a Foreign Language": On Edmond Jabès's Writing in Exile'. Dal Bo examines one of the most prolific French authors of the twentieth century, who chose to write his *oeuvre* in French despite his Jewish-Arabic origins and his fluency in both Hebrew and Arabic. In this respect, French never was a true 'mother tongue' to him but rather 'a foreign one'. This poetical choice was also instrumental to Jabès's creation of a cosmos that is very clearly defined by *la page blanche*, or the 'blank page'. His writing develops this idea, both literally and metaphorically. A blank sheet is the only thing a writer has to work with at the start of each act of writing, therefore it represents a kind of material opposition that all writers must overcome. It represents in this context an existential nothingness that precedes and simultaneously escapes both human and divine creation. In Jabès's writings, a blank page connotes both nothingness and a condition for writing. This ambivalent condition results in the paradoxical statement that his 'mother tongue is a foreign language', which he makes because the mother tongue cannot offer the same spiritual intimacy as another language, such as the Holy Language, and because the writer's 'mother tongue' — and, by extension, human language — is always impure and infiltrated by foreignness.

In his contribution, 'The Mother Tongue at School', Jakob Norberg focuses on the development of elementary education in the early nineteenth century and on a persistent problem that was posed by the nationalist valorization of the 'mother tongue', as that problem was formulated by the famous linguist Jacob Grimm. As Grimm observed the growth of a veritable army of teachers during the middle of the nineteenth century, the conflict between the mother tongue and the standardized language of the school became apparent to him. Norberg examines the fact that political rule in the modern era is acceptable only when the populace is sovereign over itself. But this contemporary idea of political legitimacy poses an issue of demarcation. What are the limits of the populace, and which law can be upheld in its name? How can the self of collective self-rule be clearly delineated? The people cannot define themselves through a democratic process since that would assume their past existence as a group that draws boundaries.

Juliane Prade-Weiss devotes her contribution, 'Scarspeak: Thinking the Mother Tongue as a Formative Mark', to the scar, which she sees as a useful metaphor for understanding how speakers relate to a particular language that is often known as their mother tongue, native language, or first language. By conceptualizing this relationship in terms of a scar, one avoids the biopolitical ramifications of conceptions that were developed within the context of family and birth and that, over the course of the nineteenth and twentieth centuries, have come to depict the notion of the mother tongue as the foundation of a nation state. Additionally, the representation of the scar avoids the linguistic hierarchy and biographical normalization that are implied by the term 'first language' and that are crucial biopolitical techniques for defining people and groups. Thinking of the mother tongue as a scar underlines the intensity of the long-lasting creation and identification that are required by the process of learning this specific language, as well as the importance of maintaining the mother tongue.

The contribution 'The Shuffling of Feet on the Pavement: Virginia Woolf on Un-Learning the Mother Tongue', by Teresa Prudente, presents Virginia Woolf's literary and linguistic experimentation as unique among coeval modernist writers. While modernist experimentation is well known for emphasizing linguistic instability, as it mixes languages and creates new linguistic codes and various forms of intermediality and transcodification, Woolf appears to stay within the confines of a single language, her mother tongue, even as she continues to violate those bounds. Through a careful and insightful analysis of Woolf's novel, *The Waves,* Prudente investigates Woolf's experimental attitude with regard to her mother tongue, language, and literature, as well as the way that Woolf's attitude is related to 'her quest for a universal language of the mind'.

In '"I know you can cant": Slips of the Mother Tongue in Fred Moten's B Jenkins', Jeffrey Champlin explores the work of Fred Moten and argues that his poetry has a way of making you feel humble while simultaneously encouraging you to work toward a better society. Its call for freedom frequently has utopian overtones since it combines high theory with the Black Arts tradition, yet it prefers language's rhythms and breaks to transcendence. In his 2007 collection *B Jenkins,* Moten literalizes the poetic appeal to the mother tongue in a way that makes it possible to recognize the mother tongue's mediated core. Champlin, by reading *B Jenkins* in connection with Friedrich Kittler's techno-psychological theory of history, interprets Moten's tuning of natural language in terms of a cultural mastery that is laced with affirmative disfluency. As a result of the cant, slang moves toward a greater understanding of the boundaries of knowledge.

In her touching contribution, 'The Mother Tongue of Love and Loss: Albert Cohen's *Le Livre de ma mère* (1954)', Caroline Sauter explores the loss of one's mother. The bare savagery of this experience will never be adequately expressed by a human being. Her ability to express the depth of love's sorrow and intensity, which came together in the instant of her mother's passing, is beyond words: a chiasmus. In the face of the most formidable, cruel, and indisputable aspect of human existence, death, crying, moaning, groaning, and sorrow are spoken acts or wordless deeds.

With his contribution, 'The Staircase Wit; or, The Poetic Idiomaticity of Herta Müller's Prose', Antonio Castore explores idioms and *Sprachbilder* as poetic views of the mother tongue. This exploration involves a special focus on Müller's Nobel lecture. While Müller frequently employs idioms in her articles, lectures, and novel titles, she never uses them in a superficial way or as a mere technique to mimic common or daily speech. Rather, as Castore argues, idioms in Müller's prose are indicative of her attitude toward language and toward the mother tongue in general. In the Nobel lecture as well as elsewhere, idioms serve a dual, occasionally conflicting purpose, combining the need for the 'singularity' of aesthetic experience with the search for a new kind of 'conventionality'.

Libera Pisano concludes the volume with a contribution, 'Wandering Words: Translation against the Myth of Origin in Fritz Mauthner's Philosophy', that examines the issue of translation as a critique of autochthony and of the correlated notion of an original state of purity and belonging. Pisano argues with Mauthner that language is rather a continuous product of borrowing, bastardization, stratification, and contingency. As a result, love of the mother tongue cannot be identified with a physical connection with the land but is rather to be appreciated as an always precarious *Heimat* (home).

But You Don't Get Used to Anything

Derrida on the Preciousness of the Singular

DEBORAH ACHTENBERG

Plurilingualism, like multiculturalism, is moving from being insurrectionary to being supportive of the dominant global neoliberal business paradigm, one which demands flexibility and mobility for its success. In a change that is a prime example of the Derridean idea of iteration and *différance*, in which ideas are repeated but the context of their utterance changes so that certain meanings are 'hollowed out' and others come to the fore, plurilingualism now is a component of global economic structures that produce a flexible but precarious workforce. Postmodern ideas of instability and deferral of meaning could be seen, as a result, as complicit in problematic aspects of global, neoliberal business as well as in the global dominance of English since the plurilingualism many are encouraged if not required to acquire is the addition of English to their repertoire. Such requirements are leading to the dominant use of English and to the decline and loss of other languages.[1]

1 See, for example, Nelson Flores, 'The Unexamined Relationship Between Neoliberalism and Plurilingualism: A Cautionary Tale', *TESOL Quarterly*, 47.3 (2013), pp. 500–20; Jan Blommaert, 'Superdiversity and the neoliberal conspiracy', Ctrl+Alt+Dem, 3 March 2006 <http://alternative-democracy-research.org/2016/03/03/superdiversity-and-the-neoliberal-conspiracy> [accessed 30 June 2017].

Can we find a paradigm for understanding the significance of language loss in our plurilingual, multicultural era? Such a paradigm would accomplish two things: (1) it would affirm flexibility, plurality, and change; and, at the same time, (2) affirm and account for the fact that loss of language and culture is indeed real loss. Jacques Derrida's work might not seem to be a likely source for such accomplishments given its association with change and difference. After all, *différance* (with an *a*) points to change, difference, and instability — even more, to the priority of change over stability and identity. It is the play of *différance* that produces differences. Are Derridean ideas unintentionally complicit with the worst aspects of neoliberal economics, then? Does his writing support and produce the kinds of people needed by the dominant economic power structure? Do his views provide justification or comfortable contextualization for a world in which more and more people are forced to accept insecurity and precarity? After all, we have learned that Derrida's ideas revalorize the rootlessness that used to be attributed to Jews and was seen as anathema to the then dominant nation-state ideal.[2] As positive as such revalorization may be, the iteration today of plurilingualism and multiculturalism has a different valence than in the past.

What such portrayals or construals of Derrida leave out is the sense of loss he expresses in his writings. New ideas are made possible by loss of old ones. There is a hollowing out of old meanings that makes room for new ones. There is an excision for every incision. In addition, there is no universal approach to universals. There is only idiomatic testimony to universal structures: such idioms are all we have.[3] They are precious, though ephemeral.

Hence the title of this essay: 'But You Don't Get Used to Anything'. In the film *Derrida's Elsewhere*, Derrida says:

---

2 See Sarah Hammerschlag's *The Figural Jew: Politics and Identity in Postwar French Thought* (Chicago: University of Chicago Press, 2010) in which she discusses the revalorization of rootlessness in Levinas, Derrida, Blanchot, and others.

3 Derrida refers to 'the enigmatic articulation between a universal structure and its idiomatic testimony'. Jacques Derrida, *Monolingualism of the Other; or, The Prosthesis of Origin*, trans. by Patrick Mensah (Stanford, CA: Stanford University Press, 1998), p. 59; Jacques Derrida, *Le Monolinguisme de l'autre ou la prosthèse d'origine* (Paris: Éditions Galilée, 1996), p. 116.

> I grew up in a country — Algeria — where you had to learn to get used to — but you don't get used to anything — to get used to the fact that all places [...] because of colonial and recent pre-colonial history [...] are, in one way or another, appropriated, expropriated, re-appropriated, closed, re-opened [...]. For example, the Great Synagogue where my father would take me and my brother on feast days was a former mosque which still had all the physical features of a mosque, became a synagogue and I know that, after de-colonisation and independence, it became a mosque again. Transitory, with provisional temporality.[4]

You get used to it — it happens frequently — but you don't get used to anything — it is a loss. This exemplifies Derrida's overall approach. Instability of meaning allows for openness to the new, but there is at the same time a loss. In the rest of this essay, I will gesture at articulating this idea further by pointing to and explicating some examples.

First example: 'circumcision, that's all I have ever talked about', Derrida says in his circumcision notebooks and quotes in 'Circumfession'.[5] What does he mean in what may appear an overstatement? Can all of Derrida's work be understood, figuratively, to focus on circumcision? 'Circumfession' is one part of a two-part work entitled *Jacques Derrida*. The work features, at the top, a stripped down or bare summary of Derrida's ideas by Geoffrey Bennington and, at the bottom, 'Circumfession', a piece Derrida wrote with the goal of surprising and adding to the summary. In 'Circumfession', Derrida portrays himself as fighting with Bennington about such a bare summary. Derrida portrays himself as fighting with Bennington about 'the crude word'. The crude word would be like crude oil. Untouched. Pure. It is 'a crudeness I don't believe in', Derrida says, not surprisingly for one who describes deconstruction as the critique of the pure.[6]

---

4 *D'ailleurs Derrida: Un film de Safaa Fathy* (Derrida's Elsewhere: A Film by Safaa Fathy) (Gloria Films, 1999).

5 Jacques Derrida, 'Circumfession', in Jacques Derrida and Geoffrey Bennington, *Jacques Derrida*, trans. by Geoffrey Bennington (Chicago: University of Chicago Press, 1993), pp. 3–315 (p. 70); Jacques Derrida, 'Circonfession', in Jacques Derrida and Geoffrey Bennington, *Jacques Derrida* (Paris: Seuil, 1991), pp. 7–291 (p. 70). He goes on: 'consider the discourse on the limit, margins, marks, marches, etc., the closure, the ring (alliance and gift), the sacrifice, the writing of the body, the *pharmakos* excluded or cut off, the cutting/sewing of *Glas*, the blow and the sewing back up.'

6 Derrida states that 'the first impulse of what is called "deconstruction" carries it toward this "critique" of the phantasm or the axiom of purity, or toward the analytical

Interestingly, though, Derrida says he dreams of such purity: 'I always dream of a pen that would be a syringe, a suction point rather than that very hard weapon with which one must inscribe, incise, choose.' He dreams of a situation in which 'the right vein has been found' and there is 'no more toil, no responsibility'.[7] But, instead, blood is mixed with prayer and tears. Derrida teaches, he says, 'so as to return in the end to what mixes prayer and tears with blood', where prayer, we may interpret, is openness to what is to come and tears express a sense of loss.[8] There is no syringe-pen, that is, but only a responsibility that comes with writing in which we must 'inscribe, incise, choose'.[9] 'As soon as there is inscription', Derrida says in *Derrida's Elsewhere*, 'there is selection — deletion, censorship, exclusion.'[10] Selection, and exclusion. Openness, and loss. Returning to his playful battle with Bennington and utilizing the trope of circumcision, Derrida refers to Bennington actually having to leave some parts of Derrida's corpus out, of having 'to let them drop like skins':

> if he has cut or lifted out some pieces, it's just so as not to keep them, to let them drop like skins useless to the understanding of my texts, to erase them in short, after having selected.[11]

Writing is incision through excision, prayer and tears, openness and loss.

In a way, the fact that openness involves loss is what Derrida is all about. It's all he's ever talked about! Hospitality, for our second example, requires inhospitality, according to Derrida, since the ethical requirements of hospitality include feasibility and feasibility is limited. You cannot open your home and its contents to everyone, despite the ethical requirement that hospitality be universal, because resources of a home are limited and would be overwhelmed. Derrida likes and uses the pun on *pas d'hospitalité*, which results from the ambiguity of *pas de*

---

decomposition of a purification that would lead back to the indecomposable simplicity of the origin' (Derrida, *Monolingualism*, p. 46; Derrida, *Le Monolinguisme*, pp. 78–79).

7 Derrida, 'Circumfession', pp. 10, 12; Derrida, 'Circonfession', p. 13.

8 Ibid., p. 20; p. 22.

9 Ibid., p. 12; p. 13.

10 *Derrida's Elsewhere*.

11 Derrida, 'Circumfession', pp. 27–28; Derrida, 'Circonfession', p. 29.

in French, meaning either 'step of' or 'no': any step taken to produce hospitality is no hospitality since the law of hospitality is 'absolute, unconditional, hyperbolical', in short, 'categorical'.[12] Any act of hospitality will fall short of absolute hospitality for it will involve conditions, norms, rights, and duties.[13] *The* law, that is, the unconditional law of hospitality, requires *laws*, that is, specific laws, rules, conditions: we will help any family, but we can only help one family; we will help you find a home, but we will not give you our home; some of us will help you, but mostly it will be those of us who are retired not those who work full-time; we will go with you to look for a job, but not if it means taking too much time off and losing our own job; we will help one family, but not several families; we will provide you with some monetary support for survival, but not so much that we ourselves will not survive and flourish; etc. The law of hospitality requires laws of hospitality since the law requires effectuation. The laws of hospitality, in turn, are inspired by the law of hospitality: 'conditional laws would cease to be laws of hospitality if they were not guided, given inspiration, given aspiration, required, even, by the law of unconditional hospitality.'[14] We are inspired by the law of unconditional hospitality just as, regarding writing, Derrida dreams of a syringe pen that could suck meaning out pure and whole. In hospitality, as in the incision that is writing, we have to select and choose.

As a home cannot be open to everyone, so subjectivity, for a third example, cannot be pure or clear — as Descartes would have it, with his famous 'clarity and distinctness' in which clarity is defined as full presence to mind — since we must utilize a background to see the foreground: 'Foreground is nothing without the background', Husserl says, and Derrida is decidedly in this phenomenological tradition.[15]

12 Jacques Derrida, *Of Hospitality: Anne Dufourmontelle Invites Jacques Derrida to Respond*, trans. by Rachel Bowlby (Stanford, CA: Stanford University Press, 2000), p. 75; Jacques Derrida, *De l'hospitalité: Anne Dufourmontelle invite Jacques Derrida à répondre* (Paris: Calmann-Lévy, 1997), p. 77.

13 Ibid., p. 77; p. 78.

14 Ibid., p. 79; p. 75.

15 Edmund Husserl, *On the Phenomenology of the Consciousness of Internal Time (1893–1917)*, trans. by John Barnett Brough (Dordrecht: Kluwer Academic Publishers, 1991), A.25, p. 57: 'Foreground is nothing without the background. The appearing side is nothing without the non-appearing side. So too in the unity of time-consciousness: the

There is no completely clear or completely present idea. There is no syringe-pen, as much as we might dream of one. We do not get a direct relation to what is. That is the point of Derrida's well-known concept of writing. In a previous epoch, he says, writing was considered secondary. For Aristotle, Derrida says, writing is secondary to voice while voice has an 'essential and immediate proximity' to mental experiences which, in turn, simply convey what is: voice 'signifies "mental experiences" (*des états de l'âme*) which themselves reflect or mirror things by natural resemblance'.[16] Moreover, the relation between mind and things is 'translation'. Voice, then, for Derrida's Aristotle, gives us the full presence of that which we understand, while writing is at a distance and does not give us full presence. For Derrida, to the contrary, even voice has the secondary relation previously attributed to writing alone and it is the privileging of the position of voice, or 'phonocentrism', that leads to the very idea of full presence, for example, to Descartes's idea of 'the self-presence of the *cogito*, consciousness, subjectivity'.[17] For Derrida, there are no acts of subjectivity that do not involve loss.

What does all of this mean for language, a fourth example and the topic of the essays in this collection? Consider Derrida's relation to one, singular language: the French language, a language he describes, in *Monolinguisme de l'autre*, as his only language, a language he inhabits as well as it inhabits him. 'I have only one language', he says, 'yet it is not my mine (*ce n'est pas la mienne*).'[18] Such loss is expressed in the statement. French was the only language he had, Derrida says in *Monolingualism*, and it was taken away. He goes further and says that he *is* that language, or at least he is that monolingualism: 'It is me. For me, this monolingualism is me.'[19] And 'I would not be myself outside it. It constitutes me, it dictates even the ipseity of all things to me.'[20] Derrida dwells in it and it dwells in him:

---

reproduced duration is the foreground; the intentions directed towards the insertion [of the duration into time] make conscious a background, a temporal background.'

16 Jacques Derrida, *Of Grammatology*, trans. by Gayatri Chakravorty Spivak (Baltimore, MD: Johns Hopkins Press, 1976), p. 7; Jacques Derrida, *De la Grammatologie* (Paris: Éditions de Minuit, 1967), p. 7.

17 Ibid., p. 12; p. 23.

18 Derrida, *Monolingualism*, p. 2; Derrida, *Le Monolinguisme*, p. 15.

19 Ibid., p. 1; p. 14.

20 Ibid., p. 1; p. 14.

> my monolingualism dwells, and I call it my dwelling; it feels like one to me, and I remain in it and inhabit it. It inhabits me. The monolingualism in which I draw my very breath is, for me, my element.[21]

Significantly, though, Derrida does not describe the loss as the loss of a mother tongue. Not for him is the colonial story of having a mother tongue that is prohibited by the colonizer. Derrida was, instead, Franco-Maghrebian by birth and, given the situation of many Algerian Jews at the time, had only one language, French, from the start. Even regarding his mother he says that she 'herself did not, any more than myself, speak a language that one could call "entirely" maternal'.[22] Algerian Jews in Derrida's milieu did not have an idiom or language all their own — no Yiddish, no Ladino — that 'would have ensured an element of intimacy, the protection of a home-of-one's-own against the language of official culture'.[23]

Language, in other words, is our dwelling, and is not our dwelling. It, like the actual dwelling Emmanuel Levinas describes in *Totality and Infinity*, is open, never closed off and finished, but a place of connection and exchange.[24] A place we enter to collect ourselves and resist incursions. In it, we can collect and, at the same time, connect. For Derrida, it is ours — and not ours, since what is in it comes from outside. Language changes by interaction and exchange. Hence, every language is a language of the other. Though the language participates in producing my identity, my ipseity, it can never be assimilated: 'anyone should be able to declare under oath', Derrida says, 'I have only one language and it is not mine; my "own" language is, for me, a language that cannot be assimilated. My language, the only one I hear myself speak and agree to speak, is the language of the other.'[25] I have a language, yet it is not my own. I have a language, yet I do not. A Derridean paradox or aporia. I have it, in that I see the world through

---

21 Ibid., p. 1; p. 13.

22 Ibid., p. 36; p. 65.

23 Ibid., p. 54; pp. 90–91.

24 Emmanuel Levinas, 'The Dwelling', in *Totality and Infinity: An Essay on Exteriority*, trans. by Alphonso Lingis (Pittsburgh, PA: Duquesne University Press, 1969), II.B, pp. 152–74; Emmanuel Levinas, 'La demeure', in *Totalité et Infini: Essai sur l'extériorité* (La Haye: Nijhoff, 1961), pp. 162–89.

25 Derrida, *Monolingualism*, p. 25; Derrida, *Le Monolinguisme*, p. 47.

it and my identity is produced in its terms. I do not have it, in that language is social and changes socially. Others use terms differently, so that their meaning changes, morphs, differs. New terms come in; old terms go out. *I* do not determine what comes in and out — or only determine it a little. Language, like *différance*, is middle-voiced. It acts on me — limits me, constrains me, enables me, produces me — and I act on it — in notable cases, by producing a new word, such as *différance*, or in ordinary cases, by using a word in a slightly different way until I am understood by some and that way becomes part of the language for us. None of this takes place except in a social context, since words must be understood if they are to signify.

For the idea of 'mother tongue', the middle-voiced quality of language means that all languages are similar to Ladino, Yiddish, Judeo-Arabic, or (to refer here to the U.S.) Spanglish. All languages, in other words, are produced in a process of interaction and exchange. But we may be as at home in these as some Jews are or were in rapidly vanishing Yiddish — Yiddish that began disappearing both with the death camps and with the decision in Israel to make Hebrew the national language. Many Jews have felt completely at home in the Judeo-German my parents referred to as 'Jewish' despite the fact that it is largely the language of a big other, the Germans. Derrida, whose family was monolingual, indicates the familiar, homey quality of languages of the other when he refers to 'some idiom internal to the Jewish community, to any sort of language of refuge that, like Yiddish, would have ensured an element of intimacy, the protection of a "home-of-one's-own" (*un chez-soi*) against the language of official culture'.[26]

The middle-voiced quality of language also means that we can feel and be bereft, lost, homeless, without a home, even when we lose a language that is not natural or maternal. We dwell in that language, Derrida says. That is, we return to the familiar in it, we pull ourselves together and produce ourselves in it.[27] And the language dwells in us, he says. It is part not only of the foreground for us, but of the background, the underground, all the grounds, frameworks, points of view, perspectives. Moreover, though it is what I am, I do not control it.

26 Ibid., p. 54; p. 84.

27 For a comment on the familiar, see ibid., pp. 45–46; p. 77.

And this is what Derrida describes, regarding his own case, in *Monolinguism*. The French language dictated the ipseity of things for him. He lived in it. He loved it. It left him, he hyperbolizes, when he was forced to leave the French school due to the *numerus clausus*, the prohibition of Jews in French schools under the Algerian version of Vichy. Derrida loved the French language, learned literature in it, was 'harpooned' by it, or by philosophy and literature written in it, was penetrated and entered by them. He also wanted to change it, to join those who have an impact on language by pushing it, pulling it, or, as he puts it, setting it on fire:

> I seemed to be harpooned by French philosophy and literature, the one and the other, the one or the other: wooden or metallic darts [flèches], a penetrating body of enviable, formidable, and inaccessible words even when they were entering me, sentences which it was necessary to appropriate, domesticate, coax [*amadouer*], that is to say, love by setting on fire, burn ('tinder' [*amadou*] is never far away), perhaps destroy, in all events mark, transform, prune, cut, forge, graft at the fire, let come in another way, in other words, to itself in itself.[28]

Levinas, in his discussion of the formation of ipseity, speaks of recurrence — a spiralling going forth and returning home that produces the self in a continuing process. With a self that is one part Abraham who goes forth (*lech lecha*, God says to him: 'go yourself forth!' (Genesis 12. 1)) and one part Odysseus who returns home (out of the pain of homecoming), thus avoiding the particularism of Odyssean Heidegger and the universalism of Abrahamic Sartre off in the non-place called the *Internationale*. What Derrida adds to this, in my opinion, salutary middle position on the self, the subject, and hospitality is — well, death, destruction, and pain! To love is to set on fire, burn, perhaps destroy. No hospitality without inhospitality! No meaning without loss of meaning — or, to be less cautious, language destruction. No comprehension without marking, transforming, pruning, cutting, forging, grafting by fire. To underscore the affinity of his autobiographical remarks and what I am saying about his thought, it is important to note that he felt both nostalgia for Algeria — 'nostalgeria' he calls it — and

28 Ibid., p. 50, square brackets in the original; pp. 90–91.

independence from it.[29] His impact on French would be like a tattoo, mixing ink and blood to reveal its colours. Ink and blood. Incision and excision. Hope and loss. Through these, meaning is revealed. Through these, the French language is produced or reproduced. Young Derrida's hope was to tattoo the language, not to bring something forth in it in a manner similar to bringing forth a baby. The penetration results from the process of tattooing, violence from without that produces something new within, new in the sense of unpredictable and unique: 'not necessarily an infant but a tattoo, a splendid form, concealed under garments in which blood mixes with ink to reveal all its colours to the sight'.[30]

What, then, does this understanding of language mean for our hopes, anxieties, and commitments in this neoliberal global age? First, language is always changing. Change in language, like change in a neighbourhood, for our fifth example, is not inauthenticity — or, at least, is no more inauthentic than anything else. Language is what it is by changing, flowing, incorporating, releasing. Second, change and loss of language is painful. It is a loss. It is an opportunity, for welcoming the new, the foreign, the stranger, the messiah, but also a risk — of loss, destruction, marginalization, loneliness, disappearance. The self, what we are, what we are being and have been, is processual and, even more, social. The self is not just ink but also blood. And, in some cases (not all), loss of blood is so great that it becomes loss of self. In other cases, the bleeding is just the bleeding required by life itself.

And that is where justice comes in. The question is not whether a language, a neighbourhood, a self is authentic but whether it is fair, whether and to what extent it manages and distributes loss and opportunity justly. Who has a right to a language? Who has a right to a neighbourhood or the city? Who bears the isolation and lack of influence caused by language loss? Who has to move — first, to the city centre when the suburbs are popular; then to the suburbs when the city centre becomes popular? Deconstruction is justice, Derrida says. If our languages are being dominated (or dominating); if our cultures are being absorbed (or absorbing); if our neighbourhoods are being over-

29 Ibid., p. 52; p. 86.
30 Ibid., p. 52; pp. 85–86.

run (or overrunning), what is the solution: to set up boundaries and restrictions to keep out those who have stepped over the boundaries of others? Or is that just a new injustice, a new imperialism? 'All culture is originarily colonial',[31] Derrida says, without wanting to diminish the distinct arrogance of, and trauma caused by, specifically colonial regimes. In other words, all cultures, all languages, all thoughts come into existence by allowing or forcing others into disuse — others just as good, or better, or different.

Derrida critiques authenticity in 'A Testimony Given ...' and in 'Abraham, the Other', the latter his response to Sartre's portrait of the Jew in *Reflections on the Jewish Question.*[32] If authenticity is being what you are all the way through, as authentic gold is gold all the way through and not just on the surface, then we simply are not authentic. Sartre, to the contrary, exhorts Jews to be authentic. Authentic Jews, according to him, choose themselves as Jews rather than being in bad faith and letting others make them what they are. The inauthentic Jew — a self-hating Jew, for example — lets the anti-Semite make him what he is, internalizing the anti-Semite's negative view of himself rather than focusing on that view and doing what is needed to resist it, internally and externally. The inauthentic Jew, for Sartre, is not what he might make of himself, a strong Jew through and through, but is what the anti-Semite makes of him, for example, inferior in various ways in the case of an inauthentic Jew who internalizes the anti-Semite's negative characterizations. For Derrida, instead, no Jew completely makes himself. No Jew is what he is all the way through. '"Authentic"', Derrida says, 'implies, in Greek as in French, the assured power, the mastery of speaking and of being oneself, the sovereign ipseity of one who is sure of oneself and of one's power to be oneself.'[33] But for

31 Ibid., p. 39; p. 68.

32 Jacques Derrida, 'Abraham, the Other', in *Judeities, Questions for Jacques Derrida*, ed. by Bettina Bergo, Joseph Cohen, and Raphael Zagury-Orly, trans. by Gil Anidjar (New York: Fordham University Press, 2007), pp. 1–35; Jacques Derrida, 'Abraham, l'autre', in *Le Dernier des Juifs* (Paris: Galileé, 2014), pp. 69–126; Jacques Derrida, 'A Testimony Given ...', in *Questioning Judaism: Interviews by Elisabeth Weber*, trans. by Rachel Bowlby (Stanford, CA: Stanford University Press, 2004), pp. 39–58; Jean–Paul Sartre, *Anti-Semite and Jew: An Exploration of the Etiology of Hate*, trans. by George J. Becker (New York: Schocken 1995 [1948]); Jean-Paul Sartre, *Réflexions sur la question juive* (Paris: Gallimard, 1954).

33 Derrida, 'Abraham, the Other', p. 25; Derrida, 'Abraham, l'autre', p. 109.

Derrida, as we saw above, what I most am is not my own. I do not have complete power over being myself.

Regarding the example of being Jewish, Derrida says to the contrary, 'the less you are Jewish, the more you are Jewish.'[34] To be Jewish is not to be Jewish through and through but is to be less Jewish. To be Jewish, for some, is to subscribe to a universal such as love of neighbour or anti-idolatry. However, for example, many ideologies, groups, and religions are anti-idolatrous. As a result, a singular focus on Judaism or Jewishness would itself be idolatrous in taking one singularization of a principle as the only such singularization. Being Jewish, then, takes you out of being Jewish. As a result, Derrida says:

> when I say 'the most jewish' (*le plus juive*), I also mean 'more than jewish' (*plus que juive*). Others would perhaps say 'otherwise jewish' (*autrement juive*), even 'other than jewish' (*autre-que juive*).[35]

These are the alternatives to Sartrean authenticity: affirming that you are Jewish and more than that; being Jewish in a different way; leaving Jewishness. Derrida identifies with the first alternative, Jewish and more than Jewish. Others might find new ways of being Jewish. Some might take on another identity. The point is that the alternatives grow out of fidelity to that to which Jewishness or Judaism is faithful in the first place.

The justice question, then, cannot be one of authenticity versus inauthenticity. It cannot simply be eating only at old mom and pop restaurants and never trying out new places on the block. It cannot simply be making old traditions persist in their old form. It cannot be keeping all the old motels and hundred-year-old Victorian houses and prohibiting all postmodern green buildings and spaces. It can be neither hypermnesia, Derrida says, nor amnesia, neither 'the madness of a hypermnesia, a supplement of loyalty, a surfeit, or even excrescence of memory' nor 'an amnesia without recourse, under the guise of a pathological destructuring, a growing disintegration' or of 'con-

34 Derrida, 'A Testimony Given ...', p. 41.

35 Derrida, 'Abraham, the Other', p. 35; Derrida, 'Abraham, l'autre', p. 126.

form[ing] to the model of the "average" or dominant French person, another amnesia under the integrative guise'.[36]

Instead, Derrida calls for an 'anamnesis of the entirely other'.[37] What would that be? Between early Sartrean amnesia and Heideggerian hypermnesia lies a different approach, a different kind of memory, whether it is the memory that is found in language, meaning, neighbourhoods, cities, or countries. It would be a remembering that is open to the coming of something new. Or an openness to the coming of something new that leaves place for recollection of what has been. An openness that leaves spaces for what has been. So, in some unexpected, undetermined way, the future will emerge from the past while including the past, interacting with it and neither simply dominating nor simply being dominated by it.

No future emerges from a past remembered entirely, however. And no future realizes all of the possibilities there were for a future. Here, too, there is selection, decision, choice, responsibility. Here, too, there will be incision and excision, selecting in and selecting out. The past is not an *archē* but an archive. The remembering that is open to something new is not a complete recall. It is not hypermnesia. We can only remember some of what has been. The openness that leaves a space for what has been is not a complete jettisoning of the old, either. It is not amnesia. Anamnesis of the entirely other must function with an awareness that, though it is remembering the past as it moves toward the new, it is only pulling together and focusing on selected aspects of the past and it is only singling out some possibilities for a future. All remembering involves forgetting. It is memory of this and not that, of foreground not background, and so on. Anamnesis of the entirely other is memory, or at least acknowledgement, of this other as well — the one left out or put in the background when one remembers some of the past in order to move into a one of a number of singular and new futures. This is how deconstruction is justice, by remaining open to what is excluded by one's efforts at inclusiveness, by keeping in mind the cut required for any inclusion.

36 Derrida, *Monolingualism*, p. 60; Derrida, *Le Monolinguisme*, pp. 116–17.

37 Ibid., p. 60; p. 117. *Anamnesis* is ancient Greek for 'recollection' or 'memory'.

Language, neighbourhoods, meaning, countries: spaces of openness that recall and include what has been; spaces of tradition that allow for the unaccountably new. Spaces of opportunity and risk, prayers and tears, incision and excision, ink and blood. With this in mind, we can propose and love fluidity and change, while recognizing and finding ways of at least more justly handling the pleasure and opportunity, and the pain and loss, that change, like life itself, inevitably involves.

Philosophy's Mother Envy

Has There Yet Been a Deconstruction of the Mother Tongue?

MICHAEL ENG

In contemporary cultural theory, one would be hard-pressed to find uncritical invocations of the mother tongue. Given the thoroughgoing critique of the will to origins, as well as the abundance of scholarship that has reconstructed the multiple ways women have been figured as mothers in the conception and reproduction of the nation,[1] and given also convincing arguments that the very idea of the mother tongue is a relatively recent invention that appeared within the intertwined machineries of modernity and coloniality,[2] there is little to convince of the idea's continuing conceptual legitimacy.

1 For an overview of the essential literature, see Alys Eve Weinbaum, 'Nation', in *Keywords for American Cultural Studies*, ed. by Bruce Burgett and Glenn Hendler (New York: New York University Press, 2007), pp. 164–70. See also Gayatri Chakravorty Spivak, *Nationalism and the Imagination* (London: Seagull Books, 2010). For an example of how the suturing of woman and nation informs the figure of the mother tongue, see Kimberly Lamm, 'Getting Close to the Screen of Exile: Visualizing and Resisting the National Mother Tongue in Theresa Hak Kyung Cha's *Dictée*', in *National, Communal, and Personal Voices: New Perspectives in Asian American and Asian Diasporic Women Writers*, ed. by Begoña Simal and Elisabetta Marino (Münster: Lit Verlag, 2004), pp. 43–65.

2 See Yasemin Yildiz, *Beyond the Mother Tongue: The Postmonolingual Condition* (New York: Fordham University Press, 2012).

Yet, while few today would uphold appeals to the mother tongue, the figure upon which that suspect concept is based — the mother — puzzlingly maintains a tenacious hold on critical thought. Or, to put it in the terms that frame this volume's collection of essays on the mother tongue, critical thought remains tied to, and tied up with, the figure of the mother.

In *The Theorist's Mother*, for instance, Andrew Parker surveys the various ways motherhood and maternity have proven troublesome for the Western philosophical tradition. What he means by this is that motherhood and maternity remain intractable, as well as elusive, problems for philosophy to theorize. The mother, Parker reminds us, has been traditionally 'put to work theoretically' by philosophy; a key example he offers involves the ways philosophy has historically used the mother 'to regulate the distinction between the literal and the figural'.[3] In so doing, however, it ends up as the origin of both the literal and the figural at once (as in the case of 'matter' being derived from *mater*, 'mother', and matter being thought of as mother of particular things).[4] The mother thus confuses the literal and the figural and undoes the theoretical distinction it was put into place by philosophy to uphold.

In his survey of the problematic nature of the maternal for philosophy, Parker dutifully includes examples from Simone de Beauvoir, Julia Kristeva, and Luce Irigaray that reveal the mother as a destabilizing category within the French feminist tradition as well. According to Parker, their writings reflect the history of feminist ambivalence with respect to maternity. A question feminist thought occupies itself with, for example, is whether or not motherhood is essential to the feminine.[5] In Parker's telling, the history of this contestation belongs to the mother's disrupting force within the Western theoretical tradition.

Yet, despite his inclusion of French feminism's guiding thinkers (Hélène Cixous makes an appearance later on as well), Parker curiously overlooks a central critique that their reflections all share: the

3 Andrew Parker, *The Theorist's Mother* (Durham, NC: Duke University Press, 2012), p. 18.

4 Ibid., pp. 18–19. In this context, Parker makes notable reference to remarks Freud makes in his *Introductory Lectures on Psychoanalysis* (1916–17) about the etymology of the Portuguese word for 'wood', *madeira*, and its derivation from *materia* and *mater*.

5 Ibid., pp. 9–11.

maternal is a problem for philosophy precisely because the feminine is only permitted to appear as a problem in philosophical discourse. The theoretical work the feminine performs for philosophy is to serve as the raw, untamed outside that threatens the symbolic philosophical order. Through shaping, taming, and ultimately mastering the feminine, the philosophical order is able to constitute and cohere itself as Subject, as 'Philosophy'.

Examples of this core critique can be found in multiple sites throughout the French feminist archive. In *The Second Sex*, Beauvoir details how the Western philosophical tradition places the feminine as intermediary between raw nature and the foreign other, standing in for both so that the masculine subject can master both by mastering her.[6] In similar fashion, Kristeva describes the feminine as serving in the role of the abject, as that '"other" without a name' that the individual must confront and subsequently separate from in order to ascend to subjectivity.[7]

However, it is Irigaray who connects the systematicity of philosophical thought to the essential role the feminine plays as both a resource for and waste product of that system. In *This Sex Which Is Not One*, she characterizes this role as serving as a mirror for philosophical speculation, that is, as the condition that makes it possible for the metaphysical subject not only to engage in reflection, but to reflect on himself engaging in reflection. The psychoanalytic term for this speculative, reflective space (which is also a space of misrecognition, and is therefore at the same time a blind spot) is the imaginary. Irigaray writes,

> the rejection, the exclusion of a female imaginary certainly puts woman in the position of experiencing herself only fragmentarily, in the little-structured margins of a dominant ideology, as waste, or excess, what is left of a mirror invested by the (masculine) 'subject' to reflect himself, to copy himself. Moreover, the role of 'femininity' is prescribed by this masculine specula(riza)tion and corresponds scarcely at all to woman's desire,

6 Simone de Beauvoir, *The Second Sex*, trans. by Constance Borde and Sheila Malovany-Chevallier (New York: Vintage, 2011), pp. 159–63.

7 Julia Kristeva, *Powers of Horror: An Essay on Abjection*, trans. by Leon Roudiez (New York: Columbia University Press, 1982), pp. 58–59.

> which may be recovered only in secret, in hiding, with anxiety and guilt.[8]

As the material condition that makes the philosophical imaginary possible, the feminine, according to Irigaray, is always-already excluded from it. As a result, the feminine is essentialized as the non-essential, as waste or by-product of speculation; she can only appear as a fragmentary being, which is to say, as no being at all. The feminine is therefore forever barred from subjectivity and is exiled in advance from the symbolic order. Consequently, not only is she prevented from having a voice, the very idea of a 'mother tongue' is a contradiction. If anything, the mother tongue is merely the name for yet one more site where the masculine subject employs the feminine as an authorizing figure for its project of self-reflection.

Accordingly, Irigaray famously plays with the figure of the mirror in her critique of philosophical speculation. This is to draw out the specular/spectacular presumptions animating speculation, as well as to connect a revealing cognate of those terms — the speculum — to the speculative act. The figure of the mirror thus emphasizes the passivity the feminine is assigned in the speculative system, the work such passivity performs as the enabling ground of speculation, and the invasive inspections to which the system subjects the female body, over which the system installs itself as master.[9] The figure of the mirror is that which undergirds the masculine figuration of the feminine in the construction of philosophical speculation.

As Irigaray has later claimed, however, her initial deployment of the mirror as speculum was not entirely negative: while the feminine historically has been assigned the task of reflecting the patriarchal imaginary back to itself in order to confirm its self-presence, Irigaray states that her invocation of the speculum was intended to introduce also the idea of a feminine reflection, of a critical reappropriation and recovery of mimesis as active production rather than as mere passive reproduction.[10]

---

8 Luce Irigaray, *This Sex Which Is Not One*, trans. by Catherine Porter with Carolyn Burke (Ithaca, NY: Cornell University Press, 1985), p. 30.

9 See Luce Irigaray, *Speculum of the Other Woman*, trans. by Gillian C. Gill (Ithaca, NY: Cornell University Press, 1985).

10 See Luce Irigaray, *I Love to You: Sketch for a Felicity Within History*, trans. by Alison Martin (New York: Routledge, 1996), pp. 59–60, and Elizabeth Hirsh and Gary A.

The speculum is a reconfiguration of the figure of the feminine as mirror. Irigaray's strategy in these early guiding texts was not simply to refuse the philosophical tradition's identification of the feminine with mimesis, but instead to repeat it, and in so doing, appropriate it as a means to rewrite philosophical speech. By taking occupation of the philosophical logos and submitting it to 'playful repetition', Irigaray intended for this strategic mimicry, as it had come to be known, to 'make "visible" [...] what was supposed to remain invisible: the cover-up of a possible operation of the feminine in language'.[11] Irigaray's own echoing of the language belonging to the Western tradition's major thinkers serves as an example of the attempt to deconstruct philosophical discourse from within, to interrupt and redirect its narcissistic self-reflections. Her echoing acts express a desire to free Echo from her role as a mere double of Narcissus and to enable Echo to sound her own voice.[12]

The question that has always haunted Irigaray's writings, however, has been whether the mimetic repetition of the philosophical logos really makes possible its deconstruction or simply reinforces it. Why does Irigaray not try to undo the identification of the feminine and mimesis? Why does she not question the figuration of the feminine as such? Why does she not try to think outside the figure? What prevents her from pursuing any of these critical approaches?

It is here, on the questions of the feminine's relation to mimesis and figuration, and the possibility of deconstructing that relation, that I wish to bring Philippe Lacoue-Labarthe's critique of onto-typology to bear on the figure of the mother tongue. What Lacoue-Labarthe contributes to an understanding of Western thought's historical suturing of the feminine to mimesis and figuration is an account of why it has been compelled to do so.

Olson, '"Je — Luce Irigaray": A Meeting with Luce Irigaray', trans. by Elizabeth Hirsh and Gaëtan Brulotte, in *Women Writing Culture*, ed. by Elizabeth Hirsh and Gary A. Olson (Albany: SUNY Press, 1995), pp. 141–66 (p. 147). Cited in Hilary Robinson, *Reading Art, Reading Irigaray: The Politics of Art by Women* (London: I.B. Tauris, 2006), pp. 72–73.

11 Irigaray, *This Sex Which Is Not One*, p. 76.

12 On Irigaray's critique of Nietzsche's repetition of the myth of Echo and Narcissus, see Ellen Mortensen, *The Feminine and Nihilism: Luce Irigaray with Nietzsche and Heidegger* (Oslo: Scandinavian University Press, 1994). See also Gayatri Chakravorty Spivak, 'Echo', in *The Spivak Reader*, ed. by Donna Landry and Gerald MacLean (New York: Routledge, 1996), pp. 175–202.

As Lacoue-Labarthe argues, the reason why philosophy has sought to master mimesis and the feminine, and the reason why they are typically sutured to one another via the figure in the history of metaphysics, is that they each challenge philosophy's sovereign ability to establish the ground of its existence. Mimesis does this by virtue of its dissimulating power to take on any identity whatsoever, thereby refusing all pretentions to fixed identities. The feminine does this by reminding philosophy that the image it has of itself as the sovereign subject of representation is ultimately fictive, that only the feminine possesses the creative power of engenderment. It is in this sense that philosophy's historical efforts to master both mimesis and the feminine through its figuration of the mother betray a profound and inconsolable desire, a mother envy.

As we just reviewed in our survey of Irigaray's critique, philosophy responds to and defends against this envy by putting the feminine to work, making it serve as the mirror for its self-speculation. But this act gives the lie to Plato's famous expulsion of mimesis from the *politeia* in the *Republic*. By subjecting the feminine to the role of mirror, philosophy has not banished mimesis; it has instead appropriated it. It then uses the power of figuration from its appropriation of mimesis to master Being as such.

The process by which philosophy attempts to master Being is what Lacoue-Labarthe calls onto-typology. It is through capturing Being in a type (*typos*) or figure (*Gestalt*) that it attempts to gain the ability to manipulate Being and thus assert its sovereignty over it. From Plato to Heidegger, he submits, the history of metaphysics is the history of the figure — Socrates, Oedipus, Spirit, Zarathustra, the Worker, *Dasein*. The figure delineates the scenography of philosophy's theorization of Being. However, to that list, we ought to add the figure of the Mother. Indeed, since Western theory is predicated on the identification of the feminine with mimesis and the figure, the Mother is the *Urgestalt* of theoretical speculation. The Mother is the name for the unconscious of Western theory.[13]

13 See Jacqueline Rose, 'Of Knowledge and Mothers: On the Work of Christopher Bollas', in *On Not Being Able to Sleep: Psychoanalysis and the Modern World* (London: Vintage, 2004), pp. 149–66.

In order, then, to deconstruct the identification of the feminine with mimesis and figuration, it is necessary to deconstruct the speculative theoretical drive, to sever what Lacoue-Labarthe, in collaboration with Jean-Luc Nancy, calls our 'affective attachment' or tie (*Gefühlsbindung*) to theory. However, as Lacoue-Labarthe's critique of onto-typology indicates, this poses a vexing problem, one that I will show especially affects any attempt to 'untie' the figure of the mother tongue. As the language of untying reveals, even simply expressing the desire to escape figuration reinforces one's capture within it. And if theoretical speculation is also fundamentally a deployment of figuration, then how is one to theorize without replicating the figurative act or without reinscribing the speculative theoretical drive?

Above all, Lacoue-Labarthe and Nancy regard the problem of theorizing an outside to theory (and thus an outside to figuration) as a political one. For example, what else is *das Volk* but a figure of community? It is only in its figural dimension that community's reliance on myth — and myth as a vehicle of identification, as in the case of the Nazi myth — can be comprehended.[14] In Lacoue-Labarthe's view, only one path remains open: following both Walter Benjamin and Theodor Adorno, he argues that critical thought must try to subject the political to *Ent-gestaltung* — *dé-figuration*, de-figuration. Along with Nancy, Lacoue-Labarthe says the task of the political will be that of following the *retrait du politique* — a 'retrace/retreat of the political' that insists on the dis-installation of the figure, on a practice of writing that effaces the figure and de-figures the appearance of the political.

Given their commitments to de-figuring the political, it is quite puzzling that in the very moment that they call for the figure's dis-installation, Lacoue-Labarthe and Nancy invoke the figure of the *outre-mère* (beyond-mother) as a way to break with the speculation/spectacularization of the political. How are we to think this figure? And what does Lacoue-Labarthe and Nancy's recourse to the Mother, even as a limit-concept or limit-figure, say about the prospects for realizing an untying of the mother tongue?

---

14 See Philippe Lacoue-Labarthe and Jean-Luc Nancy, 'The Nazi Myth', trans. by Brian Holmes, *Critical Inquiry*, 16.2 (1990), pp. 291–312.

The remainder of my remarks will be directed first at reconstructing the path that leads to this puzzle in Lacoue-Labarthe and Nancy, and then at delineating the implications of this puzzle for efforts to untie (critical thought from) the mother tongue and, ultimately, for the possibility of a re-con-figuration of the political that does not repeat the phallogocentric employment of the feminine. Although I believe Lacoue-Labarthe and Nancy's attempt to think community without appeal to a figurative/mythological — i.e., metaphysical — ground is needed now more than ever, their invocation of the 'beyond-mother' appears to be contradictory to achieving that aim. Assuming the validity of their critique of the political, is it possible to adopt their project without reinscribing the figure of the Mother and all the violences that entails?

My discussion proceeds as follows: I begin with an overview of Lacoue-Labarthe's critique of onto-typology in the history of philosophy, which he traces from Plato's theorization of mimesis to Heidegger's re-casting of truth as *aletheia*. As we will see, Lacoue-Labarthe regards Heidegger as an exemplary case of onto-typology to the extent that his fascination with National Socialism illustrates the social-political stakes of philosophy's specular capture by, and identification with, the figure.

Lacoue-Labarthe's treatment of Heidegger sets up a basis for understanding his collaborations with Nancy and their call for a de-figuration of the political. Although a number of their collective writings are concerned with this problem, I will focus specifically on their essays 'La Panique politique' and 'The Unconscious Is Destructured Like an Affect (Part 1 of "The Jewish People Do Not Dream")'. It is in those texts that they invoke the beyond-mother most explicitly.

Ultimately, my aim in this essay is a modest one. It is to introduce some hesitation into the prospect of deconstructing the Mother, and as such, into the possibility of disentangling from the mother tongue. To be sure, the political project of forging affective, non-identificatory, and non-essentialized forms of belonging relies on deconstructing both the Mother and the mother tongue. Yet, unless we inhabit first the hesitation for which I am calling, any non-metaphysical form of community, such as the one projected by Lacoue-Labarthe and Nancy, risks repeating speculative metaphysics' act of simultaneously employing the feminine, conflating it with the maternal, and burying the actual work actual women (as well as racialized others) perform in maintaining and reproducing the social.[15] So while Lacoue-Labarthe and Nancy's critique of the figure will help us move forward with engaging the seemingly intractable affective dimension of the mother tongue, capitalizing upon their critique will depend on how well we can integrate it with feminist thought and critical theories of race without repeating their re-invocation of the Mother.

PHILOSOPHY AND THE MIMETIC THREAT

In his critique of onto-typology, Lacoue-Labarthe returns to the scene of philosophy's first confrontation with mimesis, what Plato referred to and staged in the *Republic* as the ancient *polemos* between poetry and philosophy.[16] Initially, we recall, Socrates questions the place of poetry in the just polis, specifically in terms of its role in the education of the guardians. Poetry is immediately suspect because of its depictions of heroes and cowards, as well as because of what Socrates says is its false representations of the gods. This critique, offered in *Republic* II, aligns closely, though not completely, with the critique given in *Republic* X of artistic mimesis being three steps removed from the truth. What gives rise to poetry's expulsion from the *politeia*, however, is the fact that the poet often speaks in the voice of an other. When poets speak in their own voice, in the mode of diegesis or narration, everything is fine. But when poets speak in an other's voice, i.e., when they engage in mimesis, this is unacceptable. In the mimetic mode, the poet is a pantomime, occupying many roles, thus disrupting the just order of the polis, which relies on each doing their share in their assigned role.

If, politically, poetry is the threat of disorder, philosophically, it is the threat of madness. This, too, Plato pursues in such dialogues as the *Phaedrus* and the *Ion*. But as Lacoue-Labarthe argues, what we miss

15 See Kimberly Lamm, '"Mouth Work": Deconstructing the Voice of the Mother Tongue in Theresa Hak Kyung Cha's Video Art', in *Voice as Form in Contemporary Art*, ed. by Wenny Teo and Pamela Corey (= *Oxford Art Journal*, 43.2 (2020), pp. 171–83) <https://doi.org/10.1093/oxartj/kcaa011>.

16 Philippe Lacoue-Labarthe, 'Typography', in Lacoue-Labarthe, *Typography: Mimesis, Philosophy, Politics*, ed. and trans. by Christopher Fynsk (Stanford, CA: Stanford University Press, 1998), pp. 43–138.

when we take Plato's conception and critique of mimesis at face value is the fact that he gives us a theory of what, properly speaking, cannot be theorized. For mimesis, again, is, properly speaking, the improper as such. This is its threat but also the reason why it is invulnerable to the philosophical concept.[17]

It is at this point also that Lacoue-Labarthe reminds us that Plato connects mimesis's threat of madness at the beginning of *Republic* III to the threat of hysteria, which is to say, the threat of feminization.[18] Yet, while mimesis threatens philosophy with both, they are not completely the same. Madness stands for the loss of control, for the loss of the integrity of the subject; feminization reminds the philosopher (the masculine subject of representation) that he is not the origin of his own existence, despite whatever promises representation makes to him.[19] Thus, according to Lacoue-Labarthe, in response to this double-edged challenge that mimesis poses to the philosophical logos, Plato offers a theory of mimesis, thereby neutralizing its threat and pulling off what Lacoue-Labarthe describes as a speculative trick designed to ultimately master it.

As we recall, it is Book X where Plato describes the artist as having the demiurgic power of being able to recreate the world through artistic mimesis. But the example Plato calls upon in order to illustrate this power is that of someone taking a mirror and turning it around so that everything it is pointed at is reflected in it. The question Lacoue-Labarthe poses concerns the status of this mirror and the occupation of the demiurge. Which is the demiurge, the one who merely holds the mirror, or the mirror itself? Who or what is doing the work of mimesis? Where is the mimetic act to be located? How is mimesis actually 'like' a reflection in the mirror when a mirror's reflections lack permanence?[20]

As Lacoue-Labarthe argues, Plato's critique of mimesis relies on a series of mimetic gestures that elide or draw a relation of similitude between heterogeneous elements: the demiurge and the mirror; the

17 Ibid., p. 116.

18 Ibid., p. 129.

19 See Alison Ross, *The Aesthetic Paths of Philosophy: Presentation in Kant, Heidegger, Lacoue-Labarthe, and Nancy* (Stanford, CA: Stanford University Press, 2007), pp. 116–17.

20 Lacoue-Labarthe, 'Typography', p. 88.

demiurge and the artist, and; the artist and the poet. And this is all after the originary elision that serves as the condition of Plato's philosophical corpus — viz., Plato's ability to speak in the voice of Socrates (among others). This logic of substitution, which is the logic of mimesis, that one thing can stand in for an other, authorizes Plato's text in its critique of mimesis, which it then mirrors (for example, by appropriating and deploying the dialogue form and speaking in the voice of 'Socrates').[21] If Plato is exemplary of Western thought's relation to mimesis, therefore, it is because he provides the model and direction for all subsequent treatments of mimesis within the Western philosophical tradition: master, through figuration, that which undoes all forms of mastery and all stability of figures.

Yet, while *Republic* x designates the site where Plato executes his speculative sleight-of-hand by presenting the proper theory of mimesis in its threatening impropriety, it is in *Republic* II, says Lacoue-Labarthe, that Plato dramatizes philosophy's appropriation of both mimesis and the feminine/maternal labour most immediately associated with mimesis. It is at this point in the *Republic* that Socrates discusses the education of the guardians, specifically, their formation in relation to that language called myth.[22] He has not yet banished the poets from the *politeia*. In fact, quite the opposite. He argues there that the guardians ought to be told the myths that would make the desired 'impression' (*tupos*) upon their souls.[23] Explicating the passage, Lacoue-Labarthe writes that mimesis, 'imitation', involves 'the imposition of the *sign*' upon 'the infant soul. That is to say, of course, of the soul that is yet *in-fans*', without language.[24]

But Lacoue-Labarthe also observes that this site of mimetic appropriation is not without ambivalence in the Platonic text. In one respect, the infant soul's 'vulnerability to fables' makes myth a suitable tool with which to shape the future guardians' characters; in another respect, this vulnerability underscores the infant's dependency on the stories

21 Ibid., p. 135.

22 Plato, *Republic*, 376e–77b, cited in ibid., p. 126. See Plato, *Republic*, trans. by C. D. C. Reeve (Indianapolis, IN: Hackett, 2004).

23 Ibid.

24 Lacoue-Labarthe, 'Typography', pp. 126–27.

'mothers and nurses' tell.[25] Noting echoes with Lacan's theorization of the mirror stage, particularly its role in clearing the space for the emergence of the subject's aggressivity, Lacoue-Labarthe submits that this passage from the *Republic* is thus also a scene where the text of philosophy acts out its envy of and concomitant 'resentment against the original maternal domination and original feminine education'.[26] The scene is a response to a double 'panic', as Lacoue-Labarthe and Nancy characterize it elsewhere:[27] before mimesis's threat of dissolving the integrity of philosophy's subjectivity and before the maternal feminine's intimacy/identification with mimesis. Appropriating mimesis by subsuming it within the education of the guardians, philosophy masters that which threatens it with subjective dissolution, and it also claims ownership over the 'acquisition of the "mother" tongue',[28] allowing it to disavow the fact that it (i.e., philosophy) must also have received its voice by virtue of feminine/maternal labour.

As Lacoue-Labarthe argues further, the history of philosophy is nothing less than the history of philosophy's repeated disavowal and appropriation of mimesis in constituting its self-identity as 'Philosophy'. He shows that, even as they critique Platonism, both Nietzsche and Heidegger inherit and unquestioningly re-enact Plato's speculative sleight-of-hand, and with it, philosophy's narcissistic investments. Rather than a rejection of Plato's critique of mimesis, the enthusiasm for art that characterizes Nietzsche's and Heidegger's respective philosophical projects clearly amounts, in Lacoue-Labarthe's eyes, to an attempt to control mimesis and subsume it to philosophy's self-realization. Tellingly, both Nietzsche and Heidegger theorize mimesis through the figure, the former through Dionysus, and the latter through his recasting/recovery of truth as *aletheia* (unconcealment).[29] In so doing, Lacoue-Labarthe argues, they reinforce

25 *Republic*, 377c, cited in ibid., p. 127.

26 Ibid., p. 127. See Jacques Lacan, 'Aggressiveness in Psychoanalysis', in *Écrits*, trans. by Bruce Fink (New York: W. W. Norton, 2006), pp. 82–101.

27 Philippe Lacoue-Labarthe and Jean-Luc Nancy, 'La Panique politique', trans. by Céline Suprenant, in *Retreating the Political*, ed. by Simon Sparks (London: Routledge, 1997), pp. 1–31.

28 Lacoue-Labarthe, 'Typography', p. 127.

29 Ibid., pp. 61, 122, and 79–80.

their commitments to speculative metaphysics in the very moments that they call for its closure.

Yet, this mimetic repetition is just one part of Nietzsche's and Heidegger's 'mimetology': another part appears in the 'mimetic *agon*' that they sustain with the Ancients, who they posit, in a gesture Lacoue-Labarthe classifies as emblematic of modern thought, as a model both to imitate and surpass.[30] In one respect, such mimetic rivalry explains both Nietzsche's and Heidegger's reaching back to the Greeks as part of their respective critiques of modernity. In another respect, it also exposes the way art and politics are connected in terms of identification: both Nietzsche and Heidegger (and also Hölderlin) identify with the aesthetic practices of the Greeks — particularly, Plato's appropriation of mimesis in the 'political *Bildung*' of the *politeia* — in the project of calling for and identifying with a German nation to come.[31] In 'the case of Heidegger', then, his adoption of Plato's mimetology undergirds the metaphysical aspirations he pins to National Socialism (which Lacoue-Labarthe derisively refers to as 'national-Aestheticism').[32]

As we will see, Lacoue-Labarthe carries his critique of onto-typology over to his work with Jean-Luc Nancy on the *retrait* (retreat; retrace) of the political. As indicated above, their focus in their collaborations is on the affective ties that identification employs, and it is in that direction that Lacoue-Labarthe's various references to psychoanalysis, specifically Freud's theorization of group or 'mass' psychology (as in *Massenpsychologie*),[33] receive sustained development. The figure of the Mother, in the form of the 'beyond-mother', appears in this collective project as well. However, the question that emerges when we look at their investigation into the relation of identification to affect is whether Lacoue-Labarthe's attention to maternal labour also appears there, or instead becomes buried in the figure once more.

30 Philippe Lacoue-Labarthe, *Heidegger, Art and Politics: The Fiction of the Political*, trans. by Chris Turner (Oxford: Blackwell, 1990), p. 79.

31 Ibid., p. 85.

32 Ibid., p. 86.

33 Freud's *Massenpsychologie und Ich-Analyse* (1921) is a key point of departure in Lacoue-Labarthe and Nancy's 'La Panique politique' and 'The Unconscious is Destructured Like an Affect'.

IDENTIFICATION, MIMESIS, AND THE MOTHER'S RETREAT

For Lacoue-Labarthe and Nancy, psychoanalysis, particularly its realization in Freud's work, opens a new chapter in the legacy of speculative thought's project to master mimesis. On its face, since identification is central to psychoanalytic accounts of subject formation, it would seem that psychoanalysis might offer a privileged view into the mechanism by which the philosophical subject identifies with the figure. Relatedly, psychoanalysis promises to clarify also how identification works on a political level, as in Heidegger's identification with National Socialism. For while Heidegger's affiliation with National Socialism can be considered exemplary in the way that his thought combines both the philosophical and political instances of identification at once, the problem of identification is not raised by his example alone. Just how identification works — both philosophically and politically, but also in terms of how it connects the philosophical and the political — becomes the focus of Lacoue-Labarthe and Nancy's attention to the text of psychoanalysis, and specifically Freud's texts on culture: *Group Psychology and the Analysis of the Ego*, *Totem and Taboo*, and *Moses and Monotheism*.

Yet, despite this promise of psychoanalysis, what Freud's texts on culture reveal to Lacoue-Labarthe and Nancy instead is that Freud, too, participates, like Heidegger, in the Western philosophical tradition's speculative mimetic economy. As they outline in their essays 'La panique politique' and 'The Unconscious is Destructured Like an Affect (Part I of "The Jewish People Do Not Dream")',[34] Lacoue-Labarthe and Nancy show that, rather than clarify identification and the mimetic relation identification presupposes, Freud's texts on culture constitute a continuation of the attempt by speculative thought to master mimesis by proliferating the figure. Each time Freud tries to reconstruct the role of identification in constituting culture, he ends up engaging in a series of substitutions and figures that, like Heidegger

34 Philippe Lacoue-Labarthe and Jean-Luc Nancy, 'The Unconscious is Destructured Like an Affect (Part I of "The Jewish People Do Not Dream")', trans. by Brian Holmes, *Stanford Literary Review*, 6.2 (1989), pp. 191–209. (Note that this translation is only the first part of 'Le Peuple juif ne rêve pas'. For the complete essay, see Philippe Lacoue-Labarthe and Jean-Luc Nancy, *La Panique politique* suivi de *Le Peuple juif ne rêve pas* (Paris: Christian Bourgois, 2013).)

with the figure of *aletheia,* reveals a reliance on mimetic logic that obscures the workings of identification, in effect mimicking mimesis. Rather than explain culture, then, it is identification that results in need of explanation, thereby forming a lacuna in Freud's thought and exacerbating those questions the concept was projected to answer in the first place, namely: What is the relationship between individual psychology and the psychology of groups? And, how, exactly, does the group's development mirror (i.e., mimic) the individual's? For Lacoue-Labarthe and Nancy, Freud's attempts to analogize individual and group psychologies via the figure of the Father reveal how the problem of identification exposes psychoanalysis to its limit and how this limit is the political itself.

Yet, it is within this very lacuna in the psychoanalytic archive that Lacoue-Labarthe and Nancy see an opening: it is precisely in this space, where Freud's text breaks down and his attempts at theorizing identification lead to the text's 'dis-sociation', that it is possible, in one respect, to see Freud's theorization of the Father as an artefact of subjective/group 'panic' and, in another respect, to identify with the 'withdrawal' (*retrait*) of identification.[35] According to Lacoue-Labarthe and Nancy, the 'infigurable' figure of this withdrawal would be the Mother.[36]

In Lacoue-Labarthe and Nancy's reading, everything centres on the status of 'affect' (*Fühlen*) in Freud's theorization of identification. It is around *Fühlen* and its cognates, they contend, such as *Einfühlung* (empathy) and *Gefühlsbindung* (affective tie), that Freud's text both dis-sociates but also coheres.[37] Affect leads to the text's dis-sociation because, although it appears to explain the mechanism of identification, as in the 'affective tie' by which a group coheres around a figure of authority (i.e., the Father or Leader), it leads to difficulties that Freud is ultimately unable to resolve. For if his expansion of the Oedipal schema to the political plane is intended to explain the relation of the individ-

35 Lacoue-Labarthe and Nancy, 'The Unconscious Is Destructured Like an Affect', p. 201. '*Retrait*' is rendered throughout the text as 'withdrawal' in this English translation. See *Le Peuple juif ne rêve pas*, p. 72.

36 Lacoue-Labarthe and Nancy, 'The Unconscious Is Destructured Like an Affect', p. 201.

37 Lacoue-Labarthe and Nancy, 'La Panique politique', pp. 16, 19, and 20–21; Lacoue-Labarthe and Nancy, 'The Unconscious Is Destructured Like an Affect', pp. 196–97.

ual to the social, it does so by ignoring the fact that the Oedipal schema already contains this relation in theorizing the individual subject's development from the family structure. The 'sexual "integration" of the ego and socialisation', write Lacoue-Labarthe and Nancy, means that the 'integration *to* society and the integration *of* society' are essentially connected.[38] This is to say that 'the *socius* is thus in the ego'.[39]

There is thus already an irreducible intrapsychic dimension to the Oedipus complex. Consequently, Freud's theory of identification presumes social plurality as a fundamental given. In so doing, the theory of identification, whether on the individual or collective plane, ends up begging the question of the social, as well as that of affect. As a result, Lacoue-Labarthe and Nancy assess Freud's theory of identification as a kind of theoretical repetition compulsion, a compulsion that, instead of clarifying the mechanism of identification with the figure of the Father, gives way to a proliferation of figures of identification.[40]

One such figure is that of Narcissus, who, as Lacoue-Labarthe and Nancy remind us, appears in addition to or on top of the figure of Oedipus that already occupies a position in Freud's theorization of sociality.[41] Not only is the figure of Narcissus one of a number of figures installed by Freud into the matrix of the *socius*, it emphasizes the isolation of the subject and exacerbates the question of how the *socius* is held together through an affective tie. For if the social is basically a collection of 'several narcissi', including the Father, who in *Group Psychology* Freud describes as the 'absolute Narcissus', then the question remains of how these narcissi ever break out of their solipsistic confines and relate to others.[42] In their figuration and multiplication as figures, Narcissus and Oedipus are expressions of what Lacoue-Labarthe and Nancy charge is Freud's 'archeophilia', a drive to arrive at an '*arkhé*' or origin.[43] Since this drive gives rise to nothing more than 'a series of

38 Lacoue-Labarthe and Nancy, 'La Panique politique', p. 10.

39 Ibid., p. 10.

40 Lacoue-Labarthe and Nancy, 'The Unconscious Is Destructured Like an Affect', pp. 200–01.

41 See Lacoue-Labarthe and Nancy, 'La Panique politique', p. 20.

42 Ibid., p. 21.

43 Lacoue-Labarthe and Nancy, 'The Unconscious Is Destructured Like an Affect', p. 201.

[mimetic] displacements' in the form of the multiplication of figures,[44] Freud's archeophilia is also, Lacoue-Labarthe and Nancy contend, an 'egology',[45] a repetition impulse to deploy figures of identification that he shares with Heidegger and the rest of the speculative metaphysical tradition in their attempts to master mimesis. By producing and reproducing ever more figures of identification, identification in Freud simply appropriates mimesis, mimicking its movement, and in no way explains the mimetic relation of an affective tie that it posits among the multiple narcissi constituting the *socius*. The failure of identification in Freud is thus also a failed theory of mimesis.

In their reading of Freud's theory of identification as an appropriation of mimesis, Lacoue-Labarthe and Nancy imply that Freud (or at least his text) betrays an awareness that this theoretical failure also signals that psychoanalysis has encountered its limit. They consequently read Freud's proliferation of figures as a symptom of theoretical panic: when faced with the inability to explain identification and the affective tie it assumes, Freud, they assert, seeks refuge in the shelter of figuration that theory, as a mode of mimesis, provides. Installed in and through theory, Narcissus serves as a figure for the identification that *theory* furnishes. 'Freud seems never to have really shaken off this Narcissus', write Lacoue-Labarthe and Nancy. 'Even when he recognizes it as a theoretical fiction, he emphasizes all the more its function: the Narcissus is the ultimate object of the *theory*, it offers the theory its absolute figure as a *visible form*, and so assures the identity of psychoanalysis.'[46] So while the text of psychoanalysis meets its limit with identification, setting it underway towards dissociation, Narcissus, the symptom of this dis-sociation and failure of identification, nonetheless allows psychoanalysis to cohere around the figure in order to consolidate its identity as theory.

If identification's failure is one way Freud's text undergoes dissociation, then the second way it comes under dis-sociation is as an expression of a theoretical panic before identification's explanatory impotence. Curiously, this panic also announces the return of affect,

44 Lacoue-Labarthe and Nancy, 'La Panique politique', p. 15.

45 Ibid., pp. 18–19.

46 Lacoue-Labarthe and Nancy, 'The Unconscious Is Destructured Like an Affect', p. 201.

but the affective tie does not refer to the mechanism of identification within the social writ large. Rather, it refers to Freud's affective tie and identification with theory and the theoretical community that is psychoanalysis. As Lacoue-Labarthe and Nancy observe,

> identification, for Freud, is first and foremost identification with the Father — and the Father means here: he who is always-already identified, he who has presented himself before disappearing, he who has symbolized himself before being symbolic.[47]

In place of a theory of identification, Freud identifies with theory as such, and psychoanalytic theory specifically. It is an identification that consequently places Freud himself as Father and absolute Narcissus.

So, if the Father proves to be a vanishing point on the horizon of psychoanalysis, this leaves open the question of how to think the figure of the Mother. If the Father is the figure for the role of figuration in (psychoanalytic) theory, for the narcissism of theory, the narcissism that is theory, and the identification with this narcissism, then what is the status of the Mother? Does the Mother stand outside of theory? Is the Mother a figure at all? Does the Mother make possible an untying of the affective tie to theory?

According to Lacoue-Labarthe and Nancy, it cannot be as simple as a turn to the Mother once the emptiness of the Father is exposed. 'One must not, above all, simply let the original Narcissus of the Father figure return in a figure of the Mother', they caution.[48] For this reason, they eschew the terminology of 'the Mother' and refer instead to 'the maternal substance', the 'beyond-mother' (*outre-mère*) which would resist serving as yet another narcissistic figure for identification.[49] For Lacoue-Labarthe and Nancy, the beyond-mother would be the name for 'the infigurable', and the task for thought would be to identify with the beyond-mother as the withdrawal of identity.[50] With the Mother, or, to be more precise, the beyond-mother, then, there is the promise

47 Ibid., pp. 200–01.

48 Ibid., p. 202.

49 Ibid., pp. 202 and 203.

50 Ibid., pp. 201 and 203. In *Retreating the Political*, Lacoue-Labarthe and Nancy identify this withdrawal of the Mother with 'the retreat (*retrait*) of the political' (pp. 119 and 133–34).

of 'de-figuration',[51] the promise, in other words, of breaking free of the speculative metaphysical economy.

There is, however, one hazard that Lacoue-Labarthe and Nancy do not fully acknowledge. While they may recognize that this turn to the beyond-mother risks participating once more in the economy of figuration, and therefore, risks a reinscription of the speculative theoretical drive, they appear to overlook the fact that they are still putting the Mother to work. Assigning the beyond-mother the work of delineating the outside of the theoretical is no different than the reproductive labour that both French feminist thought and Lacoue-Labarthe in his earlier work proved the Mother has been assigned historically within the speculative tradition. Whether for theory or against it, the Mother still appears in order to disappear. Positing the Mother, even as the infigurable, would amount once more to appropriating the maternal and using 'her' to accomplish what theory cannot do on its own.

As it concerns the project of untying the mother tongue, Lacoue-Labarthe and Nancy's engagement with Freud's affective tie to theory shows that it is not simply a matter of dismantling the theoretical apparatus. For how would one theorize doing so without being entangled further in the affective ties that put the Mother to work? Untying the mother tongue perhaps requires then an 'other' tongue, a tongue other to and otherwise than theory. It is perhaps here that we reach the limits of Lacoue-Labarthe and Nancy's text as well and that we might realize the need to come into dialogue with those discourses that attend to actual work that actual (not only figural or theoretical) women perform in maintaining the fiction of the mother tongue and its theories.

---

51 Lacoue-Labarthe and Nancy, 'The Unconscious Is Destructured Like an Affect', p. 204.

'My Mother Tongue Is a Foreign Language'

On Edmond Jabès's Writing in Exile

FEDERICO DAL BO

If it is true that great philosophers only think one single thought throughout their lifetime, this is probably true also for great writers: they only write one single book throughout their lifetime. There is perhaps no better way to describe the long and stratified *oeuvre* of the French-Jewish poet and writer Edmond Jabès. In almost sixty years, he authored many booklets, essays, and poetry collections.[1] And yet, he never stopped spinning around the same question, over and over again: 'the question of the book'.[2]

1 His main *oeuvre* consists of three main cycles: the first cycle, called *Le Livre des questions* (Paris: Gallimard, 1963–73), consists of the seven booklets *Le Livre des questions* (1963), *Le Livre de Yukel* (1964), *Le Retour au livre* (1965), *Yaël* (1967), *Elya* (1969), *Aely* (1972), and *El, ou le dernier livre* (1973); the second cycle, called *Le Livre des ressemblances* (Paris: Gallimard, 1976–80), consists of the three booklets *Le Livre des ressemblances* (1976), *Le Soupçon — Le Désert* (1978), and *L'ineffaçable — L'inaperçu* (1980); the third cycle, called *Le Livre des limites* (Paris: Gallimard, 1982–87), consists of the four booklets *Le Petit Livre de la subversion hors de soupçon* (1982), *Le Livre du dialogue* (1984), *Le Parcours* (1985), and *Le Livre du partage* (1985). The book *Le Livre de l'hospitalité* (Paris: Gallimard, 1991) was published posthumously. This complex and stratified *oeuvre* has been translated into English only in part, as *The Book of Questions*, trans. by Rosmarie Waldrop (Middletown: Wesleyan University Press, 1976–84) and *The Book of Resemblances*, trans. by Rosmarie Waldrop (Middletown: Wesleyan University Press, 1990).

2 I am obviously alluding to Jacques Derrida, 'Edmond Jabès and the Question of the Book', in *Writing and Difference*, trans. by Alan Bass (London: Routledge, 2002), pp. 77–96. This seminal study is the blueprint for my attempt at reading Jabès's poetics.

Some inadvertent readers could dismiss this as a form of obsession. Yet, the reason that Jabès, in a metalinguistic fashion, never stopped writing his book on the question of the book was metaphysical rather than psychological. Not compulsion but rather a meta-philosophical necessity, emerging from the exhaustion of the traditional notion of the book, compelled him to deal with this question continuously, without interruption, for sixty years. Apparently, for Jabès the art of writing could no longer be accomplished with a great, single book — if this had ever been the case — but could only be disseminated in a labyrinthic series of booklets that desperately seek for unity and yet are always disparaged, scattered, and driven away. What prevented this accomplishment from taking place was — as a sort of metaphysical *a priori* — the Shoah:[3] the almost complete annihilation of European Jewry that had broken apart not only the Jewish people but also the entire Western civilization, its theodicy, and its metaphysics. In other words, Jabès's perplexity can also be phrased in one single question: if God has not saved His people from their almost complete annihilation, how is it possible to still believe in a Holy Writ?

On these premises, Jabès elaborated a strong poetics that suffered from an inescapable paradox: the tenets of traditional Judaism can no longer be upheld yet they cannot be discarded in favour of a blunt secularism. Similarly, the traditional dimension of writing has been exhausted but this does not mean that Western civilization, its theodicy, and its metaphysics have simply come to an end. It rather means that theology and secularism now overlap in a paradoxical way:

> the book answers for the book; the writer, for the words that have written him; and the Jew, for what remains always to be read in the Book of God and still to be written in the book of man.[4]

3 The history of the terminology on the genocide of the Jewish people cannot be treated in detail here. It will be sufficient to say that some early definitions as 'holocaust' and *churban* (destruction) should be avoided due to their reference to Jewish rituals and to the destruction of the Temple of Jerusalem, respectively. The use of the Hebrew term *shoah* (catastrophe) is preferable. Interestingly, Jabès appears not to refer directly to the Shoah but only to allude to it by several metaphors. For a strong criticism of Jabès's use of the Shoah in his *oeuvre*, see Berel Lang, 'Writing-the-Holocaust: Jabès and the Measure of History', in *Writing and the Holocaust*, ed. by Lang (New York: Holmes & Meier, 1988), pp. 245–60.

4 Edmond Jabès, *A Foreigner Carrying in the Crook of his Arm a Tiny Book*, trans. by Rosmarie Waldrop (Middletown: Wesleyan University Press, 1993), p. 58. See also

Jabès seems to argue that humans can no longer believe that Holy Writ is written by God and that ordinary writing can only be written by humans. This chiastic relationship between the divine and human dimensions of writing suggests that the deconstruction of the Holy Writ consists not in its end but rather in its endless dissemination by means of endless writings on a minor scale: single, erratic, and fragmented booklets. In this respect, Jabès's poetics of the book is haunted by a paradox: the inability to abide by traditional Judaism and the impossibility to simply discard it. Literature, he seems to assume, poses a much more complex question: How does one *deconstruct* the ordinary notion of a book? More specifically, this question is the task of Jewish literature: to deconstruct the Jewish notion of the Holy Writ.

This deconstruction cannot dismiss the notion of the book, which falls within a very definite boundary: *la page blanche*, the 'blank page'. Jabès's work mostly elaborates on this notion — both in an actual and a metaphorical sense. A blank page represents a sort of material resistance every writer must cope with: a blank page is all the writer — every writer, whether a divine or a human one — has at the beginning of each act of writing. In this respect, a blank page symbolizes 'blankness': an ontological void that predates and at the same time escapes the act of creation — both human and divine. In short, there are two simultaneous connotations of a blank page in Jabès's writings: a blank page that is necessary for writing and a void that metaphorically represents what inexorably eludes denomination and therefore remains silent. This all implies that both God and man find themselves as strangers in the act of writing, as if in exile.

A STRANGER TO HIMSELF I: ON GOD'S WRITING IN EXILE

The theological notion that God is exiled, while quite common in orthodox Judaism, is not an easy one. At a basic level, this notion means that God follows the Jewish people into exile after the epochal destruction of the Temple of Jerusalem in 70 CE, which took place

---

Edmond Jabès, *Un étranger avec, sous le bras, un livre de petit format* (Paris: Gallimard, 1989), p. 84: 'Le livre répond, pour le livre; l'écrivain, pour le mot qui l'a écrit et le juif, de ce qui reste, toujours, à lire dans le Livre de Dieu et de ce qui reste, encore, à écrire dans le livre de l'homme.'

during the disastrous first Jewish-Roman war. According to biblical premises, God neither interrupts His providence unto His people nor deserts them among the nations but follows them with His perduring benevolence — even at the price of following them into exile.

And yet, this quite caring though perhaps not careful notion of exile could not fully escape some more radical implications. The destruction of the Temple also implied that God's permanent residence on earth had been removed altogether. This circumstance had an unprecedented consequence: God Himself would eventually have no place to dwell on earth and would find Himself in exile. Yet, this almost literal, spatial, or cosmic notion of exile — depicting God as geographically following His people outside of the Land of Israel — would eventually be turned into an uncanny and tenebrous idea: God could only follow His people into exile if He had exiled Himself from Himself first.[5] This radical notion of exile was first introduced during the Renaissance by the famous Rabbi Isaac Luria's astonishing interpretation of the Zohar — the most important and canonical work of the Kabbalah.[6] From the Ottoman city of Safed, Luria propagated the myth of a transcendent God who had not simply followed His people into exile — into the diaspora — but had also imposed a form of exile onto Himself, as a sort of ontological condition of existence for

5 The notion of 'the Land of Israel' is modelled on the rabbinic expression *'eretz Isra'el* that was coined in post-biblical literature — especially by the Babylonian Talmud — with the purpose of emphasizing the political-theological connection between Jewish communities and the land by suggesting an 'anti-territorial' perspective to future Jewish generations. See Shlomo Sand, *The Invention of the Land of Israel: From Holy Land to Homeland* (New York: Verso Books, 2012).

6 Rabbi Isaac Luria (1534–1572) is one of the most prominent Jewish theological thinkers. His teachings were mostly transmitted orally and put into writing by his disciples, especially by Hayyim Vital (1542–1620) and Israel Sarug (1590–1610). Scholarship on the Zohar, the thirteenth-century pseudepigraphic mystical commentary on Scripture and Lurianic Kabbalah, is very vast and cannot be summarized here. For brevity's sake I will only mention this interesting introduction: Pinchas Giller, *Reading the Zohar: The Sacred Text of the Kabbalah* (Oxford: Oxford University Press, 2001). For a comprehensive review of the study of the Kabbalah, see the bibliographical collection by Don Karr, *Collected Articles on the Kabbalah* (New York: Boleskine House, 1985), which is periodically updated on Karr's personal page on the website Academia: Karr, 'Notes on the Study of Later Kabbalah in English: The Safed Period and Lurianic Kabbalah' <https://www.academia.edu/38974270/Notes_on_the_Study_of_Later_Kabbalah_in_English_The_Safed_Period_and_Lurianic_Kabbalah> [accessed 6 April 2022].

everything. Luria famously argued that the world — in essence, the reality of everything that is different from God or the non-divine reality — could exist only if it were given the opportunity or the sufficient 'space' for being. The ontological dimension that was at first saturated by the overwhelming Presence of God had to be emptied in order to allow all other entities to exist. Luria called this notion *tzimtzum* or 'contraction'.

In its simplest formulation, *tzimtzum* consisted in God's act of withholding God's creative power and allowing for ontologically inferior entities to take place. This was an act that, as the etymology of the word suggests, could also be compared to God holding His own breath or withholding the biblical 'Spirit of God', which 'hover[s] over the waters' (Genesis 1. 2). Even in its most basic sense, however, the notion of *tzimtzum* 'contraction' also suggested a darker truth, reminiscent of the Pauline notion of *kenosis* or 'God's self-effacement' (Philippians 2. 7). According to the notion of *tzimtzum*, Creation is possible only when it fills an abyssal void that precedes even the existence of God Himself — especially when He was intended as the 'Creator' of the world. This also implied the existence of a supernal dimension of the divinity that should be identified not with the Tetragrammaton — God's ineffable Name — but with a superior realm called *En Sof*, or 'Infinite'. Under these premises, a self-contracting God would allow not only for the existence of other things beside God but also for the emergence of evil. For some later commentators on the Lurianic corpus, the notion of *tzimtzum* also implied the assumption that God had retracted from the universe by 'hiding His face' (*hester panim*) and interrupting His positive influence over the world. In doing so, God had made Himself complicit with evil.[7]

7 This connection is made explicit, for instance, by the Chabad Rabbi Shneur Zalman of Liadi in his influential *Tanya*, Part I, *Likkutey Amarim*, Chapter 48 <https://www.sefaria.org/Tanya%2C_Part_I%3B_Likkutei_Amarim.48?lang=bi> [accessed 12 February 2023]. Nevertheless, they are two distinct concepts. The notion of *hester panim* (hiding of the face) derives from the biblical passage of Deuteronomy 31. 17 and designated a temporary suspension of the divine Providence. This suspension allowed the punishment of sins by the 'measure of Justice' (*middat ha-din*) to take place; such punishment would otherwise be stopped by the benevolent 'measure of Mercy' (*middat ha-rachamim*). On the other hand, the notion of *tzimtzum* designates a metaphysical event that predates Creation and is the condition for it. See Rachel Adelman, *The Return of the Repressed: Pirqe De-Rabbi Eliezer and the Pseudepigrapha*

This complex and unsettling conception of God represents the theological perimeter of Jabès's poetics of the book. In one of his later texts, Jabès is particularly explicit on the matter and mobilizes the notion of *tzimtzum* in a dialogue between two anonymous rabbis who question God's responsibility towards evil:

> 'It is time to bring up God's responsibility toward His Creation', a sage said to his disciples. 'He cannot be the only one to escape His justice.' 'He is the only one not to know it', they replied. 'Has He not, since He withdrew from the universe, been infinite Oblivion?' And the sage said: 'God is the solitude of Him who is, the only One to be in what once was.' And he added: 'What endures is powerless before what crumbles.'[8]

This frank passage shall be treated carefully. It manifests how Jabès depends on important notions from the Lurianic Kabbalah but it should not be mistaken for a theoretical text. Jabès has never intended to write a book of metaphysics alone, since the Shoah disqualified traditional philosophy and theodicy from being able to say anything meaningful on the nature of God. Jabès never considered it possible to write on metaphysics without writing on the notion of book itself. He argued that there was an uninterrupted connection between God and His Book, as each belongs to the other: 'if God is, it is because He is in the book.'[9]

The ramifications of this assumption were profound for Jabès and his poetics. This mutual association between God and His book did not simply rely on the trite monotheistic assumption that the Holy Writ had a divine origin but rather suggested, quite more radically, that

(Leiden: Brill, 2005), p. 50, and Sanford L. Drob, *Kabbalistic Metaphors: Jewish Mystical Themes in Ancient and Modern Thought* (Jerusalem: J. Aronson, 2000), p. 36.

8 Jabès, *A Foreigner Carrying in the Crook of his Arm a Tiny Book*, p. 40; translation modified. See also Jabès, *Un étranger avec, sous le bras, un livre de petit format*, p. 62: '"Il est temps d'évoquer la responsabilité de Dieu envers la Création — disait un sage à ses disciples. Il ne peut être le seul à échapper à Sa justice." "Il est le seul — lui répondirent-ils — à l'ignorer. N'est-Il pas, depuis Son retrait de l'univers, infini Oubli?" Et le sage dit: "Dieu est solitude de Celui qui est, étant seul à être dans ce qui, une fois, fut." Et il ajouta: "Ce qui perdure est impuissant devant ce qui se désagrège."'

9 For reasons of convenience, I am quoting from the French-Italian (almost) complete collection of Edmond Jabès's complex *oeuvre*: Edmond Jabès, *Le Livre des questions*, in *Il libro delle interrogazioni. Testo francese a fronte*, ed. and trans. by Alberto Folin (Milan: Bompiani, 2015), pp. 1–326 (p. 38): 'Si Dieu est, c'est parce qu'Il est dans le Livre'; all English translations are mine unless otherwise noted.

even the divine dimension of writing could not escape the abysmal reality of exile after the divine contraction of God in Himself. What form would this contraction take if God and His Book were mutually related? Jabès's implicit answer is discouraging. It would take the form of a *page blanche*, a 'blank page' that is void of writing, effaced from writing and yet dependent on it.

In this respect, divine writing underwent the same destiny as God, who had exiled Himself into Himself: words are effaced by words, not in the trite sense that words would 'overwrite' words, creating a sort of divine hypertext, but rather in the sense that writing is effaced by itself or, better put, by the perpetual mobility of the writing. In this perpetual effacement, writing also exposes the infinite blankness that structurally allows for it to be written in the first place. It is *la page blanche*, the 'blank page' that simultaneously designates the void carved out from the divine 'contraction' and the structural blankness that can be inscribed by writing. The perpetual overlapping of God and His Book describes this void as a dimension that perpetually escapes the act of Creation, and this is because the void is what poses the possibility of Creation in the first place. In both a metaphysical and literal sense, writing is only possible on a blank page, exactly because God and Book mutually belong to each other.

Yet, the exhaustion of metaphysics after the Shoah poses a serious question concerning the property of being read — or the 'readability' — of the Book. With the emergence of evil, when God has covered His face and has withdrawn Himself into Himself, a radical question arises: how can a book be read by a 'face of the non-face' (*visage du non-visage*) or, conversely, a 'non-face of the face' (*non-visage du visage*)?[10]

A STRANGER TO HIMSELF II: ON JABÈS'S WRITING IN EXILE

This radical question cannot be answered by simply relying on the metaphysical presupposition that, because God still enjoys a special relationship to His Book, these two dimensions perfectly overlap. Jabès believes that the historically unprecedented event of the Shoah also reflects a metaphysical one: it is that situation that the Lurianic Kabba-

10 Jabès, *Un étranger avec, sous le bras, un livre de petit format*, p. 62; Jabès, *A Foreigner Carrying in the Crook of his Arm a Tiny Book*, p. 40.

lah — and especially his later interpreters — has substantiated with the double connection between the 'contraction' (*tzimtzum*) into a divine exile and the 'hiding of the Face' (*hester panim*). Jabès believes that an answer to this radical question can only be achieved from the perspective of 'the Jew', who has to answer 'for what remains always to be read in the Book of God and still to be written in the book of man'.[11] Notably, this passage from the divine to the human dimension of writing is especially possible due to their chiastic relationship: humans can no longer believe that Holy Writ is written by God and ordinary writing can only be written by humans. In other words, the divine and human dimensions of writing entertain a relationship that can never be dialectical as there is no progression from one to the other but rather an unsettling mixture of the two. The Holy Writ can no longer be written — or even be read, in force of God's 'hiding of the Face' — but human writing is all that remains to man. What is this human writing exactly?

Jabès wrote *The Book of Questions* as a tragic love story of a Jewish couple after the Shoah: Yukel and Sarah. Their love story is narrated neither chronologically nor coherently but rather fragmentarily. Jabès abides by his conviction that books — as a solid chronological thread — can no longer be written, as the possibility of history has been shattered by the disruptive event of the Shoah. Therefore, he opts for a *récit éclaté*, a form of narration that is structured as a collection of: fragments from Yukel's and Sarah's diaries; imaginary dialogues between fictional rabbis; poetry; and theological ponderings. Overall, Jabès deserts the idea of narrating a love story. He rather opts for a convulsed collection of fragments. This choice entails carrying the additional burden of a theological question about theodicy and metaphysics after the Shoah. *The Book of Questions* fails at telling a love story, but this failure is intentional. It transforms the private relationship of two fictional Shoah survivors into an endless and labyrinthic meditation on Jewish existence and the emergence of evil. Jabès chooses to subvert — or rather deconstruct — every literary genre. An ordinary reader easily sees that *The Book of Questions* can be read as a poem, a fictional work, a meditation, a drama, or even a prophecy on human existence. In its most essential dimension, Jabès's book tells a tragic love story: Yukel and

11 Ibid., p. 84; p. 58.

Sarah love each other but are broken by the horrors of Nazi persecution. Sarah survived deportation but has become insane, while her partner Yukel, not accepting the idea of her madness as the only possible way out from their violent past, has committed suicide. In these terms, *The Book of Questions* desperately cries out in response to a metaphysical lack of meaning and exposes language to its fundamental inability to make sense of history.[12]

Jabès's reflection on writing essentially depends on these premises. Indeed, a subtle, non-dialectical economy governs the relation between the literal and metaphorical senses of a blank page. Writing appears to Jabès simultaneously as the actual 'product' of an individual who happens to be a Jewish writer and the horizon within which the writer's activity should be included. This same paradoxical dialectic also characterizes language, i.e. what common sense would simply understand as the means by which a writer 'produces' a piece of writing — as if there were no mystery at all in dragging something out from a dark, unexpressed dimension and delivering it to expression.

In a passage from his second cycle, *Le Livre des limites*, Jabès eloquently asserts the unfamiliar nature of his mother tongue but attributes his assumptions to an unidentified individual — 'he' — who clearly speaks on Jabès's behalf with a nameless, anonymous voice:

> 'My mother tongue is a foreign language. Thanks to her, I am on an equal footing with my foreignness', he said. And he added: 'I have patiently forged my language with foreign words to make them sister words.'[13]

It would be wrong to interpret this claim in merely biographical terms. Jabès surely had a complex and nomadic life.[14] Yet there is no doubt about his attachment to the French language — his mother's tongue and his mother tongue. As a francophone Jew growing up in Egypt, Jabès makes no mystery about his indissoluble linguistic affiliation

---

12 I am following Gianni Scalia, *Fuori e dentro la letteratura: stranieri e italiani* (Bologna: Pendragon, 2004), pp. 45–46.

13 Edmond Jabès, *Le Livre du dialogue* (Paris: Gallimard, 1984), p. 87: '"Ma langue maternelle est une langue étrangère. Grâce à elle, je suis de plain-pied avec mon étrangeté", disait-il. Et il ajoutait: "J'ai, patiemment, forgé ma langue avec des mots étrangers pour en faire des mots frères."'

14 See Didier Cahen, *Edmond Jabès* (Paris: Pierre Belfond, 1991), pp. 305–41.

to French, his only literary language, but he also acknowledges that literary intimacy is a construct that was only possible thanks to his constant effort to patiently forge his language by eliminating impurities or its constitutive foreignness. It is then quite striking that he attributes this statement to an unidentified, anonymous, and therefore nameless individual who fully retracts from the biblical custom of naming each character after their own inner qualities. On the contrary, 'one' who speaks about "one's" mother tongue has no name — exactly because one's mother tongue is a foreign language'.

What is then the meaning of Jabès's claim that his mother tongue is foreign to him? This question can be answered neither in biographical nor in psychological but rather in metaphysical terms that recall the chiastic relationship between divine and human writing. With the exhaustion of the traditional dimension of the book, Jabès acknowledges that Holy Writ can no longer be written. On the other hand, human writing remains 'still to be written in the book of man' by a Jew — like the French-speaking, exiled Egyptian writer Jabès. Yet, his mother tongue cannot offer the same spiritual intimacy as another language, such as the Holy Language. On the contrary, the writer's 'mother tongue' — and, by extension, human language — is always impure and infiltrated by foreignness. Yet, it is the only means of connection with an exiled God. In other words, when he must choose to connect to God by means of a human language, a language that is written in the void of a divine writing that can no longer be written, Jabès elects French.

In this respect, Jabès's affiliation to Judaism is a sort of a *metaphysical* fact rather than a ritual, ethnic, or social one. It is important to note that Jabès hardly received any religious education. Some volumes of the Talmud from his father's bookshelves made him curious but never really fascinated him before adulthood. Jabès addresses Judaism and the dialogical nature of the Talmud only with the years-long redaction of his *The Book of Questions* and he does it in a very personal way. This book, centred around the love story between Yukel and Sarah, is in fact also, and especially, a platform for fabricating imaginary dialogues between fictional rabbis who ponder Jewish existence, the nature of evil, and the yearning for salvation. What is then the reason for quoting fictional rabbis and insisting on Judaism as a category for understanding the act of writing?

While Jabès writes about a number of fictional rabbis, he never reads from the actual Talmud — in which non-legal portions exist but are fundamentally complementary to its main legal core — but Jabès rather ignores and replaces it with a *literary* one. The proportions of legal and non-legal texts — respectively called *halakhah*, or 'law', and *aggadah*, or 'narrative' — are put into question. Jabès writes his own Talmud and tries to make it resonate with his memories of his father. He appears to write his own 'private Talmud' yet he quotes from Jewish writers, thinkers, philosophers, and theologians — whose real names, or 'proper names', are buried under fictional ones, or, I would rather say, whose historical names are literally overwritten by literary ones. At a most superficial level, Jabès tells the story of two Jewish lovers, but this apparently simple narrative is buried under many quotes from fictional Jewish Scriptures — a kind of imaginary Bible, Midrash, and Talmud — that manifest a sort of secularization in literary form.

Of course, this means not that Jabès evacuates theology from his horizon, but rather that he treats it by means of a literature that is not necessarily *Jewish*. This is a question not of competence but of what it means to conceive Jewish identity after the Shoah. Jabès never explored the option of establishing a Jewish orthodox identity in face of the exhaustion of traditional Jewish metaphysics. In Jabès's eyes, the horrendous event of the Shoah suggested that Jewish identity could no longer be determined by the traditional tenets of orthodox Judaism, regardless of their innovation after the question of evil. Therefore, Jewish daily rituals as well as ordinary Jewish theodicy were irrevocably bracketed, if not definitely excluded, from the horizon of Jewish identity; or, better put, these were included only according to an irreversibly deconstructed paradigm. Along with other French Jewish intellectuals, he understood this choice as one that vigorously excluded other alternatives such as the quite challenging effort to explore the possibility of a modern Jewish orthodoxy after the Shoah. When Jabès implicitly opted for its impossibility, his secular Jewish background must have played a considerable role. His basic lack of education in Jewish religious texts played a role when he opted to fabricate a literary Talmud rather than read the actual one. This was a choice not to be taken lightly. It followed the circumstance that the traditional notion of the book had been exhausted and that literature represented the only option, for literature was a kind of writing that was still to be written in the book of man. Jabès was persuaded that the Holy Writ could neither be written again — not even in the sense of being inscribed in the chain of Jewish tradition — nor be read by a 'Face' that has covered Itself (*hester panim*) after God's metaphysical 'contraction' (*tzimtzum*). All this convinced Jabès that only literature could offer a way out — one that is necessarily desperate — from this cultural catastrophe. In this respect, Jabès opted not for fabricating a literary Talmud but rather for writing an *Écriture du désastre.*

To put it differently: should one still abide by the self-representation of Jewish orthodoxy as the ultimate arbiter of Jewishness or should one rather complicate the question of Jewishness by opting for a theology that has been innovated by literature? I use the verb *surviving* in its most literal sense: surviving the annihilation of European Jewry during the Nazi regime. But in addition, Jabès takes quite seriously the assumption that the Shoah has irremediably shattered traditional Jewish theology. Hence, he also takes the possibility of a new, non-orthodox theology very seriously, and argues for the potential new ground that literature implicitly offers for theological speculation. This is the ultimate reason for writing a *literary* Talmud. Since the Shoah has exhausted the traditional perimeter of theology, literature infiltrates, supplements, and possibly replaces it. In Jabès's eyes, literature can innovate the paradigm of Jewish identity more than Jewish theology itself can. Accordingly, the question of literature is not just a scholarly but a linguistic one: who is Jewish and what language should a Jew speak? These two questions also point to a third, difficult one — is it possible to write in a Jewish fashion about Jewish literature?

Jabès does not really answer these questions. He rather shows — or even displays — his own writings, full of fictional rabbis who endlessly speak and argue with one another. This *entretien infini* is implicitly a long, articulate, and rich examination of Jewish literature and its possibility of existence. Jabès does not simply offer a collection of fictional Jewish literary voices; he also offers, I am tempted to say, the deconstruction of a Jewish *archive* — which refers here, in the most genuine Foucauldian sense of the expression, to the totality of discursive practices governing a culture and its statements.[15] Jabès

15 On Foucault's notion of 'archive', see Michel Foucault, *The Archaeology of Knowledge and the Discourse on Knowledge*, trans. by A. M. Sheridan Smith (New York: Pantheon

deconstructs such an archive. He does not really appeal to Jewish tradition but rather invents one. He carves a new literary space out from an historical one: he excavates Jewish tradition and produces a singular literary space that can be experienced aesthetically as a stratified *oeuvre.* At the same time, he also puts this new formation into question and doubts its own ability to register, store, and process a new Jewish tradition.

Yet, the real question at stake here is not the fact of 'inventing' new, fictional rabbis and using them for the formation of a new Talmud — perhaps, a literary one that is entirely devoid of legal discussions. Similar collections had been written before. It is well known that the Renaissance scholars Rabbi Jakob ibn Habib and his son Rabbi Levi collected all the narrative portions from the Talmud into a new volume: the famous *'Ein Ya'akov* (Jacob's Well). Their love for 'narrative' (*aggadah*) as opposed to 'Law' (*halakhah*) reflected the Spanish Jewry's commitment to philosophy as well as their anti-Christian polemic, since these non-binding texts were used by philosophers as proof texts to confirm the rational integrity of Judaism.[16] So, collecting Talmudic narratives or even forging new ones — this was not really the question at stake. The question, more precisely, was how it is possible that Jabès could establish a new Jewish tradition in which it is assumed that someone's mother tongue is not familiar but rather 'always already' a foreign one.

Jabès was unquestionably marked by the Shoah, which he experienced only indirectly. He moved to France after the so-called 'Second Exodus' or the expulsion of Jews from Egypt after the Suez crisis in 1957.[17] Foreignness was to him not simply a cultural symbol but an actual reality. All this shows that it is not only possible but probably also necessary to write in a Jewish way *about* Jewish literature. This requires

Books, 1972), p. 129. For a deconstruction of this notion, see Jacques Derrida, *Archive Fever: A Freudian Impression*, trans. by Eric Prenowitz (Chicago: University of Chicago Press, 1996). For the use of the Foucauldian notion of 'archive' in theology, see David Galston, *Archives and the Event of God: The Impact of Michel Foucault on Philosophical Theology* (Montreal: McGill-Queen's University Press, 2011).

16 See Marjorie Lehman, *The En Yaaqov: Jacob ibn Habib's Search for Faith in the Talmudic Corpus* (Detroit, MI: Wayne State University Press, 2012).

17 See Aimée Israel-Pelletier, 'Edmond Jabès, Jacques Hassoun, and Melancholy: The Second Exodus in the Shadow of the Holocaust', *Modern Language Notes*, 123 (2008), pp. 797–818.

installing fictional rabbis within the texture of a fictional Talmud and inscribing Judaism within literature. This necessity is simultaneously moral and cultural. Judaism cannot be an object of scholarship; it must rather be the very dimension where life and literature finally meet and eventually merge in a particular — admittedly not easily accessible — style: an uninterrupted chain of aphorisms, fragmentary dialogues, and scattered voices.

Yet this is neither an effort to talk to a Jewish literary tradition, if there is one, nor to build a new one, if there is none. Jabès rather works *within* these two possibilities. His movement is based on a premise concerning the nature of Jewish literature that he might well have found in Walter Benjamin's *Auseinandersetzung* (confrontation) with Jewish tradition. What was peculiarly Benjaminian in Jabès? It was perhaps the assumption that there is no single, whole narration of the Jewish past but only an endless, potentially unrelated number of fragments that will have to be recomposed, at least tentatively, in a single work.[18]

This particular form of writing has a noble tradition that begins at the latest with the Medieval *melitzah*: a patchwork of quotations from the Holy Scriptures that are a sort of intellectual divertissement — *melitzah* also means 'joke' — and that, therefore, should not be taken too seriously.[19] In so doing, Jabès takes upon himself the burden of emending the past — its impossibility of being whole as a tradition — and offers a long, intricate, sometimes exhausting recognition of a fictional Jewish literature: quotations, mentions, digressions, quotations from quotations, and so on.

---

18 This notion does not emerge spontaneously from Benjamin's *oeuvre*; it rather emerges from the interaction between Benjamin and his close friend, the famous historian of the Kabbalah, Gershom Scholem. See Federico Dal Bo, '"Paulinism" in the *Wissenschaft des Judentums*: On Scholem's Reception of Paul in his Interwar Hebrew Lectures on Sabbatianism', in *Grey Areas — Two Centuries of Wissenschaft des Judentums* (in preparation).

19 See Moshe Pelli, 'On the Role of *Melitzah* in the Literature of Hebrew Enlightenment', in *Hebrew in Ashkenaz: A Language in Exile*, ed. by Lewis Glinert (Oxford: Oxford University Press, 1993), pp. 99–110. See also Dan Pagis, *Chidush u-Masoret be-Shirat ha-Chol ha-'Ivrit* (Jerusalem: Keter, 1976). For the notion of *melitzah* as 'joke', see Federico Dal Bo, *The Lexical Field of the Substantives of 'Word' in Ancient Hebrew: From the Bible to the Mishnah*, Abhandlungen für die Kunde des Morgenlandes, 124 (Wiesbaden: Harrassowitz, 2021), pp. 144–46 and 262–63.

Jabès's style requires a strong control over a magmatic literary material that refrains from unity and therefore never constitutes a Jewish tradition on its own. Despite his frequent indirect mentions of Jewish literature, Jabès could not acknowledge belonging to any of the several kinds of Jewish tradition: neither to the ordinary, slightly unspecified 'transmission' (*qabbalah*) of Jewish scriptures from Mount Sinai; nor to the Rabbinic 'chain of tradition' (*shalshelet ha-Qabbalah*), defined as the uninterrupted tradition of the Holy Writ together with all — past, present, and future — commentaries; nor to Gedaliah ibn Yahya ben Joseph's 'chain of tradition' (*shalshelet ha-Qabbalah*), defined as the entire history and genealogy of the Jews; nor to the mystical tradition of the *Qabbalah*, defined as an esoteric doctrine that has been emerging since Jewish antiquity.[20]

For this fundamental reason, Jabès resonates with Walter Benjamin and also transforms his vision of the past — a pile of ruins that the angel of history is melancholically contemplating — into a peculiar way of collecting texts. What matters is no longer a book but rather a collection of textual fragments.[21] Jabès makes it quite clear that this melancholic sentiment is often superseded by a more mature one — a longing for a mystical 'reparation of the world' (*tiqqun ha'olam*).[22]

20 I am alluding here respectively to: the famous passage from the Mishnah stating that 'Moses received (qibel) Torah from the Sinai and transmitted (u-msarah) it to Joshuah' (Mishnah, Tractate Avot 1. 1); the Rabbinic notion of 'chain of the tradition' (*shalshelet ha-qabbalah*) (cf. Tanna de-bey-Eliahu Zuta, 53); Gedaliah ibn Yahya ben Joseph's chronicles *Shalshelet ha-Qabbalah* Venice: Giovanni Di Gara, 1587); and the self-designation of Jewish mysticism as 'tradition' (*qabbalah*). For my own elaboration of these notions, see Federico Dal Bo, *Deconstructing the Talmud: The Absolute Book* (Abingdon: Routledge, 2019), pp. 188–93.

21 On the Pauline implications of this assumption, see Federico Dal Bo, '"L'immediata intensità messianica del cuore". Paolinismo nel *Frammento teologico-politico* di Walter Benjamin', in *Felicità e tramonto*, ed. by Gabriele Guerra and Tamara Tagliacozzo (Macerata: Quodlibet, 2019), pp. 139–52.

22 The concept of *tiqqun ha-'olam* derives from the Rabbinic expression *mipnei tiqqun ha-'olam* (for the sake of the correction of the world) and designates a secular act of social justice — a specific act, which is not strictly motivated by a Scriptural injunction but which has to be pursued for the sake of social welfare. This virtually secular concept is converted into a religious practice and then introduced as such in daily prayers and Jewish mysticism. Accordingly, the *tiqqun ha-'olam* describes the human act of emending the divine world and it is strictly associated with the performance of divine commandments. Among the large bibliography on the subject, see for instance Gilbert S. Rosenthal, 'Tikkun ha-Olam: The Metamorphosis of a Concept', *The Journal of Religion*, 85.2 (2004), pp. 214–40.

And yet this does not mean that Jabès rejects an idea of Jewish literary tradition entirely. While he has clearly relinquished the ideal that Jewish identity shall be moulded by the Jewish canon of the Holy Writ, the Talmud, and their commentaries, he cautiously holds onto the assumption that literature can supply Jewish identity. This persuasion is not an ideal that can teleologically orient someone's life but a sort of desperate effort to reconstruct Jewish identity after the Shoah. Jabès accommodates Jewish identity — by restoring and adapting it — to postmodernity. There is no legal identity based on the Rabbinic tradition, but rather something more complex — the backbone of which is literary and not theological (or at least not theological in a traditional sense).

Jewish tradition is rather a tentative and precarious product that mostly relies on the Jewish writer's syncretic power and the reader's endurance. The latter is constantly being challenged. Jabès's intertextual intricacies are eminently Jewish: they fully belong to the millenary Jewish tradition of writing, quoting, commenting, commenting on commentaries, and so on. Jabès's system of citations is recurrent in the entire text and constitutes its very literary body. There is no main 'work' but rather a 'patchwork' that holds fragments together. Despite all appearance, this is radically different from any ordinary medieval system of commentaries, commentaries on commentaries (supercommentaries), and commentaries on commentaries on commentaries (commentaries on supercommentaries). This traditional, uninterrupted 'chain of tradition' pointed to Scripture, which was the foundation of Judaism. By contrast, Jabès's Jewish literature is severed from Scripture and yet not simply secular. Jabès is rather desperate for transcendence. He clearly relaunches literature as an 'update', if not a modernization of theology. While this resonates with many post-structuralist authors, he examines messianism from the same theologically detached perspective: Scripture is no longer able to communicate a persuasive theological content and yet has transmitted this epistemological need to other modes of writing — especially literature. But how can literature substitute for theology?

Jabès refrains from posing, let alone answering this question. And yet he seems to believe that literature is the means to describe the

Jewish habit or rather the *beau risque* (fine risk) of arguing with God.[23] Judaism would then be able to ascribe a specific purpose to literature — substantiating a legal-theological faculty to litigate with God. One could therefore say that the purpose of literature is messianic insofar as messianism consists in reawakening God to His own duties.

'All Poets Are Жиды'

On the other hand, Jabès devotes the complex *Book of Questions* to a specific purpose: claiming his own identity by force of being a Jew and a writer. Is claiming to be a *Jewish writer* something peculiar, then?

This is the same question that haunted the Romanian-born Jewish poet and translator Paul Celan, who decided to write exclusively in German after experimenting with Romanian in his early poetry.[24] In an epigraph to one of his poems, Celan seems to want to communicate a secret truth about being a Jewish poet who has decided to write poetry in his own mother tongue — German. The ethical and poetic conundrum obviously is that German is the same language that the perpetrators of the Shoah spoke, a language, hence, that contributed to carrying out this *unspeakable task*, and that was manipulated to hide it from the public. Manipulation was achieved, indeed, by literally altering the nature of the German language.[25] In one epigraph to his poem 'Und mit dem Buch aus Tarussa', from his seminal poetical collection

23 There are many examples for this attitude, in both biblical and Talmudic literature. Probably one of the most famous is Abraham negotiating with God about the destruction of Sodom and Gomorrah (Genesis 18. 16–33). The notion of *beau risque* is obliquely introduced in Emmanuel Levinas, *Otherwise than Being, or, Beyond Essence*, trans. by Alphonso Lingis (Pittsburgh, PA: Duquesne University Press, 2013). See especially Paul Davies, 'A Fine Risk: Reading Blanchot Reading Levinas', in *Re-reading Levinas*, ed. by Robert Bernasconi and Simon Critchley (London: Athlone, 1991), pp. 201–26.

24 In his youth, Celan also experimented with writing poems in Romanian. See Federico Dal Bo, *Qabbalah e traduzione. Un saggio su Paul Celan traduttore* (Salerno: Orthotes, 2019), pp. 25–28. See also Barbara Wiedemann, *Antschel Paul — Paul Celan. Studien zum Frühwerk* (Tübingen: Niemeyer, 1985) and the recent monograph by Petre Solomon, *Paul Celan: The Romanian Dimension* (Syracuse, NY: Syracuse University Press, 2019).

25 The most obvious reference is to Victor Klemperer, *The Language of the Third Reich: LTI — Lingua Tertii Imperii; A Philologist's Notebook*, trans. by Martin Brady (London: Continuum, 2007).

Niemandsrose, Celan quotes (and slightly modifies) a verse from the Russian symbolist poet Marina Tsvetaeva's lyric *Poema Kontza* (Poem of the End). The epigraph is in Russian and written in Cyrillic, and therefore impenetrable to whoever is unfamiliar with Russian: 'все поэты жиды.'[26] This typographical choice makes the verse particularly enigmatic, since neither transliteration nor translation are provided. Celan's choice to repeat the Russian poet's verse in Cyrillic alphabet is in no way naive. On the contrary, Celan had a precise reason for doing so: relaunching the enigma of Jewish existence even on a linguistic level. Celan was apparently asking himself what the connection between Judaism and poetry actually was. Does one necessarily follow the other?

The question itself was already challenging, but apparently not challenging enough: Celan elaborated on it and made it even more radical — encrypted in the Cyrillic alphabet, which, like the Russian language, would have been impenetrable to most of Celan's West German readership at the time. Hence, Celan chose to keep the epigraph in Cyrillic for a profound poetic reason: to encode a message that his German readers would never be able to comprehend, unless they had departed from their own Germanness and had questioned their own identity.[27]

Digression: An Ontology of Ethnic Slurs

Perhaps it is necessary to interpret Celan's choice in yet another direction, such that it is not simply a matter of rendering the verse of the poet Tsvetaeva almost illegible to his German readers. Indeed, the use of the Cyrillic alphabet seems to obey an additional poetic task: it

26 Paul Celan, 'Und mit dem Buch aus Tarussa', in Celan, *Werke. Historisch-kritische Ausgabe. I. Abteilung: Lyrik und Prosa*, ed. by Beda Allemann and others, 16 vols (Frankfurt a.M.; Berlin: Suhrkamp, 1990–2017), VI: *Niemandsrose*, ed. by Axel Gellhaus, Holger Gehle, Andreas Lohr, and Rolf Bücher (Frankfurt a.M.: Suhrkamp, 2001), pp. 89–91 (p. 89). Cf. also *Kommentar zu Paul Celans 'Die Niemandsrose'*, ed. by Jürgen Lehmann and Christine Ivanovic (Heidelberg: Winter, 1997), pp. 353–67. Tsvetaeva's verse originally was: 'Поэты — жиды!', or 'Poets — Jews!' (Marina Tsvetaeva, *Poema Kantza* (Moscow: Directmedia, 2012), p. 149). For a more accurate translation of this verse, see below.

27 On these topics, see Dal Bo, *Qabbalah e traduzione*, pp. 63–64.

indicates, in a metalinguistic way, the most authentic content of the verse that says something about the connection between Judaism and poetry. After all, the Russian epigraph — 'все поэты жиды' — can be translated, at first, in quite ordinary terms as: 'all poets are Jews.'

Tsvetaeva wrote this verse while the Nazi armies were relentlessly pushing into Russia. The verse suggests that she identified with the fate of the Jewish people and with that of her Jewish husband, the Russian poet Sergei Jakowlewitsch Efron, who was a former officer of White Army during the Russian civil war and then agent for the Soviet secret services, and who had been executed by Soviet authorities under the false accusation of being an agent of Trotsky. One should not ignore the fact that this accusation truly was the Soviet 'translation' of anti-Semitism and that it mobilized the catastrophic prejudice against the Jews as 'agents of internationalism.'[28] In this respect, his wife Tsvetaeva was also tapping into this internationalist charge in her verse: she was claiming a universal — and, therefore, transcultural if not 'international' — stigmatization of 'all poets'. As Celan decides to mobilize this assumption in Cyrillic, a quite similar allegiance about a sort of spiritual 'internationalism' connecting all poets is at work. Yet, there is a subtle but decisive difference: this claim has been made untransparent and further encrypted within an alphabet that is impenetrable to most Western readers.

This identification, however, was not ethnic, but rather poetic. It was not a matter of circumcision — from which she would anyway be excluded as a woman — but rather a matter of understanding that poetry is necessarily condemned to persecution and rejection. Again, Tsvetaeva was not Jewish but married to a Jew. Consequently, a metaphorical interpretation of her verse, used as an epigraph by Celan, is inevitable: Tsvetaeva was not *literally* Jewish but was a poet, and therefore understood herself as *metaphorically* Jewish. The choice to report the epigraph in Cyrillic then is metalinguistic: Celan apparently used the Cyrillic alphabet to reinstitute a linguistic difference between him-

28 On this, see Paul Lendevai, *Anti-Semitism Without Jews: Communist Eastern Europe* (New York: Doubleday, 1971), and especially Cathy Gelbin and Sander Gilman, *Cosmopolitanisms and the Jews* (Ann Arbor: University of Michigan Press, 2017), pp. 189–90.

self and his readers. In so doing, he intended to underline a difference he took to be not only cultural but also ethnic.

The choice to rely not only on the Russian language but also on the Cyrillic alphabet seems to follow the desire to highlight a constitutive difference between languages — especially between the persecutors' German language and a language that is spoken by the persecuted. Only to those who can read Russian will the connotation of the epigraph be clear. Only those who know Russian well enough can understand the violence intrinsic to this verse and the derogatory use of the noun *жид* (*žid*), which can only euphemistically be translated as 'Jew' and actually is strongly pejorative in a Russian context, although it was reappropriated and used in a neutral, non-derogatory way by Ukrainian Jews.[29] Hence, Tsvetaeva's verse should rather be translated as follows: 'all poets are kikes.'[30]

Yet, this is not all. Translation can be deceiving. Slurs and profanities are usually excommunicated from poetic language but they have an intrinsic ontology that is only expressed more harshly and unforgivingly. Derogatory terms for Jews often hide a deeper quantum of violence, and this becomes particularly apparent when they are addressed from an etymological point of view. For instance, English derogatory terms for Germans and Italians might point to alimentary habits or fashion that are perceived as odd or ridiculous, as is the case with the offensive terms *kraut* or *greaseball*. As offensive as they might be, these terms imply that the lack of uniformity with 'the majority of people' mostly depends on specific habits that are stigmatized: eating too much sauerkraut or using too much hair wax. Such offensive terms might even be taken to imply that, once these obstacles have been removed, assimilation would then be possible.[31]

29 Karel C. Berkhoff, *Harvest of Despair: Death in Ukraine under Nazi Rule* (Cambridge, MA: The Belknap Press of Harvard University Press, 2004), pp. 60–61.

30 This harsh translation is uncommon among commentators, who usually read this verse euphemistically as 'all poets are Jews' or 'all poets are Yids'. I am following here Michael Eskin's suggestion in Eskin, *Poetic Affairs: Celan, Grünbein, Brodsky* (Stanford, CA: Stanford University Press, 2008), p. 192n6. See also the German translation *Alle Dichter sind Jidden*, as suggested in Wolfgang Emmerich, *Nahe Fremde: Paul Celan und die Deutschen* (Göttingen: Wallstein Verlag, 2020), p. 21.

31 On these themes, see Federico Dal Bo, *Il linguaggio della violenza. Estremismo e ideologia nella filosofia contemporanea* (Bologna: Biblioteca Clueb, 2021), pp. 21–58.

On the contrary, the derogatory terms for Jews blatantly point to ethnicity itself — the sheer fact of *being Jewish*. This is what clearly appears in many pejorative terms for 'Jew' in several European languages. For instance, the English term *kike* has an obscure etymology but was apparently used by educated American Jews to stigmatize illiterate East European Jews and was then generalized as an insult for all Jewish people.[32] On the other hand, just like the Russian *жид* (*žid*), the deeply offensive French term *youpin* as well as its variants *youp* or *youd* point directly to Jewish ethnicity and are a deformation of an abbreviated form from the Arabic-Algerian derogatory term يهودي (*yahūdiyy*).[33] Each and all of these terms only denigrate a Jew for an ontological condition — *being a Jew*.

Again, this scandalous verse stays veiled or even hidden from the general public of Celan's poem. The typographical difference imposed by the Cyrillic alphabet seems to allude to a difference with respect to other Western languages. However, one should consider the subtle transformation to which Tsvetaeva's verse is subjected, especially when it is used as an epigraph by a Jewish, German-speaking poet. On the one hand, Tsvetaeva's verse should have only a metaphorical meaning. On the other hand, Tsvetaeva's verse is quoted *in Russian* by Celan, who clearly is both Jewish and a poet — who has survived the Shoah. Hence, Tsvetaeva's verse acquires a new meaning in this context. In this respect, the use of the Cyrillic alphabet also seems to reduce Tsvetaeva's metaphorical understanding to a potentially literal one: as

32 Karen Stollznow, *On the Offensive: Prejudice in Language Past and Present* (Cambridge: Cambridge University Press, 2020), pp. 128–29. Cf. also Joachim Prinz, 'Amerika — hast Du es besser? Notizen von einer Reise', *Der Morgen. Monatsschrift der Juden in Deutschland*, 13.3 (1937/38), pp. 104–11 (p. 110). Another folk etymology suggests that the term might come from the Yiddish קיקעלע (*kikele*), 'little circle', possible designating the sign 'O', which was used by illiterate Jews who could not properly write their own name but wanted to avoid using the conventional 'X' as it would resemble a Cross. Cf. Leo Rosten, *The New Joys of Yiddish: Completely Updated* (New York: Three Rivers Press, 2010), p. 177.

33 More specifically, the French-Argot term *youpin* consists of two discrete linguistic elements: the abridgement *you* from the Arabic derogatory term يهودي (*yahūdiyy*) — also reflecting the neutral Hebrew term יהודי (*yehudi*) or the Aramaic יהודיא (*yehudaya'*) — and the Argot suffix *-pin*. Cf. Napoléon Hayard, *Dictionnaire Argot-Français* (Paris: Dentu, 1907), p. 40; cf. also Graciela Christ, *Arabismen im Argot: ein Beitrag zur französischen Lexikographie ab der zweiten Hälfte des 19. Jahrhunderts* (Berlin: Peter Lang, 1991), p. 551.

a result, there is a passage from culture to ethnicity, from the Gentiles to the Jews — the former being the persecutors and the latter being the persecuted.

Celan made a very complex poetic choice. His use of Tsvetaeva's verse in its original Russian within a German poem raises some epistemological problems. When Tsvetaeva argued that 'all poets are kikes', she was alluding to a particular ethnicity that had typically suffered from epochal persecution. At the same time, she was also generalizing that very condition to every poet by assuming, in metaphorical terms, that every poet would be persecuted as if s/he were Jewish and stigmatized for the same reason. Tsvetaeva's verse, while written in Cyrillic for Russian readers, was as transparent as it was metaphorical. The metaphorical nature of this verse — its metaphoricity — was transparent to every Russian reader. On the other hand, Celan reversed these poetical coordinates in force of his Jewish ethnicity, his personal history of persecution, and his quotation of Tsvetaeva's verse in Cyrilic as an epigraph to a German poem. This verse was now transformed into an epigraph that only few could read. Tsvetaeva's metaphorical truth on poetry was now distilled, encrypted, and turned into an almost literal statement — at least with respect to Paul Celan as a Jewish poet. Yet, this operation — reversing the poetic coordinates of Tsvetaeva's verse — was not intended to be destructive. It rather complicated or, better put, deconstructed Tsvetaeva's metaphor and distilled a new, particular truth from her generalizing verse.

When quoted by Celan with Cyrillic letters at the beginning of his German-language poem, Tsvetaeva's verse is essentially raw and impenetrable. There is a sort of a hardness to the palate that implicitly alludes to the need for maintaining a distance between the language that hosts this verse (Russian) and the language into which it could eventually be translated (German). This complexity creates an enigma: the epigraph can be read only by those who can read Russian and understand the biographical and poetic presuppositions in both Tsvetaeva and Celan. This enigma is offered to the reader and retracted from them: German is the language of the persecutors, but the content of persecution — 'all poets are kikes' — can be revealed and simultaneously hidden only in another language. Yet this other language, coming to the rescue, is also the language of the persecutor, and therefore seems, once again, to impair the persecuted: the Jew is not only a 'Jew', but above all a 'kike'. The consequences are dire: literature can only encrypt a destiny of persecution but cannot save from it.

'All Poets Are Kikes'

This long digression is instrumental in understanding the proportions of Jabès's poetics of writing and finding an implicit if not covert angle for shedding light on his implicit theology of identity as it emerges from his main character: Yukel. Despite its biblical sound, the name *Yukel* is never to be found in traditional Jewish sources. And yet, the name is not a simple invention but rather a complex wordplay on the question of Jewish identity, anti-Semitism, and poetics.

Understanding the deep theological nature of this invention also requires appreciating an intricate wordplay that has escaped the attention of many commentators on Jabès's work. Unlike Tsvetaeva, who claims that 'all poets are kikes', Jabès has never made such a bold statement and never used the equivalent derogatory French *youpin*. Yet, as a commentator suggested, the name *Yukel* would bear a small linguistic secret within it:

> this name of a foreigner opens on a rare syllable in French, *Yu*, which makes think of *Youpin* or *Yid*, a syllable that astonishes by its rarity as that which has fallen into disuse, like an old car in the Place de la Concorde. [34]

And yet, the suggestion that the name *Yukel* should be understood against the background of the French derogatory term *youpin* is not enough. This fictional name is much more than that. Indeed, *Yukel* carries a strange, provocative theophoric meaning due to its composite nature. This name joins together two different linguistic segments: the ordinary Hebrew name of 'God' (*El*) and the French derogatory term *youpin,* reduced to the unusual French syllable *yu-*. The name that emerges from this transcultural wordplay would then conflate Jewish

34 Helena Shillony, *Edmond Jabès: Une rhétorique de la subversion* (Paris: Lettres modernes, 1991), pp. 20–21. The same notion is also repeated in Emmanuel Godo, *La prière de l'écrivain* (Paris: Imago, 2000), p. 23; my translation.

identity, anti-Semitism, and poetics into a single entity — the name *Yukel* — and carry a deep theological meaning with it.

In Jabès's fiction, Yukel is a writer. One should also pay attention to Yukel's similarity to another name: *Yechiel* (God shall live). More precisely, the name *Yukel* sounds like a deformation of *Yechiel.* This old theophoric biblical name is grafted — or inscribed — with the French pejorative *youpin* and finally transformed into *Yukel.* The resulting name calls into question the nature of writing itself. Should the main character have been called after the traditional name *Yechiel,* one could easily have concluded that his profession as a writer — writing on the Book of Life and perpetuating the goodness of Creation — is quite noble. Alas, this writer is not called *Yechiel* but rather *Yukel.* So, he is called after a deformed theophoric name that has removed the original vitality of God from the act of writing. More radically, this deformation carries the stigma, humiliation, and denigration that come from the French derogatory term *youpin,* since this term has been grafted within the old theophoric name *Yechiel,* deforming it into *Yukel.* It is as if Jabès, while inventing this para-biblical name, wanted God to truly acknowledge that His people are nothing more than *youpins* — 'kikes'.

When interpreted against this grim background, the enigmatic character *Yukel* allows one to understand that Jabès too claims that 'all writers are kikes' — or, at least, that 'all writers are Jews'. This claim is maintained several times — especially when Jabès speaks about the difficulty of both being Jewish and writing:

> — I told you my words. I have spoken to you about the difficulty of being Jewish, which is confounded with the difficulty of writing; for both Judaism and writing are nothing but the same waiting, the same hope, the same attrition.[35]

The reasons for this identity are neither ethnic nor cultural but metaphysical. In this most Christian of worlds, both writers and Jews share a deserted solitude — a detachment from the world that simultaneously is the condition and the price of writing. Jabès does not thereby claim something particularly new; he rather rephrases a famous *midrash* that

35 Jabès, *Le Livre des questions,* p. 218: '— Je vous ai rapporté mes paroles. Je vous ai parlé de la difficulté d'être Juif, qui se confond avec la difficulté d'écrire; car le judaïsme et l'écriture ne sont qu'une même attente, un même espoir, une même usure.'

postulates the presence of the 'word' (*davar*) of God who 'speaks' (*medabber*) in the midst of the 'desert' (*midbar*).[36] And yet there is a supplementary similarity between Jewishness and writing, which would also clarify Jabès's previous assertion that his mother tongue is fundamentally foreign to him. Such a similarity is not explicit but only alluded to in a short, apparently occasional biographical remark:

> Born on 16 April in Cairo, my father inadvertently declared to the consular authorities charged with recording the act of my birth that I was born on the 14th of the same month. Do I unconsciously owe to this miscalculation the feeling that forty-eight hours have always separated me from my life? The two days added to mine cannot be experienced except in death.[37]

This curious mistake seems to provide Jabès with a subtle deconstruction of the Jewish notion of fatherhood and opens toward a complex appreciation of writing as a maternal dimension of existence and writing.

'The Day of My Circumcision'

At first glance, the anecdote seems to convey a trivial mistake Jabès's father made in front of an Egyptian clerk: a simple misunderstanding about his son's date of birth. And yet this mistake seems, much more profoundly, to be a parody of circumcision and its ritual arrangements.

36 These wordplays rely on the homography between the (unvocalized) Hebrew terms *davar* (word) and *dever* (plague), on the one hand, and between the Hebrew noun *midbar* (desert) and the present participle *medaber* (literally 'speaking') from the Hebrew verb *diber* (to speak), on the other hand. For a linguistic treatment of these notions see again Dal Bo, *The Lexical Field of the Substantives of 'Word' in Ancient Hebrew* and James Barr, *Semantics of Biblical Language* (Oxford: Oxford University Press, 2004). On the notion of *davar* from a theological-historical point of view, see, for instance, Piero Capelli, 'La parola creatrice secondo il giudaismo della tarda antichità', in *La parola creatrice in India e nel Medio Oriente. Atti del Seminario della Facoltà di Lettere dell'Università di Pisa, 29–31 maggio 1991*, ed. by Caterina Conio, 2 vols (Pisa: Giardini, 1994), I, pp. 155–72. For a theological treatment, see André Neher, *The Exile of the Word: From the Silence of the Bible to the Silence of Auschwitz* (Philadelphia, PA: Jewish Publishing Society, 1980).

37 Edmond Jabès, *Elya*, in *Il libro delle interrogazioni*, pp. 1020–1195 (p. 1145): 'Né le 16 avril, au Caire, mon père par inadvertance, aux autorités consulaires chargées d'établir mon acte de naissance, me déclara né le 14 du même mois. Dois-je inconsciemment à cette erreur de calcul, le sentiment que quarante-huit heures m'ont toujours séparé de ma vie? Les deux jours ajoutés aux miens ne pouvaient être vécus que dans la mort.'

What is circumcision if not the process of *inscribing* someone into the people of Israel? It is a sort of ethnic pact signed with flesh and blood. Indeed, when the father brings his son to the *mohel* (the circumciser), he does not simply indulge in an ancient tribal pact; more subtly, he delivers him to a very peculiar kind of writing that eventually inscribes his son's affiliation to Judaism by removing his foreskin — by impressing into his flesh the very same Abrahamic pact that has been marked in this fashion for many generations.

Another digression is necessary to appreciate the metaphysical nature of circumcision in Jabès and its impact on literature. I will in particular consider the figure of Elisha ben Abuyah — a master from the Talmud who was revered as a great scholar and yet apostatized, and who therefore was designated as *Acher*, or 'the other one'.[38] An impressive narrative from the Jerusalem Talmud provides a short piece of biography on Elisha that describes his father dedicating his son to Scripture for the sake of its mighty power:

> [my] daddy, Abuyah (abuyah abba), was one of the great people in Jerusalem. On the day he came to have me circumcised (be-yom she-ba le-mohaleyinyi), he called all the great people in Jerusalem and made them sit in one room [with] Rabbi Eliezer and Rabbi Yehoshua in another room. After they had eaten and drunk, they [began] stamping [their feet] and dancing. Rabbi Eliezer said to Rabbi Yehoshua: while they are keeping us busy in their way, let's keep us busy in our way, let's sit and occupy ourselves with the words of Scripture, from the Torah to the Prophets and from the Prophets to the Writings. And fire fell down from the skies and surrounded them. Abuyah said to them: My rabbis, have you come to burn my house down around me? They said to him: God forbid! Rather, we are sitting and examining the words of Scripture from the Torah to the Prophets, and from the Prophets to the Writings, and [these] words were animated as when they were given to us from Sinai and the fire shone around us as it was shone from Sinai, and principally [Scripture] was not given to us from Sinai

38 On the nature of Elisha ben Abuyah's transgression, see David M. Grossberg, *Heresy and the Formation of the Rabbinic Community* (Tübingen: Mohr Siebeck, 2017), pp. 167–92. See also Federico Dal Bo, 'Legal and Transgressive Sex, Heresy, and Hermeneutics in the Talmud: The Cases of Bruriah, Rabbi Meir, Elisha ben Abuyah and the Prostitute', in *Jewish Law and Academic Discipline: Contributions from Europe*, ed. by Elisha Ancselovits and George Wilkes (Liverpool: Deborah Charles, 2016), pp. 128–51.

> except in fire and on a mountain with flames [that reached] the skies. My daddy, Abuyah, said to them: My rabbis, if such is the power of Scripture, let's consecrate him (meprisho) [my son] to Scripture.[39]

Again, the historical reliability of this narrative is not as important as its evocative power. The narrative does not only add details to Elisha's biography; it also reports them in the first person: 'On the day he came to have me circumcised...'. An extreme perspective is then assumed here: Elisha reports in the first person the day of his own circumcision, and therefore the day in which he *was born* to the Jewish faith. Yet this event — being circumcised as an infant — cannot properly be narrated in the first-person perspective. If it is performed at the right time, on the eighth day after birth, then no one can remember the day of his own circumcision, just as no one can remember the day of their own birth. In a stringent Jewish perspective, the ritual of circumcision is to be performed shortly after birth and predates any possible experience or rather establishes the very possibility of experience of being Jewish. One's birth and circumcision are as remote and inaccessible as one's own death. There is no actual memory of any of these experiences. No *autobiographical account* — of one's own birth, circumcision, or death — is possible.

And yet the narrative from the Jerusalem Talmud is told in the first person, just as is Jabès's narrative about his father recording his birth certificate. The Talmud assumes here an extreme perspective, which is also a perspective of extremes. Circumcision should be narrated from an objective, external perspective, as a historical fact. For instance, compare what is said about Jesus: 'and when eight days were accomplished for the circumcising of the child, his name was called Jesus, which was so named of the angel before he was conceived in the womb'

39 Jerusalem Talmud, Tractate Chagigah, 2. 1, fol. 9b, my translation: 'אבויה אבא מגדולי ירושלם היה ביום שבא למוהליני קרא לכל גדולי ירושלם והושיבן בבית אחד ולרבי אליעזר ולר' יהושע בבית אחד מן דאכלון ושתון שרון מטפחין ומרקדקין א"ר ליעזר לר' יהושע עד דאינון עסיקין בדידהון נעסוק אנן בידן וישבו ונתעסקו בדברי תורה מן התורה לנביאים ומן הנביאים לכתובים וירדה אש מן השמים והקיפה אותם אמר להן אבויה רבותיי מה באתם לשרוף את ביתי עלי אמרו לו חס ושלום אלא יושבין היינו וחוזרין בדברי תורה מן התורה לנביאים ומן הנביאים לכתובים והיו הדברים שמיחים כנתינתן מסיני והיתה האש מלחכת אותן כלחיכתן מסיני ועיקר נתינתן מסיני לא ניתנו אלא באש וההר בוער באש עד לב השמים אמר להן אבויה אבא רבותיי אם כך היא כוחה של תורה אם נתקיים לי בן הזה לתורה אני מפרישו'. This passage has parallels also in Ruth Rabbah 6. 6, Qohelet Rabbah 7. 18, and only partially in the Babylonian Talmud, Tractate Chagigah foll. 15a–b.

(Luke 2. 21). The 'documentary effect' is provided by the narration in the third person. The Gospel here implicitly admits that circumcision falls beyond the limits of their own experience for whoever it befalls, even when the person it befalls is Jesus. There can be no personal narration of this event. Therefore, circumcision is an extreme experience and necessarily escapes the possibilities of any autobiography.

In contradistinction, Elisha assumes an extreme perspective on himself and explicitly speaks about the day of his circumcision as if he had witnessed it himself. Yet one should not mistake this personal narrative for ordinary biography. Circumcision does not name an ordinary date in one's life but rather posits the very 'day' (*yom*) from which one's spiritual life begins — the eighth day. Therefore, narrating one's own circumcision in the first person is not simply a rhetorical device; it constitutes a superhuman act, for it means taking for oneself the power over the *entirety* of one's *life*— from one extreme to the other, from birth to death, from spiritual birth to spiritual death, and from circumcision to apostasy. Indeed, it should not be forgotten that Elisha eventually apostatized and left Judaism, possibly following a kind of religious Gnostic conversion. The nature of Elisha's apostasy is a matter of scholarly dispute and is less relevant here than his general behaviour towards his former co-religionists, and especially towards his pupil Rabbi Meir, which is explored in yet another famous narrative from the Babylonian Talmud:

> [O]ur Rabbis taught: there was [once] a matter regarding Acher, as he was riding on a horse on Sabbath and Rabbi Meir was walking behind him to learn Torah from his mouth. [Acher] said to him: Meir, go back, because I have already measured by the paces of my horse that thus far extends the Sabbath limit. [Meir] said to him: You, too, go back! [Acher] said to him: And haven't I already said to you that I have already heard from behind the Veil: Return you backsliding children — except for Acher? [40]

40 Babylonian Talmud, Tractate Chagigah, fol. 15a; my translation: 'ת"ר מעשה באחר שהיה רוכב על הסוס בשבת והיה רבי מאיר מהלך אחריו ללמוד תורה מפיו אמר לו מאיר חזור לאחריך שכבר שיערתי בעקבי סוסי עד כאן תחום שבת א"ל אף אתה חזור בך א"ל ולא כבר אמרתי לך כבר שמעתי מאחורי הפרגוד שובו בנים שובבים חוץ מאחר'.

This is an important text since it shows that the Talmud can be quite tolerant with respect to someone's idiosyncrasies. Rabbi Meir is described as still full of reverence for Elisha and he keeps studying with Elisha, despite Elisha's apostasy and patent transgression of the Shabbat, which involves riding a horse on this holy day and also transgressing the limits of movement prescribed by Jewish law. The details about Elisha's last words are telling. At first, it seems that God Himself has spoken from beyond the Veil — a structure separating the material from the supernal world — and argued that Elisha could not repent. The Jerusalem Talmud too tells a very similar story but argues that this utterance 'from behind the Veil' (*mi-acharey ha-pargod*) actually is a 'divine voice from the Holy of Holies' (*bat qol mi-qodesh qodashim*) that explicitly exempts 'Elisha ben Abuyah' from repenting.[41]

Many commentators overlook this narrative and simply reiterate the idea that Elisha has sinned to such an extent that any repentance is no longer possible. Yet a modern commentator on the Talmud — the late Hungarian-born and Shoah survivor Rabbi Yehuda Amital (1924–2010), who was the founder and director of the Yeshivat Har Etzion (Gush Etzion, Israel), a prominent public figure in Israel, and the recipient of the Israel Prize in 1991 — offers a more intriguing interpretation of the passage. Taking into account the difference between the narratives in the Babylonian Talmud and the Jerusalem Talmud, he elaborates on Elisha's final words and especially on the assumption that Elisha could not repent, as Elisha tells his pupil. Rabbi Amital elaborates on the Hebrew expression 'except for Acher' (*chutz mi-Acher*) and interprets it literally as 'except everybody else'. Rabbi Amital argues that nobody else but Acher could actually have heard this statement about his inability to repent. Accordingly, Rabbi Amital writes: 'he alone heard this voice; he essentially convinced himself that this was his situation' (*hu mi-'atzmam shachna' et 'atzmo she-zeh matzabo*).[42] The mythological 'divine voice' speaking 'from behind the Veil' would

41 Jerusalem Talmud, Tractate Chagigah 2. 1, fol. 9b.

42 Rabbi Yehudah Amital, 'Shabbat conversation', accessible online: <http://etzion.gush.net/vbm/archive/5-sichot/48hazinu.php> [accessed 3 April 2022]. This oral interpretation was written down by Rav Matan Gliday (Yeshivat Neve Shmuel, Te'ena, Israel). I came across this commentary in a page from the prominent website *Mi Yodeya* <https://judaism.stackexchange.com/questions/104020/elisha-ben-abuya-and-repentance> [accessed 31 January 2021]. Cf. also Rabbi Yehuda Amital, *Jewish Values*

then be a sort of euphemistic expression for suggesting that Elisha has convinced himself not to be worthy of repentance, and therefore to be beyond forgiveness.

In this respect, the conviction of being beyond forgiveness was Elisha's major sin. While assuming that he had heard a 'divine voice' admonishing him not to repent, Elisha was granting to himself a divine prerogative: forgiveness. One should treat Elisha's conviction carefully. It was not humbleness that had persuaded him that he could never be forgiven for his sins. It was rather a sort of Nietzschean sentiment of loving his own life to the extreme — even more than God Himself. As he assumed that God could never forgive him, Elisha was withdrawing himself from a dimension of repentance and entering a dimension of total ownership — in the legal and theological senses of the expression. He had become the only master of his life. He was claiming his life — from the day of his circumcision to damnation — for himself and for himself alone. There was a sort of grim *amor fati* protruding from his stubborn and superb assumption that God could never forgive him. The question was not a silly one — whether there is a sin greater than God's forgiveness — but rather a radical one: should/could one claim for oneself the entirety of one's life — regardless of its negativity?

In the process of speaking about his own circumcision, Elisha stretched his self beyond his own biographical limits. He claimed the ability to fully comprehend himself as a human being, as a man of faith, and as a first-person narrator. In other words, Elisha's entire self is stretched beyond the limits of 'literature' — to which both biography and autobiography famously belong. Perhaps Derrida was right when he argued, while deconstructing Augustine's influential *Confessions* in his semi-autobiographical 'Circumfession', that biography is no longer a literary genre, although it was once the gem of classical literature.[43] Confessions, stories, biographies, and autobiographies assume that there is an unspoiled origin of life: a source from which it is possible to develop, sort out, and write down a narration about oneself or

in a Changing World (Jersey City, NJ: KTAV Publishing House, 2005), pp. 112, 139, and 223–24.

43 Jacques Derrida, 'Circumfession', in Jacques Derrida and Geoffrey Bennington, *Jacques Derrida*, trans. by Geoffrey Bennington (Chicago: University of Chicago Press, 1993), pp. 3–315.

about others. In many respects, the Writ itself is a sort of a gigantic autobiography that God delivered both to Himself and His people. The well-known radical kabbalistic assumption that Scripture would only be a single name of God is only the most conspicuous aspect of this notion, with the more subtle implication that a confession is a perpetual, interminable work.[44]

Yet there is a paradox here: there has never been an unspoiled origin for the Self. Psychoanalysis is quite eloquent about this. It has educated us to believe that Self has never been a primary entity but rather the construct of, if not the negotiation between, two unconscious dimensions: the id and the superego. In this respect, the deep nature of the mind is unconscious and therefore unsusceptible to expression in words. Consequently, there is no primordial source for narration. Therefore, each biography is structurally uncertain. In his 'Circumfession', Derrida has elaborated on the connection between biography and theology:

> Saint Augustine, of whom I read that 'having returned to God, he probably never confessed, in the modern sense of the word', never having had, any more than I, beyond even truth, 'the opportunity to confess', which precisely does not prevent him from working at the delivery of literary confessions, i.e. at a form of theology as autobiography.[45]

Derrida has shown that every biography is an art of confession to God, just as autobiography is an art of confession to oneself; he has also shown that this almost chiastic connection is not harmonious but rather interrupted by a primordial wound that is eloquently described by the homography between the Hebrew words for 'word' (*milah*) and 'circumcision' (*milah*): 'circumcision as retrenchment, mark, determination, exclusion, whence the impossibility of writing, whence the interminable reflection, whence the infinite delay'.[46]

44 See the excellent contribution Francesco Giusti, 'An Interminable Work? The Openness of Augustine's Confessions', in *Openness in Medieval Europe*, ed. by Manuele Gragnolati and Almut Suerbaum, Cultural Inquiry, 23 (Berlin: ICI Berlin Press, 2022), pp. 23–43 <https://doi.org/10.37050/ci-23_02>.

45 Derrida, 'Circumfession', pp. 86–87.

46 Ibid., p. 276.

When Elisha takes upon himself the narration of the day of his circumcision, he practices an extreme art of confession. If one joins together two narratives, as it is customary in Talmudic exegesis, one can even conclude that Elisha places himself within an impossible memory of his own circumcision while also heroically accepting his perdition as an apostate: 'haven't I already said to you that I have already heard from behind the Veil: "Return you backsliding children — except for Acher?"'. Elisha holds in his hands both extremes of his life — his own spiritual birth as well as his own spiritual death — and in this sense his apostasy is radical: he makes an example of himself; he refuses to conform to what others would call 'truth and tradition'; he rejects his own possibility of redemption.

Keeping in mind the Talmudic narrative of Elisha and the day of his circumcision, I can now return to Jabès and his anecdote about his father making a mistake about the day of his birth. From Elisha's radical perspective, it is ironic if not grotesque to read that Jabès's father made a mistake and recorded his son's birthday in the daily register of newborns as being two days earlier than it actually was. In this sense, *registering* his son's birthday — *writing* it *down* — predates the actual birth, two days later. And consider this: recording his son's birthday two days before his actual birth is not simply a serious mistake with some serious administrative ramifications; it is also, and foremost, a *deep* mistake due to the complex connection between biography and writing. Besides, registering someone's birthday is a form of an inscription that is inherently connected, in the case of Jewish male existence, once more with circumcision. Derrida eloquently wrote: 'for want of an immediately available surface of inscription, without knowing if they were being inscribed elsewhere, nor what remains once the surface of inscription has been buried, like foreskin or moleskin'.[47] When treated not as an ordinary mistake but rather as a Freudian slip, registering his own son with a false date or falsely 'inscribing' his name in the register suggests an event transcending the episodical and the individual: any kind of writing — like *recording* someone into a list of births — necessarily predates any kind of actual birth. In other terms, writing — like *recording* someone in the Book of Life

47 Ibid., p. 158.

— *anticipates* life. This constitutes then a curious inversion of two assumptions that traditionally surround the act of circumcision: that it takes place eight days *after* the actual birth and that writing — like the act of circumcision itself — can only follow an actual, biological birth.

Jabès's Mother Tongue

It is then not surprising that Jabès interprets his father's trivial mistake in metaphysical terms and possibly uses it to suggest a revolution of the ordinary notion of writing. In one of his last works, *The Book of Dividing*, Jabès briefly mentions the possibility that there is a 'maternal writing' (*écriture maternelle*) just like there is 'mother tongue' (*langue maternelle*):

> As everybody knows, there is a mother tongue, the first language we learn that is spoken by us. With this truism in mind, can we declare that there is a 'motherly' writing, a common writing, pages of our early beginnings? A child's first writings are an apprenticeship in writing and not worried about rediscovering the original text: the text that generates texts to be written, although it always escapes us, never ceases to haunt us.[48]

Again, Jabès argues here in metaphysical terms. He argues that there might be a 'maternal writing' (*écriture maternelle*) that can never be fully present to itself, that 'haunts' us while generating 'text to be written', and that is always 'escaping' us. At first, these are considerations that try to explore the dimension of writing in terms analogous to the dimension of language.

Yet, it is not difficult to appreciate here an echo of Julia Kristeva's seminal notion of *chora* and especially the distinction — or even opposition — that she has famously established between writing and

48 Edmond Jabès, *Le Livre du partage* (Paris: Gallimard, 1987), p. 46: 'Il y a — chacun le sait — une langue maternelle, la première langue apprise, parlée par nous. Fort de ce truisme, pouvons-nous déclarer qu'il y a une écriture "maternelle", un écrit commun, pages de nos premiers balbutiements? Les premiers écrits d'un enfant sont apprentissage d'écriture et non souci de redécouvrir le texte d'origine: le texte générateur de textes à écrire, bien que nous échappant toujours, ne cesse de nous hanter.'

language. In many respects, Jabès's notion of *la page blanche*, the 'blank page', owes much to Kristeva's claim that an author — a writer! — has to become anonymous, if not an absence or 'a blank space', so that text as such may eventually exist.[49] Similarly, Jabès seems to echo her assumption that the dimensions of writing and language do not overlap, since the latter is 'inscribed' in the former.[50] The dimension of writing would precisely be a 'maternal' dimension — just as the dimension of language would be a 'foreign' one. By mistakenly recording his son's date of birth, making it two days late, Jabès's father committed a serious mistake: he confirmed the impossibility of belonging to Judaism solely by means of circumcision — whose Hebrew term *milah* is a homograph that also refers to 'word', as discussed above. In this respect, there is a structural difference between a 'maternal writing' that generates texts that still have to be written and the 'word' (*milah*) by which these texts, perpetually generated by a 'maternal writing', have to be written — a word, furthermore, that can be compared to the act of 'circumcision' (*milah*). This allusion to the *milah* as both 'word' and 'circumcision' probably is the key to the enigmatic epigraph opening *The Book of Questions*: 'mark the first page of the book with a red bookmark, since in the beginning, the wound is invisible.'[51] Hence, Jabès's father made an — unconscious — mistake that proved that one belongs to Judaism specifically by means of writing a 'word' (*milah*), just as every Jewish male also belongs to Judaism by undergoing 'circumcision' (*milah*). Nevertheless, Jabès seems to argue against his father's mistake by claiming that there is a female, maternal writing that predates every spoken word — a writing that is inherently female, cut out from an incision into the flesh, just as circumcision actually is, a word carved as wound or a wound carved out as word.

And yet, the dimension of 'motherhood' should not be imagined as follows:

---

49 See Julia Kristeva, *Desire in Language: A Semiotic Approach to Literature and Art*, trans. by Leon Roudiez (New York: Columbia University Press, 1980), p. 75.

50 I am following here Steven Jaron, 'Le Remaniement', in *Edmond Jabès: l'éclosion des énigmes*, ed. by Daniel Lançon and Catherine Mayaux (Saint-Denis: Presses Universitaires de Vincennes, 2008), pp. 17–28. Cf. also Tsivia Wygoda Frank, *Edmond Jabès and the Archaeology of the Book: Text, Pre-Texts, Contexts* (Berlin: De Gruyter, 2022).

51 Jabès, *Le Livre des questions*, p. 7: 'Marque d'un signet rouge la première page du livre, car la blessure est invisible à son commencement.'

> Yukel reported the story of that blind woman who, far away from her family, raised the son who she had delivered to the world. And he compared the destiny of this woman to that of the writer and that of the Jew, bound, by a pledge, to the land of his forefathers but separated from it by the eyes and the legs…[52]

Jabès here points to the constitutive blindness of a 'maternal writing' (*écriture maternelle*) as the dark, inaccessible source for 'words' — even the words for confessing to God Himself.[53] In the unsettling metaphor, writing is a mother whose words cannot be read but only delivered and disseminated, as wounds. The metaphor does not explore the possibility that words could be written with a tactile writing system like Braille, such that the mother's words — the words of writing — could be accessed physically by touching them.

This fascinating suggestion escapes the poetic economy of Jabès, who rather conceives the dimension of writing within a stringent metaphysics of light, which obviously resonates with Scripture: 'on the threshold of the seventh day, God closed the envelope of the world, where the stars gleamed, and closed it with His seal, which man calls by the blinding name: sun.'[54] Let us consider once more the metaphor at stake here: 'maternal writing' is a blind mother who writes but will never be able to read 'her' own 'words'. If it is so, the question that arises is whether the metaphysics of light literally is the 'last word'on Creation. Apparently, Jabès does not think so. A writer is someone who inscribes words as wounds. These words, which can never be read, come from his inaccessible blind mother, who cannot see the sun as the seal of Creation. In this perspective, light is only another form of

52 Edmond Jabès, *Le Livre de Yukel*, in *Il libro delle interrogazioni*, pp. 327–590 (p. 557): 'Yukel rapporta l'histoire de la femme aveugle qui éleva, loin de sa famille, les fils qu'elle avait donné au monde. Et il compara le destin de cette femme à celui de l'écrivain et à celui du Juif rivé, par un vœu, à la terre de ses aïeux, mais séparé d'elle par les yeux et les jambes…'.

53 I cannot explore here the intriguing suggestion that, due to the complex overlapping between the voice of God and the voice of Augustine's mother Monica, 'maternal writing' may relate to the art of confession. On this, see especially Francesco Giusti, 'The Hinge of Time: Mothers and Sons in Barthes and Augustine', *Exemplaria*, 33.3 (2021), pp. 280–95 <https://doi.org/10.1080/10412573.2021.1965731>.

54 Jabès, *Le Livre des questions*, p. 118: 'au seuil du septième jour, Dieu ferma l'enveloppe de l'univers où scintillaient les étoiles et y apposa son cachet que l'homme désigna du nom aveuglant de soleil.'

inscribing a word as a wound; it is not ultimate since every word is only begotten by a 'maternal writing'. On the other hand, the constitutive blindness of a 'maternal writing' (*écriture maternelle*) is also the constitutive blindness of 'Writing' (*Écriture*) as a mother who begets her sons — Jewish 'writers' who are all that remains after the exhaustion of the Book. In this respect, 'Writing' (*Écriture*) is inherently secluded from literature, whose words written by 'Jewish writers' cannot be seen by writing, due to a structural blindness that buries writing into a tenebrous solitude:

> 'blinding a man', Reb Berre, then said, 'does that mean you deprive his soul of the sun? The world inside is a black world. Each avowal, each gesture, is a candle that burns and, while we sleep, wakes deep within us.'[55]

Jabès explicitly compares the act of writing to an unfortunate case of miscarriage: 'therefore, a stillborn child; stillborn, i.e., dead in order to be born; life denied until its birth and frozen in it, whose breath and inertia were our own' (donc, un enfant mort-né; mort-né, c'est-à-dire mort afin de naître; vie refusée jusqu'à sa naissance et figée en elle dont le souffle et l'inertie furent les nôtres).[56] In this perspective, the image of a miscarriage is eloquent enough to describe the dramatic act of writing as well as the risks of being misunderstood or, even worse, of delivering a work that is lifeless — stillborn. And yet there is something darker and uncanny at stake.

Let me insist once more on the notion of 'maternal writing'. This notion seems to object to the traditional institution of circumcision, especially because it posits writing before life whereas circumcision posits life before writing. When related to the dimension of maternity, the notion of writing is exposed to the risks of pregnancy and especially to the threat of miscarriage. Jabès's image of writing his own work projects his metaphor of a 'maternal writing' into a darker realm: if motherhood presupposes pregnancy, pregnancy might involve the risk of miscarriage. Here Jabès apparently maintains in much more radical terms that the notion of writing itself necessarily involves the event of

55 Ibid., p. 158.

56 Jabès, *Elya*, p. 1172.

miscarriage. The stillborn child carries a poignant name: Elya. Regardless of any lexicological and philological precaution, Jabès assumes the name Elya to be the anagram of his mother's name — Yael. Therefore, the miscarriage figures not simply as an unfortunate event but rather as the tragic destiny to which the act of writing is inexorably delivered. In other words, the final consequence of a fatal *mutation* is reflected in the letter *permutation* of his mother's name — from Yael to Elya. Still, this already dark dimension of motherhood does not exhaust Jabès's notions of language and writing. At first, one should recall that Jabès claims — almost in traditional, naive terms — that a writer is someone who has rediscovered the dimension of his infancy; hence, a writer would apparently be like

> [an] eighty-years old [woman] on her deathbed who, a moment before fading away, expressed herself in the language of her childhood that she had forgotten, already in her adolescence.[57]

And yet infantile words — the words of someone who cannot yet speak — are those that a writer would allegedly be required to speak again. Still, they do not appear to be mere, unoriginal repetitions of some soft 'baby talk' but rather sound like the *lamentation* of an unfortunate creature — a stillborn — who has to face a tragic destiny: being out-spoken in words and therefore destined to death. Jabès writes: 'deprived of its *r*, *la mort*, death, dies asphyxiated in the word, *mot*' (privé d'R, *la mort* meurt d'asphyxie dans le *mot*).[58]

The transparent wordplay in the original French between *mort* ('death') and *mot* ('word') manifests an intrinsic relationship of the individual act of writing with the transindividual, inexorable destiny to die — one is born to die. As a consequence, the very event of motherhood is connected to the event of death not simply as an exterior risk of miscarriage but rather as an interior will of *sacrificing* her own son. What becomes manifest on the sacrificial altar of writing is that every writer's 'word' (*mot*) is destined to 'death' (*mort*). More radically, this

57 Ibid., p. 618: '[une] octogénaire sur son lit d'agonie qui, un moment avant de s'éteindre, s'exprima dans la langue de son enfance qu'elle avait, depuis son jeune âge, oubliée'.

58 Edmond Jabès, *El, ou le dernier livre*, in *Il libro delle interrogazioni*, pp. 1474–1665 (p. 1532).

destiny is imposed as a *sacrifice* by writing itself — that is, by means of 'the sacrificed and yet always awaited word' (la parole sacrifiée mais toujours attendue).[59] In these terms, Jabès's notion of 'maternal writing' actually exhausts the patriarchal dimension of fatherhood, which is classically depicted in Scripture by means of two events: circumcision and the sacrifice of the firstborn. Besides, Abraham was the first: the first to become a Jew, the first to be circumcised, the first to offer his son as a sacrifice on an altar of fire (Genesis 22. 1–18).

By inscribing the act of writing into the dimension of sacrifice, Jabès militates for a reinstitution of traditional Jewish messianism. Yet he is well aware that this 'tradition' — the ordinary, patriarchal one — is outdated. His discomfort towards the actual Talmud, its hermeneutics, and its faith in a perpetual legal reasoning eventually brought him to write his own private Talmud — not a *legal* but a *literary* one. This fictional and yet somehow not fictitious Talmud met all the requirements for elevating Jabès's otherwise trivial discomfort for Rabbinic literature to the truly metaphysical assumption that Jewish writing is intrinsically *messianic*. A literary Talmud — populated by fictional rabbis — substantiated a radical expression of this principle: the 'inoperative nature' of Jewish Law emerges exactly when messianism is completely secularized and can no longer bear its traditional message.[60] Jabès's world is the world of revelation — from the radical perspective in which this world is returned to its own nothingness. In this respect, Jabès's notion of 'maternal writing' delivers the act of writing to the sacrificial destiny of death: 'The book is the place where the writer sacrifices his voice to silence.'[61]

Jabès's notion of 'maternal writing' replaces the traditional notion of fatherhood together with its main institutions — circumcision and the sacrifice of the firstborn. We finally understand that Jabès's claim that his 'mother tongue' is a foreign language only affirms the inability to find a centre *within* the perimeter of writing. Writing cannot provide a stable centre to those who inexorably err when disseminated in

59 Edmond Jabès, *Aely*, in *Il libro delle interrogazioni*, pp. 1196–1473 (p. 1290).

60 I am clearly alluding here to Giorgio Agamben, *Homo sacer. Edizione integrale* (Macerata: Quolibet, 2018).

61 Jabès, *Elya*, p. 1060: 'le livre est le lieu où l'écrivain fait, au silence, le sacrifice de sa voix.'

time and space. Jabès therefore delivers an uncanny diagnosis about speaking a mother tongue: the act of possessing a mother tongue cannot provide stability, and this is because one is inexorably delivered to the act of being written — and hence to die. As a consequence: 'my mother tongue is a foreign language.'

The Mother Tongue at School

JAKOB NORBERG

Political rule in the modern age is legitimate only when the people rule over themselves; the people must be sovereign. But this modern conception of political legitimacy introduces a problem of delineation. What are the boundaries of the people in whose name rule can secure legitimacy?[1] How can one draw clear lines around the self of collective self-rule? The people themselves cannot quite perform the feat of self-definition through some democratic procedure, since their prior existence as a boundary-drawing collective would then be presupposed.

In the face of this problem of definition, nationalists have stood ready to supply an answer to the question of the political unit and its coherence. The people, they claim, are already naturally given, bound together as it were by a shared history, a homeland, a common culture, but above all a language, a medium of mutual understanding that constitutes indisputable proof of cohesiveness. A minimal nationalist requirement for legitimate rule is thus that whoever rules must speak the people's language; linguistically and culturally, like must rule over like.[2] This prohibits the dominance of a foreign elite, however

1 Arash Abizadeh, 'On the Demos and its Kin: Nationalism, Democracy, and the Boundary Problem', *American Political Science Review*, 106.4 (2012), pp. 867–82 (p. 868) <https://doi.org/10.1017/S0003055412000421>.

2 Andreas Wimmer, *Waves of War: Nationalism, State Formation, and Ethnic Exclusion in the Modern World* (Cambridge: Cambridge University Press, 2013), p. 4.

advanced or enlightened. Clear linguistic and cultural discontinuity across the political hierarchy becomes discernible as a violation of national self-determination; alien rule is per definition illegitimate rule.

In the eyes of most nationalists, it is also not possible to become part of a people by working deliberately to learn their language, as this would render the people too porous. Only native speakers, only those for whom the language is a 'mother tongue', are guaranteed inclusion. National belonging is reserved for individuals who have learned the language in a natural way, as evidenced by their current mastery, free from any touch of foreign awkwardness. This delimiting and restricting notion of the mother tongue, the one special language learned early and unconsciously and therefore spoken authentically and effortlessly, borrows its plausibility from images of the maternal, icons of the mother caring for and nursing a child that imbibes both its first nourishment and its first words through a close, symbiotic relationship.[3] In the nationalist imagination, the political legitimacy ensured through the self-rule of the nationally defined people partly relies on an iconography of the singularly intimate mother-child relationship. In Germany, around 1800 in particular, the book market saw a flood of tracts and primers on maternal education, in which the mother was presented as the proper, indeed irreplaceable source of the child's linguistic ability and even alphabetization; basic cultural skills were to be taught not formally by some authority but transmitted in the medium of motherly love.[4]

But the language constitutive of the self-determining people is not really learned in the mother's embrace or from the mother's mouth. The standardized and codified national tongue, spoken by millions of individuals across several provinces, is typically taught through the institutional infrastructure of primary education, through schooling mandated by the state. The children of the nation all speak the same language and hence live in an area of mutual comprehensibility that makes them into a people insofar as they have all been exposed to the same curriculum. The school as an indispensable instrument of nationaliza-

---

3 Thomas Paul Bonfiglio, *Mother Tongues and Nations: The Invention of the Native Speaker* (New York: De Gruyter Mouton, 2010), p. 185.

4 Friedrich Kittler, *Discourse Networks 1800/1900*, trans. by Michael Metteer with Chris Cullens (Stanford, CA: Stanford University Press, 1990), pp. 27–28.

tion is hardly an unknown feature of modern nation-building,[5] and yet nationalists may prefer the image of the mother whispering to her child over the image of the schoolteacher instructing their pupils, for an honest recognition of mass schooling could suggest that the nation is a political project rather than a natural ground. An emphasis on mass instruction instead of motherly speech could disturb the nationalist conception of legitimacy, according to which political rule must trace the given boundaries among naturally living communities rather than impose unity through state-funded institutions.

The philologist Jacob Grimm (1785–1863) did more than most to promote German and reduce the use of prestigious transnational languages such as Latin or French. His collections of German folk tales, legends, myths, and legal antiquities, some of which he edited in cooperation with his brother Wilhelm, helped establish and disseminate supposedly national traditions, and his grammatical studies reconstructed the genealogy of the German language, which ultimately yielded a linguistic criterion for separating the German from the non-German.[6] A politically prominent cultural nationalist, he explicitly and influentially tied the coherence of the German people to its shared national tongue and substantiated his claim with philological studies still deemed foundational for the discipline of *Germanistik*.

Living in the era of a massive expansion of increasingly state-supervised primary schooling, Grimm also commented, rather ambivalently, on the early nineteenth-century push toward universal literacy within German-speaking territories. He welcomed the prospect of gradual unification, linguistic and therefore also political, but believed that it would occur at the expense of regional linguistic variation. Grimm, both an advocate of political unity on a cultural and linguistic basis and an expert on indigenous folk traditions rooted in particular localities, was thus compelled to reconcile his political support for the advancement of a national language with his appreciation of historical, premodern Germanic speech and present-day dialects. He

5 See for instance the recent article by Keith Darden and Harris Mylonas, 'Threats to Territorial Integrity, National Mass Schooling, and Linguistic Commonality', *Comparative Political Studies*, 49.11 (2016), pp. 1446–79.

6 Sarah Pourciau, *The Writing of Spirit: Soul, System, and the Roots of Language Science* (New York: Fordham University Press, 2017), p. 53.

had to resolve the tension between the implementation of a politically crucial transregional linguistic standard and the unplanned evolution of genuine folk idioms. To return to the nationalist iconography, Grimm's occasional writings had to suggest some way of harmonizing the institutional tool of nation-building — universal schooling — with the romanticist predilection for the icon of intimacy and naturalness, which provided a source of ideological validation — the maternal body. Grimm was, in other words, forced to present a plausible relationship between the images of the teacher and the mother.

Is there such a thing as a mother tongue in the age of mass schooling? In 1849, Grimm gave a lecture on the school, the university, and the academy at the Prussian Academy of the Sciences in Berlin.[7] The institutions listed together in the title without any mark or conjunction — 'schule universität akademie'[8] — constitute an ascending sequence of interlocking institutions: all children attend schools to learn elementary and therefore required skills; a smaller number of students go to university to explore fields of knowledge of their own choice; and, finally, an exclusive group of university-educated scholars gather in academies to exchange research findings. Each of these institutions, it turns out, also stands in a relationship to the German nation, or ought to stand in one. The university, Grimm observes, has long provided German-speaking lands with a transregional institutional network and is recognized as a particularly German achievement, the envy of competing nations. In his account, the academy, a body typically sponsored by a court, is more obviously an import from French culture and unfortunately does not quite tie the German states together. In the lecture to his peers in the Prussian Academy, Grimm thus calls for a German national academy, which would recognize institutionally that the enterprise of science is a national German endeavour.[9] The link between the

---

7 Grimm joined the Academy as a regular member in 1832 and gave twenty-three lectures, from 1842 to 1859, mostly on philological topics. See *Verzeichniss der Abhandlungen der Königlich Preussischen Akademie der Wissenschaften von 1710–1870 in alphabetischer Folge der Verfasser* (Berlin: Dümmler, 1871), pp. 93–94. The immense German dictionary, *Grimms Wörterbuch*, was begun under the auspices of the Academy. See Conrad Grau, *Die Preußische Akademie der Wissenschaften zu Berlin* (Heidelberg: Spektrum, 1993), pp. 157–59.

8 Jacob Grimm, *Kleinere Schriften: Reden und Abhandlungen*, 2 vols (Berlin: Dümmler, 1879), I, pp. 212–55.

9 The universities in Germany were very much the bases for the propagation of nationalist ideas in nineteenth-century German lands and themselves represented a

school and the nation is a little more complex and Grimm neither lauds nor calls for its complete national extension. If anything, he approaches state-mandated primary education as the relative novelty that it was, acknowledging its rapid rise in Prussia and elsewhere in German lands without quite considering its existence inevitable.[10]

Grimm opens his reflections on the school with a question, a fundamental one, namely whether schooling is or is not necessary: 'Must human beings go to school?' (musz denn der mensch zu schule gehen?).[11] His answer to this question is no. Human beings do not in fact have to go to school, since they can learn plenty of things, all that they really need, at home, from their parents, their siblings, and their neighbours. The son of the farmer learns to work on the farm, the daughter in the household learns how to manage it, and both learn how to speak the language of their environment. No pedagogically informed instruction outside of the familial unit and hence no public institution staffed by a distinct group of instructors is needed for children to learn the tongue spoken by the parents, the language which could legitimately be called the mother tongue.

German-national network with national scientific journals and professional congresses. See Charles McClelland, *State, Society, and University in Germany 1700–1914* (Cambridge: Cambridge University Press, 1980), p. 9. Grimm himself was an active member in the university networks, as a practitioner and proponent of *Germanistik*, the fledgling German national (and nationalist) philology. He had a prominent role at the first national congresses of Germanists in the 1840s. See Katinka Netzer, 'Die Brüder Grimm und die ersten Germanistenversammlungen', in *Die Grimms – Kultur und Politik*, ed. by Bernd Heidenreich and Ewald Grothe (Frankfurt: Societätsverlag, 2008), pp. 290–326.

10 Schools were in no way a nineteenth-century invention. Richard Gawthrop describes a school-driven literacy campaign in Germany that went on for about two centuries and points to examples such as the establishment of hundreds of schools in Prussia in the 1730s and of laws that made schools compulsory in the eighteenth century. See Richard L. Gawthrop, 'Literacy Drives in Preindustrial Germany', in *National Literacy Campaigns: Historical and Comparative Perspectives*, ed. by Robert Anrove and Harvey Graff (New York: Plenum, 1987), pp. 29–48. Still, Gawthrop's editors mention that Prussian military defeat contributed to a renewed and intensified emphasis on the achievement of mass literacy via schooling after 1807. See Robert Arnove and Harvey Graff, 'Introduction', in *National Literacy Campaigns*, ed. by Anrove and Graff, pp. 1–28 (p. 4). And schooling also changed, in that a focus on religious conformity under church supervision was replaced, in the nineteenth century, by a creation of a national body of literate and loyal citizens. It is this state-organized schooling that is Grimm's concern.

11 Grimm, *Kleinere Schriften*, I, p. 222. All translations are by the author unless otherwise stated.

And yet human beings do go to schools, and Grimm knows well the rationale behind compulsory education in nineteenth-century Europe, namely the achievement of universal literacy. The basic aim of mass schooling is to ensure that all children 'without exception' (ohne ausnahme) learn how to read and write in a medium of communication with a wide, national reach; this set of skills has become so vital that Grimm does not quite feel the need to outline its particular purpose.[12] His silence indicates perhaps that literacy no longer possesses one exclusive purpose, such as the religious one of basic access to the Bible, but rather constitutes a fundamental general requirement in the institutional and media landscape of the day.[13] Yet the language that the pupil is supposed to learn to read, write, and properly speak in school as a future member of a literate national citizenry is not exactly the mother tongue, but rather the language of the schoolteacher, which, for Grimm, in no way ranks as of superior quality. On the contrary, he claims, native rules of language, the 'angeborne sprachregel', are routinely abused by teachers.[14] Compulsory primary education organized by states has become inescapable, Grimm concedes, but does not, from a purely linguistic standpoint, constitute an advance.

Grimm recognizes the general importance of teaching rudimentary reading and writing, although he objects to frequent and perhaps ineliminable flaws in instruction. The unity of a written German language, Grimm announced in a preface to the 1822 edition of his *German Grammar*, is indispensable[15] for it serves as a continual reminder of a shared German descent and a medium of present German

12 Ibid.

13 Michael Mann provides a basic list of eighteenth- and nineteenth-century institutions and societal fields that in some way required and promoted literacy: the military and navy supplied officers with manuals and maps; merchants dealt with contracts and accounts; the legal profession and any encounter with it involved paperwork; and, finally, paperwork was also required by state administration. Of course, people of the age also saw a rapidly increasing volume of newspapers, periodicals, pamphlets, handbooks, and novels. See Michael Mann, *The Sources of Social Power*, 2 vols (Cambridge: Cambridge University Press, 1986–93), II: *The Rise of Classes and Nation-States, 1760–1914* (1993), pp. 37–38.

14 Grimm, *Kleinere Schriften*, I, p. 229.

15 Jacob Grimm, *Deutsche Grammatik*, ed. by Wilhelm Scherer and others, 4 vols (Berlin: Dümmler, 1870–98), I (1870), repr. in Jacob and Wilhelm Grimm, *Werke*, ed. by Ludwig Erich Schmitt and others, 47 vols (Hildesheim: Olms, 1985–), X: *Deutsche Grammatik I*, ed. by Elisabeth Feldbusch and Ludwig Erich Schmitt (1989), p. xiii.

community. Such linguistic unity could hardly be achieved without mandatory schooling, since the school introduces it to the totality of the nation's children. Even when it is taught imperfectly, instruction in, and use of, German across all institutions of education, from primary school to the university, represents for Grimm a triumph of the national over the foreign and the classical.[16]

Many decades before his lecture to the Academy in Berlin and some years before he commenced his grammatical studies, however, the young Jacob Grimm was less willing to accept the intrusion of teachers into a spontaneous familial and social process of language learning. In a letter that he wrote as a young man to his mentor Friedrich Carl von Savigny, the era's prominent authority on the history of Roman law and Grimm's mentor from his earliest university days, one encounters a slightly more principled resistance to instruction in German to German-speaking children. Educational reform, he writes in 1814, means that the natural linguistic competence fostered in small-scale communities may well be disturbed. To learn a language at school is to learn to apply a set of rules, whereas the language spoken at home is learned naturally, without the mediation of explicitly stated conventions. Those who go to school, Grimm writes, learn to read and write their supposed 'mother tongue' as an explicit set of rules and begin to see their language as if it were foreign, while simultaneously being deprived of their local dialect.[17] It is appropriate to learn Latin or Greek in school, he claims, since the acquisition of these traditionally taught languages does not disturb the automatic absorption of local speech, but that which is already one's own should not be presented, through formalized teaching, as if it came from without. The native, 'das einheimische', does not amount to a kind of knowledge or defined skill to be acquired; it comes, it should come, as naturally as breathing.[18] The German native tongue is rendered alien by the teacher.

But when Grimm is speaking to the Academy in Berlin in 1849, this early opposition to the teaching of German seems to have faded. In his estimation, inadequately trained schoolteachers corrupt young

16 Grimm, *Kleinere Schriften*, I, p. 233.

17 Jacob and Wilhelm Grimm, *Briefe der Brüder Grimm an Savigny aus dem Savignyschen Nachlaß*, ed. by Wilhelm Schoof (Berlin: Erich Schmidt, 1953), p. 170.

18 Grimm and Grimm, *Briefe an Savigny*, p. 170.

speakers with their faulty teaching of grammar, but there is no longer any debate over alternatives. It is evidently not too late to pose a fundamental question — must human beings really go to school? — and yet much too late to believe in a society without national schooling; the question of schooling has become philosophical and anthropological rather than political, for the political battle against universal schooling, if there ever was one, has already been lost. By the second decade of the nineteenth century, after Grimm's letter to Savigny, German liberals and conservatives, that is, figures across the political spectrum, had come to accept mandatory schooling as a basic feature of society and an instrument for (liberal) reform or (conservative) social control.[19] The educable masses and the schooled society were no longer, as they had been in the eighteenth century, visions or ideas; they were realities to be shaped or modified but no longer to be eliminated.

Instead of demanding limits to the school system and its curriculum, the older Grimm marvels at its sheer scale in the mid-nineteenth century. There are, he writes in his 1849 address, 15 million people in Prussia, and 30,000 schoolteachers, roughly one for every group of 50 pupils according to his calculations. The other German-speaking lands employ around 50–60,000 teachers, a figure that Grimm believes may be larger than in other European countries and hence testifies to the pan-German commitment to schooling: 'Deutschland ist ein wahres land der schulmeister.'[20] All in all, about 80–90,000 schoolteachers contribute to the rise and dominance of a more or less uniform national language.

Against this backdrop, Grimm has ceased to question the institution of the school and chooses instead to focus on the political fights that have emerged within it.[21] In particular, he wants to make sure that the comparatively low status of the elementary schoolteachers is

---

19 Karl Schleunes, *Schooling and Society: The Politics of Education in Prussia and Bavaria 1750–1900* (Oxford: Berg, 1989), pp. 96–97.

20 Grimm, *Kleinere Schriften*, I, p. 229.

21 For an overview of German and specifically Prussian teachers' socio-political situation, including their struggle for an elevated reputation, the gulf between schoolmasters and credentialized academics, the subordination under local pastors, the poor teacher training, and the reluctance of communities to pay for instruction, see Anthony La, *Prussian Schoolteachers: Profession and Office, 1763–1848* (Chapel Hill: University of North Carolina Press, 1980).

maintained, against the efforts of the group's more restless and radical representatives, whose alleged ties to communists Grimm deems quite plausible.[22] As a delegate to the Frankfurt assembly in 1848, Grimm reports, he found himself inundated with schoolteacher requests for higher pay and elevated legal standing, both of which he considers unsuitable to the important but still modest schoolhouse tasks. Human beings must go to school and hence there must be tens of thousands of primary schoolteachers and yet this stubborn fact about German society does not, Grimm feels, need to be glorified in a way that would suggest any meaningful social proximity of the schoolteacher to the educated teachers in the much more selective and demanding institutions of the gymnasium and the university. In some way, the gradually fading importance of Latin in higher education, of which Grimm's own efforts in Germanic philology were perhaps a symptom, was blurring the social border between the *literatus* and the simple teacher.[23] Yet maintaining the barrier is clearly important to Grimm. The poorly trained schoolteacher, he insists, does not deserve the status of a civil servant employed by the state.[24]

In 1849, then, Grimm seems to have partially overcome some of his anti-institutional impulse, his emphasis on the natural, the native, and the local, and come to recognize an accomplished fact: that schools and schoolteachers are everywhere, in every German land, province, and village, and that Germany is well on its way to being a fully 'schooled society', in which school attendance has been installed as a non-negotiable obligation.[25] The ubiquity of the school

---

22 Grimm, *Kleinere Schriften*, I, p. 228.

23 For the role of Latin as a conspicuous social border around the learned in a traditional European society composed of legally constituted estates, see Heinrich Bosse, 'Gelehrte und Gebildete – die Kinder des 1. Standes', *Das achtzehnte Jahrhundert*, 32.1 (2008), pp. 13–37 (p. 14).

24 When elementary education was a responsibility of the church, in the seventeenth and eighteenth centuries, the pastor would usually hand the task of this mostly religious instruction to (only rudimentarily trained) sextons, and the position of the teacher for a long time remained associated with the simplest of artisans, without social standing in the community. Despite the rise of state-mandated schooling and dedicated teacher seminars in the nineteenth century, the teacher remained a low-status figure, worlds apart from the prestige of university professors. See for instance Hans-Ulrich Wehler, *Deutsche Gesellschaftsgeschichte 1700–1815* (Munich: Beck, 1987), pp. 284–88.

25 Thomas Nipperdey, *Deutsche Geschichte 1800–1866: Bürgerwelt und starker Staat* (Munich: Beck, 1983), p. 451.

does not, however, suddenly render it a more appropriate vessel for the mother tongue. For Grimm, the separation between the genuine 'Muttersprache', simply absorbed within the natural confines of the family, in proximity to the loving mother, and the schoolmaster's rigidly taught idiom remains in force. Still, the older Grimm tries to soften the sharp opposition between the two figures. Rather than posit a clear polarity of mother and teacher, he searches for some way to let one approximate and take the place of the other.

The schoolteacher is not the mother and yet, it turns out, is not far removed from the maternal body. In his 1849 lecture, Grimm likens the schoolteacher to another figure, the 'Amme', the wet nurse, the woman who provides the child with nourishment and comfort, breastfeeds it and cares for it, but is not the birth mother:

> such a teacher, who like a wet nurse holds her breast toward the infant, pours the still simple food of the first knowledge into the boy, nourishes, prepares, and instructs him in all things
>
> solch ein lehrer, wie die amme ihre brust dem säugling hinhält, flöszt dem knaben die noch leichte speise des ersten wissens ein, nährt, baut auf und meistert ihn in allen dingen.[26]

This is in no way a slip on Grimm's part, but an attempt, however awkward, to give the teacher a place in relation to the nationalist iconography of the mother tongue. The teacher cares for and fosters the child and provides it with the first light serving of knowledge — this is the gist of Grimm's more accommodating treatment of the school. Hallowed words for teaching and instruction in classical languages, he then points out in a footnote, derive from ancient terms for wet nurse; the position of the teacher as the substitute for the mother has an ancient pedigree.[27]

The metaphor of the 'Amme' is meant to sanctify the local (male) teacher, without of course granting him a more elevated social status vis-à-vis instructors in the higher levels of the educational apparatus. Grimm means to establish the teacher's relative nearness and closeness rather than his intrusiveness and strangeness, and does so by feminizing him. Yet following the logic of Grimm's image, we could say that at

26 Grimm, *Kleinere Schriften*, I, p. 224.

27 Ibid.

school the children learn not a mother tongue, but the tongue of their surrogate mother. After the introduction of state-mandated education in the mid-nineteenth century, after the establishment of schoolhouses in each and every German town, all of which provide training in the reading and writing of a transregional language, the population learns to write and perhaps also to speak neither a genuine mother tongue nor an essentially foreign language, but some close substitute for the most natural idiom.

Grimm's attempt to mediate between the mother tongue and the school takes the form of a trope: teaching involves the substitution of the mother, and the language taught is a surrogate mother tongue. This addition of the wet nurse to the iconography of the maternal seems like a necessary compromise. The age had installed the mother as the primary source of a child's early language acquisition and even as the guide to alphabetization, and Grimm then complies with this logic by calling schoolteachers surrogate mothers: the two figures emerge as aspects of a maternal instructor — the mother teaches lovingly, and the teacher is like a mother. The ideological motivation for this arrangement ought to be clear: if the age of mass schooling and its proliferation of teachers puts some pressure on the iconography of the mother-child relationship that is supposed to anchor the naturalness and intimacy of the mother tongue, then the unity of the nation, and with it the idea of legitimate political rule in the era of the nation state, can be preserved by the extension of the maternal through the presentation of the teacher as wet nurse, the traditional replacement for the mother as the icon of intimacy and naturalness. At the moment that the Romantic vision of the 'Muttersprache' is brought into contact with the fact of mass schooling, the teacher must appear as a motherly figure — such is the form of Grimm's solution.

'Must humans go to school?' The answer is no if humans are to learn to speak their mother tongue, but the answer is yes if they are to become members of a nation millions of people strong. And the answer is emphatically yes if they are to become loyal subjects of a state willing to take up arms to defend its integrity. In an early nineteenth-century Germany shaken by Napoleon's victories and occupations, mass schooling emerged as a potentially effective means of forging a more compact and disciplined citizenry, in a manner analogous to the way that ecclesiastical authorities has used education as a device to ensure conformity with proper religious beliefs.[28] And mass education remains a preferred instrument for governments who want to

> indoctrinate previously unschooled populations into a coherent, shared national identity and establish a common, durable, national loyalty that supersedes previous ethnic, family, and kinship ties, inoculates the population from external agitation, and ensures resistance to alien rule.[29]

The sociologist Ernest Gellner ranks the importance of the state's monopoly over the means of instruction higher than its monopoly over the means of coercion, for the former establishes a common standard of linguistic proficiency and cultural competence that facilitates communicative ease across a large region and in the process builds a widely shared attachment.[30]

But attachment to what? Co-nationals, Gellner writes, are loyal not to the same king or the same God but essentially to the same school culture, which formed them and to which they owe their social membership. This may have been an intuition shared by nineteenth-century governing elites that found themselves increasingly reliant on armies raised by conscription rather than on mercenaries. Facing the threat of defeat and dissolution, these elites set about expanding the school system, partly in order to provide a public good to a population on which they now depended militarily, partly to homogenize that population's varied cultures and give a consistent national shape to its allegiances.[31] The school system represents a historical bargain between rulers and populations through which schooled subjects achieve literacy and numeracy of increasing utility within a national territory, but are also introduced to standardized nationalist narratives designed to ensure the uniform cultural identity of these subjects.

---

28 Gawthrop, 'Literacy Drives', p. 41.

29 Darden and Mylonas, 'National Mass Schooling', p. 1447.

30 Ernest Gellner, *Nations and Nationalism* (Ithaca, NY: Cornell University Press, 1983), pp. 34–37.

31 See Alberto Alesina, Bryony Reich, and Alessandro Riboni, 'Nation-Building, Nationalism and Wars', National Bureau of Economic Research, Working Paper 23435 <http://www.nber.org/papers/w23435.pdf> [accessed 1 June 2017].

Early German nationalists certainly observed the close link between universal schooling and state loyalty. The school as an instrument of military preparation appears in Johann Gottlieb Fichte's *Addresses to the German Nation,* delivered in French-occupied Prussia in 1807, which the young Grimm was moved to hail as one of the finest books ever written.[32] A system of national education supervised by the state rather than by the church or local authorities, Fichte claims, would undoubtedly be a costly enterprise and yet it would prove an exceptionally wise investment in that state's future military capacity. With great confidence, Fichte envisages a straight path from the state schools to the military barracks; a properly schooled people would be a people ready for mobilization and unyielding in war.[33] Around the time that Fichte gave his nationalist lectures, Prussian elite reformers explored the possibility of a large-scale expansion and reform of schooling after the humiliating defeat to Napoleon in 1806; they, too, considered investments in primary education a means to winning future wars. Schools could increase fighting incentives by linguistically integrating and instilling patriotism in an otherwise scattered, culturally fragmented, and hence reluctant population.[34]

In contrast to Fichte, Grimm exhibits no overt militarism in his 1849 lecture on educational institutions, but does understand the school curriculum as a means to reduce foreign influence on German culture and chooses to express this view in martial rhetoric. Cultural and literary accomplishments, he writes, must be achieved with one's 'own weapons' (eigenen waffen), that is, in and with the national lan-

32 Grimm and Grimm, *Briefe an Savigny,* p. 73. Fichte did not discover the link between schooling and national loyalty. According to Heinrich Bosse, discussions of a system of national education (*National-Erziehung*) took place among governing elites in the Holy Roman Empire, as well as among academics in the so-called *Polizeywissenschaft* as early as the 1770s. See Heinrich Bosse, *Bildungsrevolution 1770–1830,* ed. by Nacim Ghanbari (Heidelberg: Winter, 2012), p. 59.

33 Johann Gottlieb Fichte, *Reden an die deutsche Nation,* ed. by Alexander Aichele (Hamburg: Felix Meiner, 2008), p. 182.

34 Philippe Aghion, Torsten Persson, and Dorothee Rouzet, 'Education and Military Rivalry', National Bureau of Economic Research, Working Paper 18049 <http://www.nber.org/papers/w18049> [accessed 1 June 2017]. The authors note that literacy rates in Prussia were very high prior to 1800 but that illiteracy became virtually negligible in the male cohort born between 1837 and 1841; the post-defeat push of the state administration mattered.

guage rather than a classical or transnational one.[35] And the emergence of German as a fully developed literary language, which culminates in distinctive masterpieces such as Goethe's poems, justifies the desired dominance of the vernacular across the institutions of learning, including the university.

But the idea of a nation in arms has not disappeared completely from Grimm's lecture on education. The most revealing moments may be those when he calls the tens of thousands of schoolmasters a vast army of teachers, 'ein heer', and mandatory primary education the 'heerstrasze für alle kinder', the military road for all children.[36] At the level of metaphor at least, the agents of instruction are associated with the massive armies that first appeared in the Napoleonic age; if nothing else, scale allows for an association between the school and the military.

We could say that Grimm pictures the individual schoolteacher in the era of mandatory schooling as both a surrogate mother and a member of a military-scale collective, a wet nurse and a foot soldier. This oddly split characterization of the teacher, dispersed across the pages on primary education, is not an unfortunate case of mixed metaphors but reflects the necessary ideological construction of nationhood. The national subjects taught at school are the potential members of a future army ready to battle and die for their nation — one prominent ideological aim of education was and is to generate a loyal national citizenry. At the same time, the national language must remain a mother tongue, that is, the linguistic criterion of this national membership must be naturalized in such a way that the national collective, however large, retains the semblance of a familial community. The schoolteachers of the nation prepare the children for the defence of the state and must in precisely this capacity plausibly stand in for the mother as the icon of symbiotic intimacy, for the maternal body that guarantees the depth and authenticity of national belonging. Given nationalism's double preference for the maternal and the martial, it is ideologically fitting that Grimm's schoolteacher appears over the course of the lecture as both a substitute mother and an infantry soldier.

---

35 Grimm, *Kleinere Schriften*, I, p. 233.

36 Ibid., pp. 229 and 222.

Through his constellation of metaphors, Grimm captures the paradoxical task of the school to sustain the idea of an intimate linguistic communion and community across generations while also preparing large cohorts for military duties in the service of the state. If anything dampens his enthusiasm for schooling, it is, again, its deleterious effect on local habits of speech; it is primarily as a scholar of folk tradition that Grimm deems the price of mandatory education high. As mentioned, Grimm noticed early on how schooled children tended to unlearn the dialect that may have been almost entirely incomprehensible to German speakers of other regions, and the older, distinguished member of the Prussian Academy remains aware of the fact that the schoolteacher's tongue amounts to a sustained assault on local cultural integrity in the considerably varied German lands.[37] An early linguist, Grimm views schooling as something that is accompanied by the threat of a future retreat and even extinction of the linguistic variety internal to Germany.[38] The consolidation of a single national language, which he clearly embraces, must ultimately happen at the expense of an existing welter of dialects, a loss that he regrets. And something of a political motive may play a subdued role in Grimm's hesitation. Fearful of the cultural uniformity enforced by a coercive state eager to dissolve the semi-opacity of local communities and integrate them into a larger collective, Grimm knows that the language of the schooled nation is never introduced into a linguistic vacuum but does damage, irreparably, to existing linguistic subgroups for the sake of their greater transparency to a centralized authority.[39] 'Of all state simplifications', James Scott writes, 'the imposition of a single, official language may be the most powerful' — and such an imposition is made possible by means of schooling.[40]

37 To root out dialects, some so coarse as to be considered animal-like, and replace them with a purer national idiom was often the expressed aim of education. See Kittler, *Discourse Networks*, pp. 37–38.

38 For an evocative study of linguistic extinction in modern Europe, see Barry McCrea, *Languages of the Night: Minor Languages and the Literary Imagination in Twentieth-Century Ireland and Europe* (New Haven, CT: Yale University Press, 2015).

39 Grimm read and was inspired by Benjamin Constant's discussion of modern political uniformity in *De l'esprit de conquête et de l'usurpation, dans leur rapports avec la civilisation européenne* (1814). See Roland Feldmann, *Jacob Grimm und die Politik* (Kassel: Bärenreiter, 1970), p. 151.

40 James Scott, *Seeing Like a State: How Certain Schemes to Improve the Human Condition Have Failed* (New Haven, CT: Yale University Press, 1998), p. 72.

But Grimm's reserved stance is still most obviously motivated by a scholarly concern for the preservation of his research material. Grimm notes in his lecture that the academic achievements of comparative grammar and mythology depended partly on the turn to scorned idioms, allegedly unsophisticated languages, and neglected folk traditions, which helped uncover a more complete picture of linguistic change.[41] Grimm thought that dialects embodied regional diversity and, because they had been relatively untouched by elites, preserved archaic linguistic forms with greater fidelity.[42] From the point of view of the grammarian and cultural historian, local variation is to be salvaged and cherished, not smoothed out. The achievement of national literary and cultural greatness does require the spread of a standardized literary German throughout educational institutions, but this very standardization marginalizes and endangers the local material necessary for the comparative grammarian's exploration of linguistic history. A comprehensive German school system that would teach all its pupils to read and recite Goethe poems, which is Grimm's prime example of canonical vernacular literature, would at the same time contribute to the gradual elimination of rich local dialects and speech patterns and hence attenuate connections to the past and deprive grammatical studies of important clues.

The nationalist cause of achieving German literary and cultural greatness is at odds with the linguist's and folklorist's interest in maintaining or at least honouring a historical-cultural diversity of German culture. But where we can discern an obvious tension between nationalist and localist causes, or a conflict between the aims of national-literary competitiveness in a European cultural space, on the one hand, and antiquarian or scientific motives, on the other, Grimm chooses instead to see a coordinated process of nation-building in which the school system can contribute to both the homogenization of the vernacular *and* the preservation or perhaps the musealization of linguistic remains. Yet again, Grimm seeks to accept and accommodate the school system without betraying his appreciation of the local, native, and intimate.

---

41 Grimm, *Kleinere Schriften*, I, p. 216.

42 Tuska Benes, *In Babel's Shadow: Language, Philology, and the Nation in Nineteenth-Century Germany* (Detroit, MI: Wayne State University Press, 2008), p. 135.

What reconciles Grimm to the reach of the school system is at least partly the problem of collecting. Several times over his career, Grimm announced or sought to initiate collaborative projects of folklore collection in order to expand the archive of neglected and endangered traditions of German poetry. One year before the two Grimm brothers published their very first volume of folk tales in 1812, for example, Jacob drafted a call, an 'Aufforderung', for materials, including traditions, legends, fairy tales, proverbs, poems, or really any fragment of a genuine folk literature, that would allow him and others to conjure up a richer image of old German poetry.[43] In the call, Grimm makes apparent why such an enterprise cannot be completed by a few scholars alone. The desired materials, Grimm writes, and especially the purest samples of folk literature, treasures undistorted by any 'false enlightenment', will likely be found in the most remote and even hidden regions of Germany — in mountain regions, closed valleys, and small villages unconnected to major thoroughfares.[44] For this reason, only a considerable number of geographically dispersed collaborators will ever be able to gather the necessary volume of valuable folk expressions. Since specificity and locality was of utmost importance to Grimm, he also encourages the future volunteers to transcribe dialects faithfully, without correcting perceived errors made by uneducated informants, and to record the precise place of transcription; only in this way would scholars be able to piece together a more comprehensive picture of the variegated cultures of Germany. For reasons of completeness, Grimm expresses the hope that they would find a knowledgeable liaison in every single area of Germany.

The large numbers of eager amateur collectors never materialized, at least not to serve Grimm's preferred cultural-nationalist research project, but the vision of an associational infrastructure for collecting folk materials resurfaces in his lecture on the school, university, and academy. Grimm sees that the thousands of German schoolteachers cannot avoid serving as agents of cultural and linguistic homogenization, insofar as they teach a language that is a more or less uniform

43 Jacob Grimm, 'Aufforderung an die gesammten Freunde deutscher Poesie und Geschichte erlassen', in Reinhold Steig, *Clemens Brentano und die Brüder Grimm* (Bern: Lang, 1969), pp. 164–71.

44 Steig, *Brentano und die Brüder Grimm*, p. 165.

national language across different provinces, but he also states that the school system that puts a teacher in every village could also allow for the systematic collection of linguistic and narrative materials so valuable to research in the field of *Germanistik*.[45] Schoolteachers could retrieve, record, and pass on local speech and tradition from all corners of the German-speaking lands to some centre of study. The mass of teachers clearly contributes to the consolidation of German across regions but they could, Grimm suggests, also be preparing the 'artifactualization' of folk culture, the conversion of oral tradition and local habits into objects of scientific study.[46] And the arrangement and ordering of such materials, already conducted with exemplary zeal by Grimm himself, would in turn help provide the nation with a cultural-historical depth that would otherwise be lost.

Grimm imagines the schoolhouse as the site for an exchange of great value to the nation-building project. The schoolteachers are primarily tasked with the dissemination of an increasingly widely read and understood national tongue, but ideally they should also be transferring now-endangered folkloric forms to some centre of research devoted to the scholarly excavation of the varied national past. The rural idioms, local dialects, and travelling stories that Grimm knows will likely vanish over time, not least because of mass schooling, could nonetheless be preserved and moved into the publications of researchers, thanks to the combined efforts of schoolteachers everywhere. If this came to pass, the myriad local mother tongues that would soon cease to be spoken could at least be transcribed and eventually put on display in anthologies and studies of German linguistic history, much like the magnificent historical objects for which we no longer have actual use, such as royal insignia, are not discarded but moved into the space of the history museum in order to support the constitution of a shared historical identity. Boris Groys has claimed that museums, and by extension anthologies of linguistic and literary materials such as the ones Grimm produced, are tools of cultural recycling that convert the materials marginalized by supposed historical progress into building blocks for a common identity.[47]

45 Grimm, *Kleinere Schriften*, I, p. 230.

46 Susan Stewart, *Crimes of Writing: Problems in the Containment of Representation* (Durham, NC: Duke University Press, 1994), p. 105.

47 Boris Groys, *Logik der Sammlung: Am Ende des musealen Zeitalters* (Munich: Hanser, 1997), pp. 46–47.

It is partly thanks to this double function, this bi-directional traffic between the peripheral school, on the one hand, and the centres of state administration and research, on the other, that Grimm views the school as a crucial institutional device for nation building. Its agents do work that replaces dialects with standardized German and yet they could also collect samples of local speech to be presented as historical evidence of the gradual emergence of a (surrogate) mother tongue. In Grimm's vision, the army of German teachers will prepare their pupils for a national future and, on the side, help retain for this unified people relics of a national past.

Scarspeak

Thinking the Mother Tongue as a Formative Mark

JULIANE PRADE-WEISS

This chapter proposes the scar as a productive image to conceptualize the relation of speakers to the particular language that is otherwise called *mother tongue, native* or *first language*. Thinking of this relation in terms of a scar avoids the biopolitical implications of concepts derived from the context of family and birth that have, throughout the nineteenth and twentieth centuries, come to present language as basis of a nation state. Furthermore, the image of the scar also avoids the biographical normalization and linguistic hierarchization that are implied in the term *first language*, as both are equally important biopolitical strategies of forming individuals and communities. Thinking of the *mother tongue* in terms of a scar emphasizes the intensity of lasting formation and identification entailed by acquiring this particular language, and it highlights the violence, inherent to these processes, that tends to be covered up by the naturalizing and family-related imagery of *native* or *mother tongue* as well as by the favour implied in the term *first language*. A mother tongue is neither a birthmark nor an open wound, rather, it is formed by intentional intervention into natural structures, and thus resembles scarification.

The chapter proceeds in four steps: First, it will outline more clearly why an alternative conceptualization of the mother tongue appears necessary; second, it will call attention to theoretical approaches to language and language acquisition that allow for a conceptualization of the primary language as scar; third, it will specify the notion of the scar (explaining, not least, why this is not a trauma theory) with a short reference to Franz Kafka's 'Red Peter'; finally, it will read passages from two literary texts that portray the acquisition of the respective language they speak as a process of scarification: Joyce's *A Portrait of the Artist as a Young Man*, and Aglaja Veteranyi's *Why the Child Is Cooking in the Polenta* (*Warum das Kind in der Polenta kocht*).

Reconceptualizing the relation of speakers to the language that seems to have shaped them most, that they identify with, and/or that they are identified by, appears necessary as the common terms *mother tongue* and *native* or *first language* have, throughout the nineteenth and twentieth centuries, come to be used with the sociopolitical aim of forming homogenous nation states — which entails the further aims of forming monolingual speakers and distinguishing one national language and linguistic community from all other ones. Even in studies on multilingualism, it is everything but commonplace to presume that languages are not distinct and countable like apples, and that translingualism is a fundamental feature of language rather than an exceptional trait of an author's biography. For acquiring a mother tongue means altering this language so that it is, in fact, not congruent with the mother's language. As Jakobson has shown, the phonetic variations of infantile language acquisition change a language's phonetic structure.[1] This model can be expanded to include lexical and grammatical changes children introduce to a language, so that individual language acquisition and overall historical language change appear as one process: Children do not merely accept and imitate the words they learn but, rather, form the language anew, and thereby change it. 'The child creates as [it] borrows', Jakobson notes.[2] By the time a child has acquired fluency in its mother tongue, this language is no longer the language of the child's mother or father, no longer the language the child had been taught. Therefore, a mother tongue always remains an 'other' tongue insofar as it comprises forms other than the familiar

1 Roman Jakobson, *Child Language, Aphasia and Phonological Universals*, trans. by A. R. Keiler (The Hague: Mouton, 1968), pp. 13–18.

2 Ibid., p. 14.

ones: unknown words, unheard pronunciations and expressions, as well as relations to other idioms in loan words or homonyms. Just as in a foreign language, there always remains a realm yet to be explored in the first language — which is, therefore, not one singular, homogeneous language, but a plurality of possible expressions, and hence a different tongue for every speaker. The notion of the homogeneity of a so-called natural language is thus a hypothesis that ignores basic structures of language but that is, still, unavoidable when using a dictionary. The structural character of the distinction between languages appears, paradoxically, as one of precise uncertainty: It is precise insofar as it can be exemplified with an indefinite number of words and phonetic, grammatical, semantic, or syntactic rules; yet the differentiation between languages remains uncertain because it cannot be abstracted from these examples as would be imperative for any other terminological distinction. Since the clear distinction between languages is a claim rather than an empirical observation, it keeps calling for decisive, violent acts that draw — or, rather, cut — dividing lines.

Developed with the idea of national languages, the notion of distinct, homogeneous languages still strives in what appears (in economical, ecological, and many political terms) rather as a post-nation state world. This pressure might even contribute to making the mother tongue a decisive cultural identifier and mark of social classification. The proposed notion of language acquisition as scarification, and of the mother tongue as a scar, seeks to reflect the violence inherent to the logic of identification as well as to education and formation.

Thinking of the forming and identificatory function of the primary idiom in terms of a scar means employing a metaphor, of course, but so does speaking of *mother*, *tongue*, and *native*. Speaking of a *first language* presupposes that there is a chronology of acquisition and/or an order of usage, while many structures of multilingualism provide parallelism and functional separation. What this shows, on a fundamental level, is that the relation to a system of symbolization can only be named in transferred terms, not 'as such', since it is only this very system that allows the employment of any terms. Therefore, every denotation will be misleading in some respects, not solely in English: the identificatory primary idiom may, as in classical Latin, be called 'father tongue', *sermo patrius* or *lingua patria*,[3] which is the tongue that comes with the (per se) paternal heritage and the 'homeland' (*patria*) — yet this language is not necessarily learned from the father. Alternatively, it can be called mother tongue, a term to which Latin shifted in the wake of Christianization[4] — still, it is not inevitably the mother's first language or taught by the mother. In Russian, it can be called 'native tongue' (*rodnoj jazyk*), the language associated with birth and 'origin' (*rody*) as if it was the language one is born to speak — when it is not necessarily the (sole) language native to the place where one is born and where the language is learned. Even the biographical approach of defining a first language leaves room for doubt. In his autobiography, Nabokov — usually considered a native speaker of Russian — insists that when he was six years old, 'my brother and I could read and write English but not Russian (except the words KAKAO and MAMA).'[5] The term *first language* does not solve all the complications evoked by the attempt to distinguish one primary and principal language from others, but opens up more questions: Is it the chronologically first language or the one primarily used? In speaking or in writing? And in writing what: texts for publication or just any scribbling? The more precisely the difference between the mother tongue and other languages is to be defined, the more this distinction appears to disperse.

The notion of the scar reflects the formative and identificatory function of the primary idiom — not in contrast to other languages (as the term *first language* does), but as an experience of the individual (instead of taking the point of view of those passing it on, as in *mother tongue* or *lingua patria*), and as a process involving incontrollable (mental, emotional, etc.) as well as controllable (cultural, social, etc.) factors (instead of viewing language as a given, as the terms *native* suggests).

Numerous theoretical approaches to language allow for a conceptualization of the primary language as scar insofar as they highlight

---

3 Horace, *Ars Poetica*, in *Epistles Book II and Epistle to the Pisones ('Ars Poetica')*, trans. by Niall Rudd (Cambridge: Cambridge University Press, 1989), pp. 58–74 (57); Ovid, *Tristia*, ed. by John Barrie Hall (Stuttgart: Teubner, 1995), 4.4.5.

4 Leo Spitzer, 'Muttersprache und Muttererziehung', in *Essays in Historical Semantics* (New York: Russell & Russell, 1948), pp. 15–65.

5 Vladimir Nabokov, *Speak, Memory: An Autobiography Revisited* (New York: Putnam's, 1966), p. 28.

the violence inherent in both language acquisition and symbolic substitution. The formative violence of language features prominently in approaches that apply a strategy popular at least since the eighteenth century, which conceptualizes structures of language by way of imagining a scenario of the origin of language (an approach still popular with evolutionary models of language development). Language, several such scenarios suggest, originates in a traumatizing strike that leaves a formative mark.

In his groundbreaking text, *The New Science*, Vico pictures language as a means for responding to overwhelming experiences of nature. The first word and thus language arose when 'the sky fearfully rolled with thunder and flashed with lightning' (il Cielo [...] folgorò, tuonò con folgori, e tuoni spaventosissimi).[6] The 'beastlike pre-humans' (*bestioni*), Vico explains, took these strikes, parallel to their own inarticulate utterances, as expressions of a superior being who 'was attempting to tell them something'.[7] Their response, and first word, is a name: in Latin *Ious* (as in Jove) after the crashing of thunder, or in Greek *σίζ* (as in Zeus) after the hiss of lightning, or in Hebrew *Ur* after the burning fire.[8] Vico's classical preference for Greek and Latin, and, to some extent, Hebrew as original languages notwithstanding,[9] Vico's multilingual primal scene of language corresponds to what Cathy Caruth calls the conventional definition of trauma:

6 Giambattista Vico, *The New Science*, trans. from the 3rd edn by Thomas Goddard Bergin and Max Harold Fisch (Ithaca, NY: Cornell University Press, 1948); Giambattista Vico, *Principi di scienza nuova*, 3rd edn, 2 vols (Naples: Stamperia Muziana, 1744), II, p. 377.

7 Vico, *Principi di scienza nuova*, II, p. 377; my translation.

8 Ibid., p. 447. This passage appears as a 'scientific' re-rendering of the Israelites' fear at the theophany at Mount Sinai, when God dictates the Ten Commandments, in Exodus 20. 18–19: 'When all the people witnessed the thunder and lightning, the sound of the trumpet, and the mountain smoking, they were afraid and trembled and stood at a distance, and said to Moses, "You speak to us, and we will listen; but do not let God speak to us, or we will die."' See *The New Oxford Annotated Bible: New Revised Standard Version with the Apocrypha*, ed. by Michael Coogan, 5th edn (Oxford: Oxford University Press, 2018). I thank Dominik Markl for making me aware of this background.

9 Others favour Hebrew, such as the influential Dante Alighieri, *De vulgari eloquentia*, trans. by Steven Botterill (Cambridge: Cambridge University Press, 1996), p. vi.

> the response to an unexpected or overwhelming violent event or events that are not fully grasped as they occur, but return later in repeated flashbacks, nightmares, and other repetitive phenomena.[10]

Hardly any phenomenon is as repetitive as language. Even more important than repetition, however, is the role of the strike in Vico's account: The names imitate the sounds of thunderstorm, yet the origin of language is not onomatopoeia. The first word is a reproduction of a deafening crash that also 'flashes' and 'dazzles' (*folgolare* means both) — which is to say that rather than arising from a particular perception of the senses, the first word arises from a defeat of perception. The crash causes a rupture in the continuum of sensual perception that permits abstraction, projection, and imitation, which is impossible without a rupture between original and copy. Crucial to conceptualizing language acquisition as scarification is Vico's apotropaic notion of language: originating in an overwhelming attack on the senses, and thus incomprehensible, speech appears as a means for averting the fear of destruction by a superior force and, at the same time, for accepting the shock as an authority's call, and answering it. The original shock, however, evades full comprehension as it precedes, and installs, language as a means for comprehension. The language thus formed testifies to the original strike, it still carries a rupture between signifier and signified; any linguistic representation necessarily differs from the entity it refers to, just as the first words differ profoundly from the thunderstorm they respond to and imitate.

Condillac, Rousseau, and Herder imagine similar origins of language: for each of them, language originates in averting the fear of being overcome. Condillac pictures the origin of language in 'cries' (*cris*) of two infants abandoned in the desert: First, they use these 'natural signs' (signes naturels) in order to soothe the passions aroused by their needs, later they use these 'natural cries' (cris naturels) as models for the 'arbitrary signs' (signes arbitraires) of a new language.[11] Adopting the idea

10 Cathy Caruth, *Unclaimed Experience: Trauma, Narrative, and History* (Baltimore, MD: Johns Hopkins University Press, 1996), p. 91.

11 Etienne Bonnot de Condillac, *Essai sur l'origine des connoissances humaines*, in *Œuvres philosophiques de Condillac*, ed. by Georges Le Roy, 3 vols (Paris: Presses universitaires de France, 1947–51), I (1947), pp. 1–118 (pp. 60–61).

of an original 'cry of nature' (cri de la Nature),[12] Rousseau points out what Condillac's scenario implies: an articulate language of arbitrary signs appears hardly necessary in the communication between mother and child, especially given that the infant has more to point out to the mother than she might have to say,[13] so that the pedagogical relation implied in the term *mother tongue* appears questionable.[14] For Rousseau, symbolic substitution, rather, originates from a Vico-like encounter of 'a primitive man' (un homme sauvage) with unknown others, first taken to be, and thus called, 'giants' (géans), but later comprehended to be equals.[15] Arising from an original error, language according to Rousseau is, as Derrida outlines,[16] an original prosthesis that, as de Man has shown,[17] hardly permits a profound distinction between proper and transferred sense. Thinking of the primary idiom as a scar connects to this assumption of a profound metaphoricity of language. In Rousseau, the founding error results from fear, which makes man see other men as larger and stronger than himself.[18] Hence in Rousseau as in Vico, language arises, as an apotropaic means, from the fear of being overcome and defeated. Herder adopts this notion and locates the first origin of language in every animal's expression of pain. Reflection and symbolic substitutes have a different origin, yet the primary purpose of language, according to Herder, is overcoming the panic of being overcome by the world, and making room to breathe by means of a cry. [19]

---

12 Jean-Jacques Rousseau, *Discours sur l'origine et les fondements de l'inégalité parmi les hommes*, in *Œuvres complètes*, 5 vols (Paris: Gallimard, 1959–95), III (1964), pp. 111–223 (p. 148).

13 Ibid., pp. 146–47.

14 On Rousseau's exclusion of the mother from the discourses on the mother tongue, see Anne Berger, 'The Popularity of Language: Rousseau and the Mother-Tongue', in *The Politics of Deconstruction: Jacques Derrida and the Other of Philosophy*, ed. by Martin McQuillan (London: Pluto, 2007), pp. 98–115.

15 Jean-Jacques Rousseau, 'Essai sur l'origine des langues', in *Œuvres complètes*, V (1995), pp. 371–429 (p. 381).

16 Jacques Derrida, *Monolingualism of the Other; or, The Prosthesis of Origin*, trans. by Patrick Mensah (Stanford, CA: Stanford University Press, 1998).

17 Paul de Man, *Allegories of Reading* (New Haven, CT: Yale University Press, 1979), pp. 135–59.

18 Rousseau, 'Essai', p. 381: 'Sa frayeur lui aura fait voir ces hommes plus grands et plus forts que lui-même.'

19 Johann Gottfried Herder, *Treatise on the Origin of Language*, in *Philosophical Writings*, trans. by Michael N. Forster (Cambridge: Cambridge University Press, 2002), pp. 65–164 (pp. 65–66).

Fear, it should be noted, is both a key factor in directing these primal scenes and a driving force for the systematic exclusion of women from the origin(s) of languages. The reduction of the female to an allegorical, inarticulate 'Nature', as in Rousseau and Herder,[20] appears as an overdetermined flipside of the subsequent Romantic reliance solely on the mother to build the mother tongue as a both natural and cultural basis of the nation state (in which she has no say).[21]

In Modern thought, more conventional than an apotropaic concept of language is, of course, the notion of language as a means for marking and appropriating objects, as for instance Smith's account of the first formation of languages depicts it.[22] Walter Benjamin, however, comes back to thinking origin as a structural rather than historical concept in his discussion of the primal scene of language depicted in the biblical book of Genesis,[23] and so does Gershom Scholem, who seeks to continue Benjamin's essay on language with the short text 'On Lament and Lamentation', an epilogue to his translation of the biblical book of Lamentations, or *Eikha* in the Hebrew Bible.[24] The five songs of lamentation, Scholem says, only raise their voice in order to fall back to silence, because the movement of falling silent is the adequate way of tonguing mourning — the state of refuting any symbolic substitution for what is absent, or lost.[25] Reading Benjamin and Scholem, Agata Bielik-Robson schematizes two notions of language that differ profoundly in how they deal with the trauma that originates symbolic substitution. She labels them, for the sake of brevity, as Greek *logos* on the one hand, and Hebrew *kinah* (lament) on the other. '*Logos*', Bielik-Robson explains, 'protects itself against its traumatic origins by producing a plethora of meaning that immediately repairs the broken

---

20 For Rousseau, see note 14; Herder, *Treatise on the Origin of Language*, pp. 68–69.

21 Friedrich Kittler, *Discourse Networks 1800/1900*, trans. by Michael Metteer with Chris Cullens (Stanford, CA: Stanford University Press, 1990), pp. 25–69.

22 Adam Smith, 'Consideration Concerning the First Formation of Languages', in *Works*, 5 vols (London: Cadell & Davies, 1811), v, pp. 3–48 (pp. 3–4).

23 Walter Benjamin, 'On Language as Such and on the Language of Man', in *Selected Writings*, ed. by Michael W. Jennings and others, 4 vols (Cambridge: Belknap, 2004–06), i (2004), pp. 62–74; with reference to Genesis 2. 19–20.

24 Gershom Scholem, 'On Lament and Lamentation', trans. by Lina Barouch and Paula Schwebel, *Jewish Studies Quarterly*, 21 (2014), pp. 1–12 (p. 5).

25 Ibid., pp. 7–9.

world — while *kinah* [...] delays the moment of sense-bestowing.'[26] Language can be a reparation for damage, a rather Smithsonian notion, but just as well a means for perpetuating and conveying damage. The point is not to decide between the two, but to see the less reassuring notion of a remaining damage as complementing the commonplace view of symbolic substitution in terms of reparation and compensation. The notion of the scar embraces both aspects, the restoration by way of symbolic substitution as well as the remaining traits of damage.

Individual language acquisition — rather than a speculative common origin — has become the prominent scene for the study of the general structure of language in the twentieth century. The original traumatizing strike that necessitates, installs, and shapes language is to be found in the ontogenetic primal scene of speech and symbolization, too. An example that might seem unusual in this context still serves well to illustrate the structural point. Freud's case history of the so-called 'Wolf Man' hints at a traumatic notion of the acquisition of the primary idiom: the patient consults Freud because the world seems veiled to him unless, all too rarely, he is relieved of his intestinal contents.[27] Freud finds this complaint — both the symptom and the wording — to be an adaptation of the patient's mother's complaints about a different condition, expressing and at the same time suppressing the infantile wish to replace her in the intercourse with his father,[28] and thus to overcome the father's preference for the patient's late sister, whom the grown up patient cannot mourn.[29] Nicolas Abraham and Maria Torok's reanalysis of the case expounds a translation not only of a primal scene to dreams and symptoms, but also of a nanny's complaint about child abuse from (the nanny's) English to (the mother's) Russian to (the analyst's) German, and of the mother's denial of the

26 Agata Bielik-Robson, 'The Unfallen Silence: *Kinah* and the Other Origin of Language', in *Lament in Jewish Thought: Philosophical, Theological, and Literary Perspectives*, ed. by Ilit Ferber and Paula Schwebel (Berlin: De Gruyter, 2014), pp. 133–52 (p. 135).

27 Sigmund Freud, 'From the History of an Infantile Neurosis', in *The Standard Edition of the Complete Psychological Works*, trans. by James Strachey and others, 24 vols (London: Hogarth, 1953–1974), XVII (1973), pp. 1–124 (pp. 74–75). Freud calls the patient 'Wolf Man' in 'Inhibitions, Symptoms and Anxiety', in *The Standard Edition of the Complete Psychological Works*, XX (1973), pp. 75–176 (p. 105).

28 Sigmund Freud, 'Neurosis', pp. 76–101.

29 Ibid., pp. 21–23.

charge.[30] The report of the seminal wolf dream might thus be based on an echo of the English words *witness,* and *son,*[31] in the Russian *vidietz son* (видеть сон), literally 'seeing a dream'.[32] The 'Wolf Man's' patho-logical mother tongue, however, is none of these natural languages but rather the idiom of complaints learnt from his mother, with the key phrase claiming, announcing, and lamenting that one 'cannot go on living like this'.[33] Just as his mother speaks several languages, the 'Wolf Man's' mother tongue of complaints can be articulated in different natural languages (even Latin and French).[34] It is, however, not a language to lament over others or to connect and communicate with others, but a medium to demean oneself, to replace oneself with others, and thus to restage the traumatic primal scene. The scene's specific character remains forever unknowable as it exceeded the infant's comprehension. Therefore, it remains a shapeless wound within his psyche that starts to organize his wishing and thinking as soon as he acquires speech, the means for comprehension. Crucial, here, is that what is transmitted from the mother to the son is neither the cause nor the referent of the ceaseless complaints (these differ), but a symbolic organization that allows one to deal with the wound.

In the case history of the 'wolf man', language marks an individual trauma, but the mother tongue of complaining is also acquired as a transgenerational trauma. And transgenerational tradition is indispensable to any notion of language. Yet while the view of language as a cultural asset and identifying possession is a phantasm, and while, furthermore, the concept of trauma may seem to fit well a reflection of the formative and identificatory violence linked to the primary idiom, simply arguing for a general link of language to trauma is too easy for a topic this serious. Transgenerational traumata are mostly marked by speechlessness, and although the 'wolf man's' mother tongue of complaining enables him to deal with his trauma, this *dealing* cannot at all be called *coping,* since he remains seriously sick and dysfunctional, as

30 Nicolas Abraham and Maria Torok, *The Wolf Man's Magic Word: A Cryptonomy,* trans. by Nicolas T. Rand (Minneapolis: University of Minnesota Press, 1986).

31 Freud, 'Neurosis', pp. 28–29.

32 Abraham and Torok, *The Wolf Man's Magic Word,* p. 110.

33 Freud, 'Neurosis', p. 76.

34 Ibid., p. 39.

Freud notes.[35] *Scar* seems to be a more appropriate term than trauma for grasping the formative and identifying dynamics of the first idiom as outlined by Vico and others. Before reading texts that portray the acquisition of a mother tongue as lasting scarification, it is necessary to specify the notion of the scar.

Medicine views scar tissue as 'of inferior functional quality' compared to other skin.[36] This secondary quality represents, on the one hand, the limitation of the notion of the primary idiom as a scar, for we cannot know, or even ask, what communicative structure there would be without articulate language. On the other hand, inferior supplementarity — be it compared to a hypothetical natural expression, or to mere presence — is the canonical resentment against symbolic substitution in general and written language in particular.[37] And scars are, indeed, not solely somatic phenomena, but have 'medical, psychological, social, political [and] moral aspects', too.[38] Etymology makes this apparent: The ancient Greek ἐσχάρᾳ (*eschara*), literally 'fireplace',[39] denotes the 'trace of a healed wound, sore, or burn',[40] such as the brand used to mark slaves.[41] Intentional scarification is often used as an identifying mark, be it with the aim of inclusion and decoration, signifying maturity and capability, such as duelling scars, or be it with the aim of exclusion and stigmatization,[42] which testify, for instance, to the torture of being whipped in slavery.[43]

35 Ibid., p. 6: Freud describes him as 'entirely incapacitated and completely dependent upon other people when he began his psycho-analytic treatment'.

36 N. L. Occlestone and others, 'The Discovery and Development of New Therapeutic Treatments for the Improvement of Scarring', in *Advanced Wound Repair Therapies*, ed. by David Farrar (Oxford: Woodhead Publishing, 2011), pp. 112–29 (p. 112).

37 Plato, *Phaedrus*, in Plato, *Lysis. Symposium. Phaedrus*, ed. and trans. by Chris Emlyn-Jones and William Preddy (Cambridge, MA: Harvard University Press, 2022), pp. 344–531 (274c–d).

38 Dagmar Burkhart, 'Narbe: Archäologie eines literarischen Motivs', *arcadia*, 40.1 (2005), pp. 30–60 (p. 30).

39 *A Greek-English Lexicon*, ed. by Henry G. Liddell and Robert Scott, 9th edn (Oxford: Clarendon, 1961), p. 699.

40 Scar, n. 2, in *OED Online* (Oxford: Oxford University Press, 2020) <https://www.oed.com/view/Entry/171985> [accessed 13 June 2017].

41 Burkhart, 'Narbe', p. 34. Hence Odysseus's scar is called differently. Homer, *The Odyssey with an English Translation by A. T. Murray*, 2 vols (Cambridge, MA: Harvard University Press, 1919), II, 19. 391–93.

42 Burkhart, 'Narbe', p. 49.

43 Jennifer Putzi, *Identifying Marks: Race, Gender, and the Marked Body in Nineteenth Century America* (Athens: University of Georgia Press, 2006), pp. 102–09; Susan

A scar is thus as much a somatic phenomenon, most notably of the skin, as a cultural one. It is what Turner calls 'the social skin'.[44] For no matter whether it was caused intentionally or accidentally, and regardless of its particular appearance, every scar can be read as an indexical sign referring to a cause. Moreover, as Burkhart points out, scars are a phenomenon of chronemics, that is, of the semiotics of time: in their retrospective aspect, scars refer back to a wound and strike, while in their prospective aspect, they refer to the course of (further) healing.[45] These two temporal aspects are crucial to the narrative of Odysseus's scar.[46] Testifying to an episode from Odysseus's childhood, the scar identifies the guest in the house of Ithaca as the 'changeful', 'much-wandered', πολύτροπος (*polytropos*) head that had left it.[47] The narrative reminisces, among other things, about how one sang to the wound to promote its healing.[48] Being read and revealed, the scar forebodes the end of the suitors waiting for Penelope to choose one among them. Both temporal aspects are crucial to thinking the primary idiom in terms of the scar: the retrospection onto an original strike, or shock, as well as the outlook for healing. The mother tongue is taught with the intention of training future speakers, and once the language is acquired, it is a means for speaking of this formation, and for being identified with reference to it. Kafka's 'A Report to an Academy' expounds the violence inherent to the formative and identifying processes of language acquisition.

Corey, 'Toward the Limits of Mystery: The Grotesque in Toni Morrison's Beloved', in *The Aesthetics of Toni Morrison: Speaking the Unspeakable*, ed. by Marc C. Conner (Jackson: University Press of Mississippi, 2000), pp. 31–48 (pp. 34–36).

44 Terence T. Turner, 'The Social Skin', in *Not Work Alone: A Cross-Cultural View of Activities Superfluous to Survival*, ed. by Jeremy Cherfas and Roger Lewin (Beverly Hills, CA: Sage, 1980), pp. 112–40.

45 Burkhart, 'Narbe', p. 35.

46 Homer, *Odyssey*, XIX. 390–92. Terence Cave, in *Recognitions: A Study in Poetics* (Oxford: Clarendon, 1988), p. 23, is right to insist that only the narrative makes the scar a signifier: 'the scar, then, is more than a sign by which Odysseus is recognized. It composes his identity by calling up retrospectively a fragment of narrative, since only narrative can compose identity as continuity once a severance has occurred, and the scar here may well look like a sign of the wound, the hiatus, the severance constituted by Odysseus' wanderings.'

47 Homer, *Odyssey*, I. 1.

48 Ibid., XIX. 457.

Requested to give an account of 'the life [he] formerly led as an ape',[49] Red Peter tells of how he came to be able to speak. He received two shots: one 'left a red scar' on his cheek, earning him his name; the other shot hit him 'below the hip', left him limping,[50] and is as important as the first one for his introduction to human language:

> I read an article recently by one of the ten thousand windbags who vent themselves concerning me in the newspapers, saying: my ape nature is not quite under control; the proof being that when visitors come to see me, I have a predilection for taking down my trousers to show them where the shot went in. The hand which wrote that should have its fingers shot away one by one. As for me, I can take my trousers down before anyone if I like; you would find nothing but a well-grown fur and the scar made — let me be particular in the choice of a word for this particular purpose, to avoid misunderstanding — the scar made by a wanton shot. Everything is open and aboveboard; there is nothing to conceal.[51]

For Red Peter, Walter Sokel remarks, 'identity is performance. It is not a static essence, a given, but a constantly reenacted self-presentation.'[52] There is nothing ape-like about this insight, as the parallel narrative of Odysseus's scar makes clear. Each is identified by the representation of his past'. Yet while Odysseus can rely on an authoritative narrator to make sure 'everything is visible', as Auerbach says,[53] Red Peter has to tell the story of his formative scar himself. Yet what the scar testifies to is the absolute abandonment of his life as an ape, which he can remember as little as humans are able to recall their infancy. What Red Peter performs is, thus, language as a scar: As if to disprove the scar in his face, he puts the place of the second shot on display, where there is no scarlet mark, but fur and a healed wound. This scar is crucial to his self-performance because it is as secondary as

49 Franz Kafka, 'A Report to an Academy', in *Complete Stories*, trans. by Willa Muir and Edwin Muir, ed. by Nahum N. Glatzer (New York: Schocken, 1971), pp. 250–67 (p. 250).

50 Ibid., p. 251.

51 Ibid., pp. 251–52.

52 Walter Herbert Sokel, *The Myth of the Power and the Self: Essays on Franz Kafka* (Detroit, MI: Wayne State University Press, 2002), p. 283.

53 Erich Auerbach, 'Odysseus' Scar', in *Mimesis: The Representation of Reality in Western Literature*, trans. by Willard R. Trusk (Princeton, NJ: Princeton University Press, 2003), pp. 3–23 (p. 3).

scar tissue: Testifying to the second shot that hindered him from running, the mark below the hip is not free for everyone to see, but subject to willing exposure by Red Peter, who let go of the animal fur in favour of the human concept of nakedness without clothing. The exposure of the second scar, and its narrative, explain the facial mark, and all these elements together identify him. Yet even as it is retrospective in gesturing back towards the shots leading to captivity, Red Peter's identifying performance is also prospective: The violence of the original blows is perpetuated when he tells of how language was his way out of panic and fear of death. 'The ape's name', Carolin Duttlinger writes, 'is itself a kind of scar, a reminder of the violence which catapulted him out of his animal existence into the world of language' as 'he did not choose his own name', but was named by his captors.[54] The violence of being given a name before being able to have a say in it, and thus being marked for life, however, is what Red Peter has in common with most name-bearers. And he also shares the narrative use of language in response to the imperative to claim an identity. Although an unusual speaker, Red Peter's experience of being forced into language, and submitted to symbolic substitution, is perfectly ordinary. The common scarification of language acquisition is put on display by the uncommon details of his story. Language is a scar for Red Peter because symbolic substitution by way of arbitrary signs did away with any original inviolacy so profoundly that it cannot be recalled, and thus has to be reconstructed endlessly. 'The human straightjacket', Paul North writes, 'in which he is already pinned when the story begins may as well have always been his.'[55] In order to prove that he has stopped being an ape, and to be himself, he has to display the scar and language, which are the reasons why he cannot know what being an ape is like. Speech and scars are concomitant for Red Peter — they are aspects of one phenomenon, hence his aggressive insistence on not being silenced and on displaying his scar.

---

54 Carolin Duttlinger, *The Cambridge Introduction to Franz Kafka* (Cambridge: Cambridge University Press, 2013), p. 78.

55 Paul North, *The Yield: Kafka's Atheological Reformation* (Stanford, CA: Stanford University Press, 2015), p. 222.

Words and wounds, as Geoffrey Hartman alliterates,[56] maintain a relation well scrutinized in criticism, concluding: 'where there is a word cure, there must be a word-wound.'[57] The paradigm of such readings is, more often than not, the talking trauma as outlined by Caruth: 'the story of a wound that cries out, that addresses us in the attempt to tell us of a reality or truth that is not otherwise available'.[58] Scarification is rarely taken into account, even though it is the regular prospect of wounds. To be sure, an open wound may seem more evocative of a talking mouth than of a closed wound. The disregard of the scar in the critical imagery of trauma is still surprising, given that trauma studies have shifted their focus from the causes to the aftermath of traumatization, as Hartman notes. Scars come in the aftermath of wounds. And the regard for scarification is all the more necessary as the shift of attention to the aftermath often results in an unsettling 'structural equivalence' of individual and communal traumata, which may have very different causes, as Hartman continues: a careless word or even an intentional insult evokes, and permits, other reactions than war and genocide.[59] Thinking of the mother tongue, and of language acquisition, in terms of a scar or scarification seeks to avoid such uneasy equivalence while still reflecting the violence inherent to the processes of formation and identification. Thus, the notion of the scar seeks to balance in between the simplistic extremes of, on the one hand, a generalization of the concept of trauma so that it embraces every kind of shock, and, on the other hand, a celebratory emphasis on healing that integrates even events of psychic destruction into a developmental narrative of 'experience'. Suffice it to say that while, somatically, scars are closed wounds, semantically, these closures are often regarded as grotesque, that is, as permeating the boundary between corporeal inside and outside in a way that Bakhtin has conceptualized as carnivalesque.[60] Scarification

56 Geoffrey H. Hartman, 'Words and Wounds', in *Saving the Text: Literature/Derrida/Philosophy* (Baltimore, MD: Johns Hopkins University Press 1981), pp. 118–67.

57 Ibid., p. 123.

58 Caruth, *Unclaimed Experience*, p. 4.

59 Geoffrey H. Hartman, 'Wörter und Wunden, bei Wordsworth und Goethe', in *Grenzwerte des Ästhetischen*, ed. by Robert Stockhammer (Frankfurt a.M.: Suhrkamp, 2002), pp. 164–85 (pp. 165–66); my translation.

60 Burkhart, 'Narbe', pp. 31–32; Mikhail Bakhtin, *Rabelais and his World*, trans. by Helene Iswolsky (Bloomington: Indiana University Press, 1984), pp. 303–67.

allows for survival, yet with their readability scars put the individual on display, so that the marks prolong the violence of the original strike into the future. Besides the initial infliction of the logic of symbolic substitution, the lasting inclusion into a particular cultural, social, historical (national, religious, etc.) discourse, and the identification with reference to that discourse, there comes with language acquisition an eminent, both scaring and scarring, violence. This violence may be addressed through accounts of language acquisition provided by Joyce and Veteranyi.

The first section of Joyce's *Portrait of the Artist as a Young Man* portrays the 'features of infancy' commonly omitted in portraits, as Joyce notes elsewhere.[61] What is at stake is the infancy not of a particular speaker, but of language. The first stage of language acquisition is an onomatopoetic encounter with a 'moocow' in a tale of the father, explicating the claim of words — such as 'cow' — to refer to something that sounds utterly different — more like 'moo'.[62] While this tale serves as a gentle introduction to the structure of reference and arbitrary signs, the second stage of language acquisition outlines how symbolic substitution works, and it is rather traumatic. In one act, the child is given a name and threatened with being silenced:

> He hid under the table. His mother said:
> — O, Stephen will apologise.
> Dante said:
> — O, if not, the eagles will come and pull out his eyes.
>
> Pull out his eyes,
> Apologise,
> Apologise,
> Pull out his eyes.

61 James Joyce, 'A Portrait of the Artist', in *The Workshop of Daedalus: James Joyce and the Raw Materials for 'A Portrait of the Artist as a Young Man'*, ed. by Robert E. Scholes and Richard M. Kain (Evanston, IL: Northwestern University Press, 1965), pp. 60–68 (p. 60).

62 James Joyce, *A Portrait of the Artist as a Young Man*, ed. by Jeri Johnson (Oxford: Oxford University Press, 2008), p. 5: 'Once upon a time and a very good time it was there was a moocow coming down along the road and this moocow that was coming down along the road met a nicens little boy named baby tuckoo. … | His father told him that story: his father looked at him through a glass: he had a hairy face. | He was baby tuckoo.'

Apologise,
Pull out his eyes,
Pull out his eyes,
Apologise.[63]

The mother's imperative 'Stephen will apologise' evokes Stephen in order to accuse him of owing an apology without explaining what he is guilty of. The child is thus baptized by the order to apologize, and it might be no coincidence that *Stephen* is the name of the first Christian martyr.[64] The threat following the mother's order varies a line from the biblical book of Proverbs: 'the eye that mocketh at his father, and despiseth to obey his mother, the ravens of the valley shall pick it out, and the young eagles shall eat it.'[65] The obedient child, this is to say, follows blindly. The mother's incomprehensible order, however, cannot be followed because it does not explicate the subject of the offence, or the addressee of the apology. It imposes onto the child a guilt to which no apology can ever correspond: The order 'Stephen will apologise' predicts a compensation by way of the *logos*, language and rationality, so that Stephen will always have to go on speaking in his defence, and will have never said enough.

What makes the order a traumatizing blow is that, unlike the father's infantile tale of the 'moocow', the mother's proper usage of what just now becomes the child's mother tongue does not explicate the referential connection between name and named. Neither the name *Stephen* nor the words of the order and threat comment on the referential gap. Reference is not explained but dictated — because there is no way to explain arbitrary signs, as even the gentle tale of the 'moocow' demonstrates. While the first encounter with naming gestures towards the named *cow* by way of onomatopoeia (*moo*), the second encounter with language is shocking as it points out that this is not how language usually works. The mother and her duplicate do not even need to see the child under the table in order to name it, to threaten it, and to tell it what to do. The shock is that the name is arbitrary and that there is, still, no way to escape from being named and

63 Ibid., pp. 5–6.

64 Cf. Acts 6. 5–8. 4.

65 Proverbs 30. 17. *The Bible: Authorized King James Version with Apocrypha*, ed. by Robert Carroll and Steven Prickett (Oxford: Oxford University Press, 1998).

thus evoked. Names make things that are not visible, such as Stephen, and that are not even there, such as 'the eagles', appear. The answer to the shocking strike is given in lines that look like a playful song the child sang earlier,[66] which makes apparent that Joyce read Vico.[67] The song featuring the rhyme 'eyes'/'apologise' is an apotropaic echo that responds to the rhyme of the order and threat by repeating the only thing about them that can be grasped. The lines are not taken seriously enough by Derek Attridge, who says that in the song the sound of language 'overwhelms its rational communicative function: words are progressively emptied of their meaning.'[68] Thomas Docherty equally states that 'in the corporeality of the word, understanding is lost'.[69] The distinction between sound and sense is vain when there is nothing to understand. In the apotropaic echo of the order and threat, 'sense' is restored by way of forming a 'sound' — a strategy that employs a basic principle of articulate speech in order to cope with the shock of being subjected to language. The sound effect of the rhyme entails semantic effects. The song voices the requested apology. In its repetitive structure, however, the song also depicts the blinding, separately for every eye. Ignoring all grammatical subjects just as the child under the table was ignored, the song voices the violence that intends to silence the child by means of an order that leaves no room for an answer.

With this traumatic scene of language acquisition, Joyce's *Portrait* outlines an ambiguity that is also to be found in the speech of Kafka's 'recent human',[70] Red Peter. In comparison to individual sounds and natural noises, codified articulate language comes as a shock, and is acquired as a means to respond to this violence. Joyce's *Portrait* analyses not how but why the highly regulated human language is acquired.

---

66 'He sang that song. That was his song. | *O, the geen wothe botheth*' (Joyce, *Portrait*, p. 5).

67 Richard Ellmann, *James Joyce*, new and rev. edn (Oxford: Oxford University Press, 1982), p. 340.

68 Derek Attridge, 'Language, Sexuality, and the Remainder in *A Portrait of the Artist as a Young Man*', in *James Joyce and the Difference of Language*, ed. by Laurent Milesi (Cambridge: Cambridge University Press, 2003), pp. 128–41 (p. 135).

69 Thomas Docherty, '"sound sense"; or "tralala"/"moocow": Joyce and the Anathema of Writing', in *James Joyce and the Difference of Language*, ed. by Laurent Milesi (Cambridge: Cambridge University Press, 2003), pp. 112–27 (p. 124).

70 North, *The Yield*, p. 222.

What he points out is not the infant's will to communicate (sound structures seem to suffice for that) but the necessity of finding a means of resistance against assaults of being named and told what to do, or be, that is: a remedy against the panic language causes. Joyce's *Portrait* thus suggests that a mother tongue is as little a first *language* as it is *native*, and that it is not so much taught as it is inflicted on a child, like a wound, regulating later communication by leaving a scar — to talk about as a personal, never fully comprehensible history. Yet that very scar also provides the symbolic means for standing up to this and later traumatic blows, such as when Stephen later confronts English for being a colonial language in Ireland.[71] The traumatic origin of language therefore does not remain a wound but becomes a scar. In Joyce, the two structural notions of language that Bielik-Robson differentiates complement one another: Articulate language provides the means for compensating the damage caused by its acquisition, and it does so in such a way that language keeps testifying to the initial trauma. Insofar as articulate language forces one to take one thing for another in order to be a social being, and provides no explanation or defence that was not already based on this principle of symbolic substitution, each language is a *scarspeak*.

One important aspect, however, is still missing in order to think the mother tongue in terms of a scar: any concept of language pertains to communities as much as it does to individuals. Thinking of language acquisition as scarification allows one to reflect the political aspect of community-formation particularly well, given that the intentional infliction of scars is just as much a means of distinguishing communities as it is differentiating between languages is. Veteranyi articulates the tension between traumatic individual and marginalized group history as well as the violence at the basis of individualization and community. Escaped into exile from Communist Romania at the age of five, Veteranyi was raised in the circus around the world, speaking Romanian and Spanish, and was temporarily schooled in Switzerland, yet remained illiterate until her late teen years. Published in 1999, *Why*

71 Joyce, *Portrait*, p. 203: 'My ancestors threw off their language and took another, Stephen said. They allowed a handful of foreigners to subject them. Do you fancy I am going to pay in my own life and person debts they made?'.

the Child Is Cooking in the Polenta traces her childhood, including the stages of language acquisition.[72] The text's childlike speech echoes her parents' terms and concerns. Oral internalization as a technique of comprehension features prominently in her work; it complements verbal expression and resonates strongly with psychoanalytic accounts of sign development out of the need to fill the empty mouth:[73] 'I know my [...] country only by smell. It smells like my mother's cooking' (Mein Land kenne ich nur vom Riechen. Es riecht wie das Essen meiner Mutter).[74] Unlike the gaze that allows one to tell the viewer apart from the viewed, the sense of smell does not evoke clear distinctions. Antitheses of home and foreign country, inside and outside, although often evoked, appear to be as volatile as smell:

> Mein Vater hat eine andere Muttersprache als wir, er war auch in unserem Land ein Fremder.
> Er gehört zu den anderen, sagt meine Mutter.
> Im Ausland sind wir aber keine Fremden untereinander, obwohl mein Vater hier fast in jedem Satz eine andere Sprache spricht, [...]
> Seine Muttersprache klingt wie Speck mit Paprika und Sahne. Sie gefällt mir, aber er darf sie mir nicht beibringen.
> Wenn er mit uns reden will, soll er unsere Sprache sprechen, sagt meine Mutter.
> Mein Vater stammt aus einem Vorort von Rumänien, ich glaube, daß er deshalb zornig ist, weil wir aus der Hauptstadt kommen.
>
> (My father has a different [mother tongue] from us; even in our own country he was a foreigner.
> He [belongs to the others], my mother says.
> In foreign countries we're not foreigners to one another, though, even if my father does speak almost every sentence in a different language [here]; [...]
> His [mother tongue] sounds like bacon with peppers and sour cream. I like it, but he's not allowed to teach it to me.
> If he wants to talk to us, he should speak our language, my mother says.

72 Aglaja Veteranyi, *Why the Child Is Cooking in the Polenta*, trans. by Vincent Kling (Champaign, IL: Dalkey Archive Press, 2012); Aglaja Veteranyi, *Warum das Kind in der Polenta kocht* (Stuttgart: Deutsche Verlags-Anstalt, 1999).

73 Sigmund Freud, *The Interpretation of Dreams*, in *The Standard Edition of the Complete Psychological Works*, v (1973), pp. 565–66; Nicolas Abraham and Maria Torok, 'Mourning *or* Melancholia: Introjection *versus* Incorporation', in *The Shell and the Kernel: Renewals of Psychoanalysis*, trans. by Nicholas T. Rand (Chicago: University of Chicago Press, 1972), pp. 27–128.

74 Veteranyi, *Why*, p. 8; Veteranyi, *Warum*, p. 10.

> My father comes from [some] suburb in Romania; I think he's so angry because [we] come from the capital.)[75]

On the one hand, it is obvious and consistent that the father should have a mother tongue on his own, for he has a different mother than the narrating child. The explication of the distinction the child's mother draws so rigorously between the two of them and the father, on the other hand, points out that what is at stake is no peculiar, culinary concept of language or family ties. The child voices a quite ordinary discourse of social exclusion that the mother brought along into exile, a discourse that employs any linguistic, geographical, or other dichotomy that promises to prove superiority. The vehemence of the distinctions suggests that she considers the father Rom or Sinto.[76] Yet instead of establishing clear-cut distinctions, the mother's discourse outlines the inconsistency of all qualifications of things as *own* as opposed to *foreign*: It suggests that even the father is not family, but 'belongs to the others', only less so when the family is in a foreign country — that the homeland is not the father's land, even if it is called *patrie* in Romanian — and that although it is the opposite of 'foreign countries', Romania is itself split up into realms of different quality.

In an attempt to compensate for the contempt, exclusion, and continuous loss en route,[77] the child is regularly told that as members of a circus, 'we're international!' (wir sind international!).[78] Yet few things, she finds, are truly in between the nations, and beyond their differentiation. Suffering and eating are among them: 'BEING SLAUGHTERED THE CHICKEN SCREECH INTERNATIONALLY, WE UNDERSTAND THEM EVERYWHERE' (BEIM SCHLACHTEN KREISCHEN DIE HÜHNER INTERNATIONAL, WIR VERSTEHEN SIE ÜBERALL).[79] Fear of death appears as *lingua franca* in

75 Veteranyi, *Warum*, p. 50; Veteranyi, *Why*, p. 46 (translation modified).

76 'My sister is good-looking like a man; she gets into fights with all the other children. She's a Gypsy. | I WANT TO BE A GYPSY TOO' (Veteranyi, *Why*, p. 27); 'Meine Schwester ist schön wie ein Mann, sie prügelt sich mit allen Kindern. Sie ist eine Zigeunerin. | ICH WILL AUCH EINE ZIGEUNERIN SEIN' (Veteranyi, *Warum*, p. 31).

77 'WE MUST NEVER GROW FOND OF ANYTHING' (Veteranyi, *Why*, p. 15); 'WIR DÜRFEN NICHTS LIEBGEWINNEN' (Veteranyi, *Warum*, p. 18).

78 Ibid., p. 53; p. 57.

79 My translation, cf. ibid., p. 14; p. 17.

Veteranyi. Not wanting to die and perish — of hunger or terror, in incomprehensible institutions, in abusive families, or in a soup — seems to be the only thing that lasts, and that is there to be understood. While making clear that it is not just any *others* in some *outside* who exercise cruelty, but everyone, the preparation and consumption of food still reveals stability amidst the ever-changing accommodations, languages, and identifying distinctions. The distinction of the mother's tongue drawn — or, rather, cut — so violently establishes no sense of belonging but an analytic distance, leaving the never voiced but abundantly thematized Romanian language as a scar within Veteranyi's utterly (Swiss) German discourse, a scar that necessitates and shapes the narrative.

These short readings may serve to outline that thinking of the mother tongue as a scar aims not at replacing other metaphors — Kafka, Joyce, and Veteranyi evoke the notions of *mother, father, native,* and *first* language — yet the notion of the scar contributes to comprehending the violence that these common concepts entail.

The Shuffling of Feet on the Pavement

Virginia Woolf on Un-Learning the Mother Tongue

TERESA PRUDENTE

Modernist experimentation has famously emphasized linguistic instability by means of a focus on the mingling of different languages, the coining of new linguistic codes, and the forms of intermediality and transcodification. Within such forms of overt experimentation, Virginia Woolf sets a rather different case, by seemingly remaining within the boundaries of one single language, her mother tongue, while performing constant processes of transgressions of those boundaries.

Woolf's experimentation has been related to her will to undermine the patriarchal nature of her mother tongue, thus allowing the maternal (i.e. feminine) qualities of language to emerge. My essay focusses on Woolf's processes of deconstructing her mother tongue from a different perspective, relating the writer's reflection on and experimentation with language to her quest for a 'universal' language of the mind. In particular, Woolf's novel *The Waves* can be seen as a culminating point of the author's search for a new narrative form capable of conveying 'some continuous stream, not solely of human thought, but of the ship, the night, all flowing together'.[1] The novel's focus on the six characters' development from childhood to adult life offers a symbolic reconfiguration of the process of language acquisition, which is portrayed as

1 Virginia Woolf, *The Waves* (Oxford: Oxford University Press, 2014), p. 52.

reversing linear development. The process moves from the characters' fictive linguistic hyper-competence in childhood to their final longing for 'some little language such as lovers use, broken words, inarticulate words, like the shuffling of feet on the pavement', rather than for 'phrases that come down beautifully with all their feet on the ground'.[2]

Woolf's essays, as well as her connection to Coleridge's views on language, suggest that we can read her experimentation as redefining and even reinventing the notion of mother tongue. Woolf's stress on a dynamic, ever-moving conception of language, as well as her view of ancient Greek as an ideal lost language capable of bringing the meaning 'just on the far side of language',[3] reveal her questioning of the idea of a culturally homogeneous and monolith language. In Woolf, the notion of a mother tongue is reconfigured in terms of a dreamed and imagined ideal language combining familiarity and foreignness, reality and ideality, exactness and perpetual deferral of meaning.

MOTHER TONGUE AND NATIVE SPEAKER: QUESTIONING THE MYTHS

Since the 1960s, linguistic reflection on the concept of mother tongue has undermined common assumptions in the field, such as the linguistic competence of native speakers vs non-native speakers, coming ultimately to question the very foundation of the concept. The stress has been especially on the idea of mother tongue as an artificial construct, as suggested by inquiries incorporating the perspective of the history of language(s). Giulio Lepschy's analysis of the etymology and usage of the two terms *mother tongue* and *native speaker* in English, German, and Italian has pointed out their late incorporation into dictionaries and their varied origins.[4] In the same line, Thomas Bonfiglio has underlined the absence of such notions in ancient Greece and the Roman Empire, thereby calling attention to 'the submerged racial, ethnic, and gender ideologies present in the concept of mother

2 Ibid., p. 143.

3 Ibid., p. 27.

4 Giulio Lepschy, 'Mother Tongues and Literary Languages', *The Modern Language Review*, 96 (2001), pp. 33–49.

tongue and the native speaker'.[5] Gender, especially, has entered the picture in the 1970s with the work carried out by feminist linguists to deconstruct the gender-biased and sexist implications in the expression 'mother tongue'. In particular, Alette Olin Hill refers to the idea of mother tongue as part of an analysis in which she draws on and advances Robin Lakoff's seminal singling out of the specificities of women's language.[6] Intending to push the debate forward by debunking the stereotypes connected to women and language, Olin Hill challenges the two images of *mother tongue* and *father time*, seeing them as embodying the sexist dichotomy of patriarchal culture that associates women with the corporeal and men with abstract thinking.[7]

As I intend to show in this paper, all the above-mentioned issues acquire complex and contradictory implications when related to the way the notion of mother tongue features in Virginia Woolf's work. An initial problematic consideration derives from the way that feminist thought has disputed the stereotypical implications in the feminine/maternal component of the notion. Drawing on Woolf's affirmation that 'a woman writing thinks back through her mothers',[8] feminist perspectives on the author embarked on a conceptual path that was the opposite of the above-mentioned questioning of the expression 'mother tongue' as implying a patriarchal stereotype. Seminal feminist essays on Woolf, such as those by Jane Marcus and Frances Restuccia, refer to the idea of mother tongue as pivotal to the writer's 'effort to valorise female difference',[9] and to her attempt at 'untying the Mother Tongue, freeing language from bondage to the fathers and returning it to women and the working class'.[10] This discloses how contemporary feminist studies tended to undertake opposing directions in relation to

5 Thomas Paul Bonfiglio, *Mother Tongues and Nations: The Invention of the Native Speaker* (New York: De Gruyter Mouton, 2010), p. 3.

6 Robin Lakoff, *Language and Woman's Place* (New York: Colophon Books, 1975).

7 Alette Olin Hill, *Mother Tongue, Father Time: A Decade of Linguistic Revolt* (Bloomington: Indiana University Press, 1986), pp. xi–xvii.

8 Virginia Woolf, *A Room of One's Own* (London: Hogarth, 1935), p. 146.

9 Frances L. Restuccia, '"Untying the Mother Tongue": Female Difference in Virginia Woolf's *A Room's of One's Own*', *Tulsa Studies in Women's Literature*, 4 (1985), pp. 253–64 (p. 254).

10 Jane Marcus, 'Thinking Back Through our Mothers', in *New Feminist Essays on Virginia Woolf*, ed. by Jane Marcus (London: MacMillan, 1981), pp. 1–30 (p. 1).

the notion of mother tongue, which, on the one hand, was employed to reaffirm the matriarchal cultural lineage suppressed by patriarchal society, while, on the other, was stigmatized as an implicit validation of patriarchal oppression. To add further complexity to the issue, feminist criticism during the 1970s and 1980s also proved divided on whether Woolf's texts were meant to value the notion of female difference, or rather that of the gender-blind synthesis of the 'androgynous mind'.[11] Yet rather than pointing at irreconcilable views, this division shows how the complex and multilevelled nature of literary texts tends to perpetually defy rigid categories.

Another example relevant to our topic is Marcus's remark that Woolf's writing had the underlying intent of empowering two oppressed categories: women and the working class. The tie established between the two is significant considering that if the Woolfian notion of the female subject and the 'motherly' implications of language represents a complex crux, her role as a writer portraying inequalities in society is even more debated. Famously, Woolf long suffered from the stereotype of a snobbish author unable to incorporate in her writing the diversity of social groups and a true-to-life representation of the lower classes. The point has often been made in comparison to the way the linguistic experimentation of other modernist writers, like Joyce, recombined languages and codes with overt political and societal implications. *Mrs Dalloway* may be taken as paradigmatic in this field, given that Woolf's intent with the novel was not only to 'give life and death, sanity and insanity side by side', but also 'to criticize the social system, and to show it at work at its most intense'.[12] Class differences dramatically emerge in the dynamics between Septimus and the two doctors examining him, as well as in his specular relation with the character of Clarissa Dalloway. Nonetheless, such differences, oppositions, and inequalities are not conveyed via linguistic variations in the characters' speeches and thoughts; furthermore, interestingly

11 Woolf, *A Room of One's Own*, p. 148. In light of the connection that I will draw later it is worth remembering that Woolf quotes Coleridge on the issue: 'Coleridge perhaps meant this when he said that a great mind is androgynous' (ibid.). On the different perspectives in Woolfian feminist criticism see Restuccia, 'Untying the Mother Tongue', pp. 253–55.

12 *The Diary of Virginia Woolf*, ed. by Anne Olivier Bell, 5 vols (London: Penguin Books, 1980–85), II (1981), p. 248.

for our topic, the character of Rezia, Septimus's Italian wife, manifests estrangement from the foreign culture she lives in, but her speech and thoughts show no linguistic mark of her condition as a non-native English speaker. Yet it is precisely such overt violation of verisimilitude that suggests how the (apparent) homogeneity of the language employed by Woolf can hardly be seen as proof that she was unable or unwilling to provide genuine diverse voices for her characters; rather, the writer seemed to follow the specific intent of creating an anti-mimetic 'universal' voice for consciousness. A whole line of inquiry into Woolf's exploration of the relationship between language, mind, and experience has stressed the *intentionally fictive* quality of her representation of consciousness, ranging from Auerbach's remarks on the anti-mimetic perspective from which the reader is given access to consciousness in her novels,[13] to Ann Banfield's linguistic examination of Woolf's techniques as revealing 'the essential fictionality of any representation of consciousness, of any approximation of words to thought, even of our own.'[14]

In the following analysis, I will focus on how learning and unlearning language (and literary language) is explored in *The Waves*, where the overt fictionality of the Woolfian language of consciousness radically emerges. My aim will be to show how Woolf's emphasis on the conventional, fictitious nature of language represents a powerful, though oblique, challenge to linguistic myths. More specifically, Woolf's experimentation proves to inscribe the myth of the mother tongue — the existence of a language to which we adhere and in which we best express ourselves — into the wider questioning of how and to what extent language is capable of providing expression for our thoughts and experience. In this respect, the elements that I intend to highlight in Woolf's reconfiguration of linguistic competence in the transfigured terms of her 'play-poem' show convergence with Lepschy's powerful point that 'no one is a native speaker of the language of poetry.'[15]

13 Erich Auerbach, 'The Brown Stocking', in *Mimesis: The Representation of Reality in Western Literature*, trans. by Willard R. Trusk (Princeton, NJ: Princeton University Press, 2013), pp. 525–53.

14 Ann Banfield, *Unspeakable Sentences: Narration and Representation in the Language of Fiction* (London: Routledge, 1982), p. 260.

15 Lepschy, 'Mother Tongues and Literary Languages', p. 48.

UNFINISHING SENTENCES: LEARNING AND UN-LEARNING LANGUAGE IN *THE WAVES*

Conceived by Woolf through a complex process of revision, the 'abstract mystical eyeless' novel *The Waves* came to acquire, in its final version, the form of a 'play-poem' structured on 'a series of dramatic soliloquies'.[16] Innumerable epistemological and aesthetic implications arise from the highly experimental form of the work, which Woolf came to consider capable 'to embody, at last, the exact shape my brain holds. What a long toil to reach this beginning — if *The Waves* is my first work in my own style!'.[17] I will focus here on those elements that specifically connect to the relationship between language and experience, with reference to how the issue is conveyed in the novel as an ever-evolving and contradictory process. In particular, I will underline those instances in *The Waves* that point to language seen, simultaneously, as *the* instrument for elaboration and expression of experience, and as a limited and limiting tool. This, as we will see, is symbolically mirrored in the novel by the portrayal of language acquisition as paradoxically entailing both *learning* and *un-learning*.

As mentioned, *The Waves* can be seen as paradigmatic of Woolf's anti-mimetic poetics, not only for its abstract, anti-conventional structure, but also for the way the six (or seven, counting the immaterial presence of Percival) characters are portrayed. Woolf's project was to 'do away with exact place & time' as well as to move towards a polyphonic narration that works as a 'gigantic conversation' and that includes not only human consciousness but also, as it happens in the interludes, the natural world: 'some continuous stream, not solely of human thought, but of the ship, the night&c, all flowing together'.[18] Woolf's challenge with this work was to build narration on the deconstruction and gradual reconstruction of the essential elements of linguistic expression, starting with the key anchoring provided by deixis.[19] At the beginning of the novel, after the first interlude, the

16 *The Diary of Virginia Woolf*, III (1982), pp. 203 and 312.

17 *The Diary of Virginia Woolf*, IV (1983), p. 53.

18 *The Diary of Virginia Woolf*, III, pp. 230, 285, and 139.

19 As per John Lyons's classical definition: 'by deixis is meant the location and identification of persons, objects, events, processes and activities being talked about, or

characters are introduced as isolated perceptual subjects deprived of a clear spatio-temporal location: time is suspended in the perpetual present of the language of description, and no elements of spatial deixis anchor the voices to a setting. Time and space appear gradually and in a fragmented form: the passage of time is first introduced via the shift from the present simple to the present perfect tense ('Biddy has smacked down the bucket on the kitchen flags'),[20] while Bernard's act of pointing ('Look at the spider's web'),[21] although still not locating the voices, opens a space of shared deixis among the characters. However, as I will show later, the most radical deconstruction is operated in relation to person deixis, in line with Woolf's intention to portray in this work the constant symbolic merging of different consciousnesses:

> 'But when we sit together, close', said Bernard, 'we melt into each other with phrases. We are edged with mist. We make an unsubstantial territory.'[22]

The reference to 'phrases' is crucial here, as it is via the interaction of their soliloquies that the characters merge, but language also defines the borders of one's identity thus separating the subject from both the world and the others:

> But we were all different. The wax — the virginal wax that coats the spine melted in different patches for each of us. [...] I made notes for stories; drew portraits in the margin of my pocket-book and thus became still more separate.[23]

The dynamics between merging and separation are conveyed, especially, in the process that brings the characters to move from their osmotic perception in childhood to an acknowledgement of their individual identities, a turning point recalled by Bernard in the final section

referred to, in relation to the spatiotemporal context created and sustained by the act of utterance and the participation in it, typically, of a single speaker and at least one addressee.' See John Lyons, *Semantics* (Cambridge: Cambridge University Press, 1977), p. 637. For deixis in narrative, and in particular the notion of deictic shift, see *Deixis in Narrative: A Cognitive Science Perspective*, ed. by Lynne E. Hewitt, Judith F. Duchan, and Gail A. Bruder (Hillsdale, NJ: Lawrence Erlbaum Associates, 1995).

20 Woolf, *The Waves*, p. 7.

21 Ibid., p. 5.

22 Ibid., p. 11.

23 Ibid., pp. 202–03.

of the novel: '"therefore", I said, "I am myself, not Neville", a wonderful discovery.'[24] Nonetheless, the time span following the characters from childhood to adult life is not depicted as a linear progression, but rather as a contradictory movement also entailing regression and loss:

> We saw for a moment laid out among us the body of the complete human being whom we have failed to be, but at the same time, cannot forget. All that we might have been we saw; all that we had missed, and we grudged for a moment the other's claim, as children when the cake is cut, the one cake, the only cake, watch their slice diminishing.[25]

The reversal is actually anticipated in the opening chapter, where the characters are portrayed as small children showing an unrealistic linguistic competence. This appears to align their complex sensorial experience to language, thus filling that gap between perception and expression typical of childhood.[26] In the novel, such a (fictive) ideal state of felicitous matching of words and experience becomes lost in the process of building — via language and its conventions — one's identity ('some crack in the structure — one's identity') and, in this sense, the work appears to trace, while also questioning it, the entire parabola of language acquisition.[27]

Particularly revealing on the topic is the second chapter, where the children are portrayed as entering school. This entails their gendered separation — the boys in one college and the girls in another — as well as the 'orderly progress' of formal education.[28] Differences among the characters acquire here a more distinct shape, in line with Bernard's remark on how the emergence of one's identity implies a process of differentiation. Distinctions had however already surfaced in the first section:

---

24 Ibid., p. 201.

25 Ibid., p. 231.

26 Virginia Woolf, 'A Sketch of the Past', in Woolf, *Moments of Being*, ed. by Jeanne Schulkind (New York: Harcourt Brace, 1985), pp. 61–160 (p. 67): 'Perhaps this is the characteristic of all childhood memories; perhaps it accounts for their strength. Later we add to feelings much that makes them less strong; or if not less strong, less isolated, less complete.'

27 Woolf, *The Waves*, p. 94.

28 Ibid., p. 25.

> 'I will not conjugate the verb', said Louis, 'until Bernard has said it. My father is a banker in Brisbane and I speak with an Australian accent. I will wait and copy Bernard. He is English. They are all English. Susan's father is a clergyman. Rhoda has no father. Bernard and Neville are the sons of gentlemen. Jinny lives with her grandmother in London.'[29]

Louis's sense of estrangement is determined by his different cultural and linguistic background but, as it happens with Rezia in *Mrs Dalloway*, this is not rendered by linguistic marks like the phonetic rendering of his accent, but only via the content of his soliloquy. Rezia's marginalization comes from her different mother tongue, while Louis embodies, long before the theorization of World Englishes, the sociocultural stratifications active in each single language: 'I am now a boy only with a colonial accent.'[30] Significantly, Louis welcomes the order and hierarchy of institutional (religious) education, which allows him to feel as part of an indistinct homogeneous group:

> 'Now we march, two by two', said Louis, 'orderly, processional, into chapel. I like the dimness that falls as we enter the sacred building. I like the orderly progress. We file in; we seat ourselves. We put off our distinctions as we enter. I like it now, when, lurching slightly, but only from his momentum, Dr Crane mounts the pulpit and reads the lesson from a Bible spread on the back of the brass eagle. I rejoice; my heart expands in his bulk, in his authority.'[31]

By contrast, the feeling of melting into a crowd is experienced by Rhoda as a destabilizing deprivation of identity ('But I am nobody. I have no face. This great company, all dressed in brown serge, has robbed me of my identity'),[32] and Neville resents the oppressive authority symbolized by Dr Crane's sermon:

> The brute menaces my liberty [...] when he prays. Unwarmed by imagination, his words fall cold on my head like paving-stones, while the gilt cross heaves on his waistcoat. The words of authority are corrupted by those who speak them.[33]

29 Ibid., p. 30

30 Ibid., p. 40.

31 Ibid., pp. 25–26.

32 Ibid., p. 25.

33 Ibid., p. 26.

Bernard's reaction to the sermon is equally negative, and, in line with the character, especially pointed towards the linguistic distortion operated by Dr. Crane:

> He sways slightly, mouthing out his tremendous and sonorous words. I love tremendous and sonorous words. But his words are too hearty to be true. Yet he is by this time convinced of their truth.[34]

The disjunction between language and truth, leading to deceptive and self-deceptive rhetoric, is amplified by the fact that the adjective 'sonorous' was present also, a few lines before, in Neville's soliloquy:

> those are laboratories perhaps; and that a library, where I shall explore the exactitude of the Latin language, and step firmly upon the well-laid sentences, and pronounce the explicit, the sonorous hexameters of Virgil, of Lucretius; and chant with a passion that is never obscure or formless the loves of Catullus, reading from a big book, a quarto with margins.[35]

Formal education is embodied here first by the official places where knowledge is acquired — laboratories, library — and then by the unequivocal language ('never obscure or formless') of the classical heritage preserved and transmitted in beautifully authoritative publications ('a big book, a quarto with margins'). Latin language is portrayed as combining the famous 'granite & rainbow' pair,[36] which recurs in Woolf's writing: a language endowed with 'exactitude', solid syntactical structures, and a regular versification in poetry ('hexameters'), all elements capable of providing the dynamic and sensorial elements of experience ('explicit', 'sonorous', 'passion') with a neat form. Nonetheless, the fact that the adjective 'sonorous' is employed in the two instances with opposite implications discloses the novel's focus on the double nature of language: the sonorous quality may render words exact by resorting on the phono-symbolic potentialities of language, but it may also lead language to the opposite, the twist of authenticity

34 Ibid., p. 24.

35 Ibid., p. 23.

36 This is the title of one of Woolf's collection of essays: Virginia Woolf, *Granite & Rainbow* (London: Hogarth, 1960).

via rhetorical emphasis. This is further reinforced by the fact that Virgil is mentioned also by Louis with reference again to his desire to see his physical and linguistic features ('my large nose, my thin lips, my colonial accent') blur into the new identity granted him by education: 'I am then Virgil's companion, and Plato's.'[37]

In this sense, the path of education travels along *The Waves* in a double-faceted fashion, representing both the building of a structure providing individual personalities with solidity and a cultural background, and, at the opposite, a dangerous blurring of differences, of individualities, as they merge into the formal, institutional, and canonical ordering of language and culture. With reference to the ordering potentiality of language, at the end of the sermon Bernard imagines storing the details of the episode for his future writing, in the paradoxical intent of cataloguing experience in the form of phrases meant to fix the moment in its definitive form — the one that would provide it, once for all, with its exact description:

> I note the fact for future reference with many others in my notebook. When I am grown up I shall carry a notebook — a fat book with many pages, methodically lettered. I shall enter my phrases. Under B shall come 'Butterfly powder'. If, in my novel, I describe the sun on the window-sill, I shall look under B and find butterfly powder. That will be useful. 'The tree shades the window with green fingers'. That will be useful.[38]

Bernard's cataloguing project is however contradicted not only by his flying mind ('But alas! I'm soon distracted'),[39] but also by the process he operates in storing the phrases: reference is not direct, but it rather works via metaphorical transferral, connecting 'butterfly powder' to the description of 'the sun on the window-sill'. In search of an impossible exactitude ('there is about both Neville and Louis a precision, an exactitude, that I admire and shall never possess'),[40] Bernard will be 'eternally engaged' in 'finding some perfect phrase that fits this very moment exactly'.[41] The perfect 'phrase', however, will

37 Woolf, *The Waves*, p. 41.

38 Ibid., p. 27.

39 Ibid.

40 Ibid., p. 54.

41 Ibid.

always escape him, and he will be instead 'breasting the world with half-finished sentences',[42] or, as he will describe them in the last chapter, 'unfinishing' phrases.[43]

In the last chapter, which is entirely devoted to Bernard's soliloquy, the need and desire for a less structured language is made explicit. In the character's perception, the above-mentioned 'well-laid sentences' have become a mystification that orders experience in falsifying 'neat designs of life': 'how tired I am of stories, how tired I am of phrases that come down beautifully with all their feet on the ground!'.[44] In contrast, Bernard begins to 'long for some little language such as lovers use, broken words, inarticulate words, like the shuffling of feet on the pavement',[45] 'a painful, guttural, visceral, also soaring, lark-like, pealing song to replace these flagging, foolish transcripts',[46] as 'what is the use of painfully elaborating these consecutive sentences when what one needs is nothing consecutive but a bark, a groan?'.[47] The radical questioning of language unfolding in the last chapter brings to a climax the confrontation between words and experience lying at the core of *The Waves*. Language is disclosed by Bernard as an imperfect tool:

> my book, stuffed with phrases, has dropped to the floor. [...] What is the phrase for the moon? And the phrase for love? By what name are we to call death? I do not know. I need a little language such as lovers use, words of one syllable such as children speak when they come into the room and find their mother sewing and pick up some scrap of bright wool, a feather, or a shred of chintz. I need a howl; a cry. When the storm crosses the marsh and sweeps over me where I lie in the ditch unregarded I need no words. Nothing neat. Nothing that comes down with all its feet on the floor. None of those resonances and lovely echoes that break and chime from nerve to nerve in our breasts, making wild music, false phrases. I have done with phrases.[48]

42 Ibid., p. 55.

43 Ibid., p. 236.

44 Ibid., p. 199.

45 Ibid.

46 Ibid., p. 209.

47 Ibid., pp. 209–10.

48 Ibid., p. 246.

The structured form of language proves incapable of conveying the unstructured, primordial aspects of experience: the resonances, the echoes, the subtle, nuanced, and inexplicable sensations appear unfit to be categorized via the consecutive and well-structured form of language:

> but it is a mistake, this extreme precision, this orderly and military progress; a convenience, a lie. There is always deep below it [...] a rushing stream of broken dreams, nursery rhymes, street cries, half-finished sentences and sights.[49]

The most symbolic character, in this sense, appears to be Rhoda, with her inability to fix her perception in the stability of language:

> Louis writes; Susan writes; Neville writes; Jinny writes; even Bernard has now begun to write. But I cannot write. I see only figures. The others are handing in their answers, one by one. Now it is my turn. But I have no answer. [...] The figures mean nothing now. Meaning has gone. [...] 'There Rhoda sits staring at the blackboard', said Louis, '[...] her mind lodges in those white circles, it steps through those white loops into emptiness, alone. They have no meaning for her. She has no answer for them. She has no body as the others have.'[50]

Melting with the others and the world, perpetually traversed by 'the arrows of sensation',[51] Rhoda will ultimately prove unable to sustain perception and, as hinted by the other characters, will commit suicide. Bernard, the writer, will instead finally revert to silence, overwhelmed by the inability of language to catch the fluid and sensorial aspects of life:

> but how describe the world seen without a self? There are no words. Blue, red — even they distract, even they hide with thickness instead of letting the light through. How describe or say anything in articulate words again? — save that it fades, save that it undergoes a gradual transformation, becomes, even in the course of one short walk, habitual — this scene also.[52]

49 Ibid., p. 213.
50 Ibid., pp. 15–16.
51 Ibid., p. 200.
52 Ibid., p. 239.

Yet *The Waves* appears to trace not a path of progressive disenchantment towards language, but rather a circular process bringing the characters back to the ideal synergy between mind, senses, and language that was depicted at the beginning. As previously mentioned, the opening of the book is entirely structured on I-centred perception:

> 'I see a ring', said Bernard, 'hanging above me. It quivers and hangs in a loop of light.'
>
> 'I see a slab of pale yellow', said Susan, 'spreading away until it meets a purple stripe.'
>
> 'I hear a sound', said Rhoda, 'cheep, chirp; cheep chirp; going up and down.'
>
> 'I see a globe', said Neville, 'hanging down in a drop against the enormous flanks of some hill.'
>
> 'I see a crimson tassel', said Jinny, 'twisted with gold threads.'
>
> 'I hear something stamping', said Louis. 'A great beast's foot is chained. It stamps, and stamps, and stamps.'[53]

Woolf's exploration in this work of I-less perception requires her to confront the challenge of registering the 'unrecorded', 'unattended', 'unfeeling universe' via the unavoidably I-centred tool of language.[54] In line with this, the opening portrays the characters as the overt deictic centres of their utterances. Their linguistic acts convey what may be seen as the origin of the encounter between the subject and language, when no meanings, interpretations, and not even descriptions are attached to the choice of words, which appear to register the sensorial ('I see', 'I hear') encounter between the subject and the world. This is depicted as an agglomerate of figures ('a ring', 'a loop', and 'a globe'), colours ('yellow', 'purple', 'crimson', and 'gold'), and sounds ('cheep', 'chirp', and 'stamping'). As anticipated, subtle shifts in the utterances progressively come to build the narrative setting by adding the spatial and temporal coordinates. In terms of person deixis, an essential shift is operated when the *I-origines* become implicit and language takes the form of pure description:

---

53 Ibid., p. 5.

54 Ibid., pp. 214, 239, and 234. On this point see, especially, Ann Banfield, *The Phantom Table: Woolf, Fry, Russell and the Epistemology of Modernism* (Cambridge: Cambridge University Press, 2000).

> 'The leaves are gathered round the window like pointed ears', said Susan.
>
> 'A shadow falls on the path', said Louis, 'like an elbow bent.'
>
> 'Islands of light are swimming on the grass', said Rhoda. 'They have fallen through the trees.'
>
> 'The birds' eyes are bright in the tunnels between the leaves', said Neville.[55]

Interestingly, when the characters shift from I-centred to object-centred description figurative language is employed, first in the explicit form of similes ('like pointed ears' and 'like an elbow bent') and then in that of metaphors ('islands of light are swimming on the grass swimming').[56] Shortly later, in the scene that sees the children gathered around a table for a lesson, the words that they are learning undergo the same figurative transformation and are rendered in synaesthetic terms:

> 'Those are white words', said Susan, 'like stones one picks up by the seashore.'
>
> 'They flick their tails right and left as I speak them', said Bernard. 'They wag their tails; they flick their tails; they move through the air in flocks, now this way, now that way, moving all together, now dividing, now coming together.'
>
> 'Those are yellow words, those are fiery words', said Jinny. 'I should like a fiery dress, a yellow dress, a fulvous dress to wear in the evening.'[57]

In the process of learning, words enter the perception of the children as objects: rather than being mere tools of expression, they are felt by the characters as living elements possessing the same physical qualities as the other objects they are encountering, and are thus equally expressed via figurative language, in an endless self-reflective process. This living

55 Woolf, *The Waves*, p. 5.

56 I have explored the different implications of Woolf's employment of metaphors and similes in *The Waves* in Teresa Prudente, 'From "The Aloe" to "Prelude" and from *The Moths* to *The Waves*: Drafts, Revisions and the Process of "Becoming-Imperceptible" in Virginia Woolf and Katherine Mansfield', *Textus: English Studies in Italy*, 27.3 (2015), pp. 95–118.

57 Woolf, *The Waves*, pp. 14–15.

quality also coincides with the conception of language to which Bernard finally longs to return:

> the crystal, the globe of life as one calls it, far from being hard and cold to the touch, has walls of thinnest air. If I press them all will burst. Whatever sentence I extract whole and entire from this cauldron is only a string of six little fish that let themselves be caught while a million others leap and sizzle, making the cauldron bubble like boiling silver, and slip through my fingers.[58]

In this sense, *The Waves* represents a poignant and radical rediscussion of any idea of a language capable of expressing with exactitude the subject's relationship with the world. The symbolic parabola of language acquisition traced by the novel discloses Woolf's questioning of the myth of exact referentiality implied in our language learning processes: 'but meanwhile, while we eat, let us turn over these scenes as children turn over the pages of a picture-book and the nurse says, pointing: "That's a cow. That's a boat."'[59] As I will show in the last section, the issue traverses Woolf's writing, building a complex design touching upon essential cruxes in the philosophy as well as in the history of language, and hinting at what I propose to read as Woolf's redefinition of the expression mother tongue and its implications.

'GREEK IS THE ONLY EXPRESSION': REINVENTING THE MOTHER TONGUE

The elements that I have underlined in *The Waves* show how in Woolf there appears to be a constant, pervasive hint at, and struggle for, an ideal universal language — one capable of connecting mind and senses as well as one subject to others. It is in this sense, I argue, that the notion of mother tongue becomes in Woolf rediscussed and, ultimately, redefined in terms that actually do appear to tie the notion of mother/origin and that of tongue/language — only in complex and reversed terms with respect to their traditional interpretation.

To explain this point better, I will widen the angle of that circular design that ties together, in *The Waves*, beginning and end: the first

58 Ibid., p. 214.
59 Ibid., p. 200.

encounter, in childhood, between language and experience and the longing, in adulthood, to disarticulate language in order to return to that same fluid, osmotic, and mythic coinciding. In order to do so, it is necessary to place *The Waves*' portrayal of language acquisition and (symbolic) dis-acquisition in the context of Woolf's view on the history of language(s), for which her 1925 essay 'On Not Knowing Greek' proves revealing. The lack of knowledge of ancient Greek to which Woolf points in the title is in fact not a lack derived from not knowing the language, but rather the perpetual separateness we experience from a language and culture we will never be able completely to appropriate:

> we do not know how the words sounded, or where precisely we ought to laugh, or how the actors acted, and between this foreign people and ourselves there is not only difference of race and tongue but a tremendous breach of tradition.[60]

Woolf's emphasis on the fact that Greek literature represents impersonal literature discloses the strong nexus between the essay and *The Waves*, or, better, once again clarifies how the 1931 novel condensed the many intricate directions of her thinking and experimentations.[61] Greek literature is for Woolf an 'imaginative literature, where characters speak for themselves and the author has no part, the need of that voice is making itself felt'.[62] This quality derives for Woolf from the language itself and, more specifically, from the feeling of distance that we, modern readers, experience and that mirrors our distance from *the origin*, the (mythical) point in time when things were experienced for the first time:

> a fragment of their speech broken off would, we feel, colour oceans and oceans of the respectable drama. Here we meet them before their emotions have been worn into uniformity. Here we listen to the nightingale whose song echoes through English literature singing in her own Greek tongue.[63]

60 Virginia Woolf, 'On Not Knowing Greek', in *Collected Essays*, 4 vols (London: Hogarth, 1966–67), I (1966), pp. 1–13 (p. 1).

61 Ibid., p. 1.

62 Ibid., p. 6.

63 Ibid., p. 5.

As I have underlined in *The Waves*, the mythical origin coincides for Woolf with the initial true encounter between the subject, experience, and language, before habits, repetition, conventions come to order and uniform experience and its expression: 'those habitual currents in which after a certain time experience forms in the mind, so that one repeats words without being aware any longer who originally spoke them'.[64] In Woolf these hints at an idealized initial coinciding between words and things, an oblique and revisited version of the pre-Babelian myth, prove to coalesce with a multitude of further elements, among which are those coming from the philosophy of language contemporary to her, as well as from the tradition of Romantic poetry. As Ann Banfield has singled out,[65] Woolf's treatment of language appears to be strongly influenced by Bertrand Russell's theory of descriptions, which represented a fundamental step in the logico-philosophical reflection on language that departed from Frege and culminated in Wittgenstein's *Tractatus*. But Woolf's focus on the opposition between the conventional and the genuine quality of language also seems to incorporate the redefinition of language proposed by Romantic poets and, above all, by S. T. Coleridge.

The living quality of words underlined by Woolf in *The Waves* is stressed by Coleridge in his *Aids to Reflection*:

> Horne Tooke entitled his celebrated work, *Ἔπεα πτερόεντα*, winged words: or language, not only the vehicle of thought but the wheels. With my convictions and views, for *ἔπεα* I should substitute *λόγοι*, that is, words select and determinate, and for *πτερόεντα ζώντεσ*, that is, living words.[66]

For Woolf, words cannot be fixed, pinned down, 'because the truth they try to catch is many-sided, and they convey it by being themselves many-sided, flashing this way, then that'.[67] Yet words are also solid,

---

64 Virginia Woolf, *To the Lighthouse* (London: Penguin, 1996), p. 233.

65 Banfield, *The Phantom Table*.

66 Samuel T. Coleridge, *Aids to Reflection*, in *The Complete Works of Samuel Taylor Coleridge with an Introductory Essay upon his Philosophical and Theological Opinions*, ed. by William Greenough Thayer Shedd, 7 vols (New York: Harper & Brothers, 1853–54), I (1953), p. 114.

67 Virginia Woolf, 'Craftsmanship', in *The Crowded Dance of Modern Life: Selected Essays*, 2 vols (London: Penguin, 1993), II, pp. 137–43 (p. 143).

both for Coleridge ('not only the vehicle of thoughts but the wheels') and for Woolf:

> they are the wildest, freest, most irresponsible, most unteachable of all things [...] And how do they live in the mind? Variously and strangely, much as human beings live, by ranging hither and thither, by falling in love, and mating together.[68]

As Woolf writes in 'The Man at the Gate' (1940), the 'labyrinth of what we call Coleridge' is characterized by a verbal abundance that ignites infinite multiplications ('the innumerable, the mutable, the atmospheric') and that becomes however ultimately distilled in poems 'in which every word is exact and every image as clear as crystal'.[69]

There is a striking resemblance between the words employed by Woolf to convey Coleridge's language and the ones we find in *The Waves*. At the end of the novel, the crystal comes to embody life itself ('the crystal, the globe of life'),[70] but the image rapidly transforms into that of a malleable nucleus that loses its hard quality to become porous and expand to the bursting point ('has walls of thinnest air. If I press them all will burst').[71] Thus the hard, stable, multifaceted crystal reverses back to the globe, the image present at the beginning of the novel: '"I see a globe", said Neville, "hanging down in a drop against the enormous flanks of some hill."'[72] The globe is however in its turn a transformation of the very first image opening *The Waves*: '"I see a ring", said Bernard, "hanging above me. It quivers and hangs in a loop of light."'[73] In the last part of the novel, even the solidity of the globe is in fact revealed to be a convention, the epistemological mystification we build in order to understand and communicate our experience:

> let us again pretend that life is a solid substance, shaped like a globe, which we turn about in our fingers. Let us pretend that we can make out a plain and logical story, so that when one

68 Ibid., pp. 141–42.

69 Virginia Woolf, 'The Man at the Gate', in *The Death of the Moth and Other Essays* (New York: Harcourt, 1974), pp. 104–10 (pp. 104 and 110).

70 Woolf, *The Waves*, p. 214.

71 Ibid.

72 Ibid., p. 5.

73 Ibid.

> matter is despatched — love for instance — we go on, in an orderly manner, to the next.[74]

What recurs in the novel as an alternative to the globe is the thinner and more stylized figure of the ring:

> that is, I am fiercer and stronger than you are, yet the apparition that appears above ground after ages of nonentity will be spent in terror lest you should laugh at me, in veerings with the wind against the soot storms, in efforts to make a steel ring of clear poetry that shall connect the gulls and the women with bad teeth, the church spire and the bobbing billycock hats as I see them when I take my luncheon and prop my poet — is it Lucretius? — against a cruet and the gravy-splashed bill of fare.[75]

Significantly, it is here Louis — the character whose socio-linguistic estrangement we have mentioned — that dreams of the 'steel ring of poetry' capable of holding together the several contradictory elements of human experience. Reference is again to the heritage of the classics, Lucretius, and a hint of the above-mentioned 'sonorous' quality of Latin language is rendered via the polyptoton playing on the plosive sound ('the apparition that appears'). The 'steel ring of clear poetry' — not a globe but a thin, resistant structure encapsulating a portion of emptiness[76] — appears however to result precisely from the opposite of rhetorical excess, for it stems from that process of depurating and distilling that brings us back to Coleridge and Greek ('words select and determinate').[77]

Within the wider context of the Romantic poets who redefined language by rejecting rhetorical artifice insofar as it was employed ex-

74 Ibid., p. 210.

75 Ibid., p. 105.

76 I have explored the interplay between ecstasy and emptiness in Teresa Prudente, *A Specially Tender Piece of Eternity: Virginia Woolf and the Experience of Time* (Lanham, MD: Lexington Books, 2009), pp. 45–67.

77 Coleridge, *Aids to Reflection*, p. 114. For this process in Woolf see especially *The Diary of Virginia Woolf*, III, p. 209: 'The idea has come to me that what I want now to do is to saturate every atom. I mean to eliminate all waste, deadness, superfluity: to give the moment whole; whatever it includes.'

clusively 'as a mechanical device of style',[78] Coleridge holds a special position in virtue of the ample angle of his reflections. Dynamically engaging with the empiricist and idealist philosophical traditions, Coleridge's positions on language represent a complex and multifaceted stage in the evolution of the philosophy of language.[79] The poet appears to signal a way out from the Lockean affirmation of the arbitrariness of language not so much by insisting on a lost mythical stage of coincidence between words and things but, on the contrary, through a diachronic perspective unfolding the history of words — the multidirectional paths of significance that they undertake in time. Thus, Coleridge's method constantly refers back to the etymology of words in order to seek their origin: the first encounter between words and experience, which does not, however, point to a static coincidence of signifier and signified, but rather — as it happens at the beginning of *The Waves* — to the process allowing things to come into existence by being named:

> The name of a thing, in the original sense of the word name (*nomen, νούμενον, τὸ intelligibile, id quod intelligitur*), expresses that which is *understood* in an appearance, that which we place (or make to *stand*) *under* it, as the condition of its real existence, and in proof that it is not an accident of the senses, or affection of the individual, not a phantom or apparition [...]. Thus, in all instances, it is words, names, or, if images, yet images used as words or names, that are the only and exclusive subjects of understanding. In no instance do we understand a thing in itself; but only the name to which it is referred.[80]

Although Coleridge's apparent one name-one thing association may seem the opposite of Woolf's emphasis on the ever-moving quality of words, the two perspectives actually converge into the project of freeing language from the conventions that have grown about words

78 William Wordsworth, 'Preface (to the Second Edition)', in William Wordsworth and Samuel T. Coleridge, *Lyrical Ballads: 1798 and 1802*, ed. by Fiona Stafford (Oxford: Oxford University Press, 2013), pp. 95–116 (p. 100).

79 See William Keach, 'Romanticism and Language', in *The Cambridge Companion to British Romanticism*, ed. by Stuart Curran (Cambridge: Cambridge University Press, 2010), pp. 95–118.

80 Coleridge, *Aids to Reflection*, pp. 248–51.

and of reviving their ever-living, generative power. Woolf underlines how words tend progressively to lose their meaning as

> words, English words, are full of echoes, of memories, of associations — naturally. They have been out and about, on people's lips, in their houses, in the streets, in the fields for so many centuries. And that is one of the chief difficulties in writing them today — that they are so stored with meanings, with memories, that they have contracted so many famous marriages.[81]

Woolf's idea is then to free words from established associations and to bring them back to life by allowing them to live not in dictionaries, but 'in that deep, dark and only fitfully illuminated cavern in which they live — the mind',[82] so as to restage, every time, that genuine encounter between the mind, experience, and language. In this sense, the exactness to which Woolf refers both in *The Waves* and in her essay on Coleridge may actually coincide with the opposite of the idea of one single, static, codified language, in the same way Coleridge insisted on the infinite variations of language.[83] In 'Craftsmanship', the emphasis is again on the idea of reversing back to an extraverbal system of communication, and, especially, on the power of suggestion of words: the set of associations, memories, images that they suggest as they 'combine unconsciously together'.[84] For Woolf, each word contains 'so many sunken meanings', and it is necessary 'to allow the sunken meanings to remain sunken, suggested, not stated'.[85] In this sense, an exact language would need to retain that power of suggestion, similar to how the 'buzz of words', the 'hypnotic fume' of Coleridge's language, ultimately results into the clear crystal of his poetry where 'meaning dwindles and fades to a wisp on the mind's horizon'.[86]

---

81 Woolf, 'Craftsmanship', pp. 140–41.

82 Ibid., p. 142.

83 Samuel T. Coleridge, *Biographia Literaria, or Biographical Sketches of My Literary Life and Opinions* (New York: Wiley & Putnam, 1847), p. 170: 'Every man's language varies according to the extent of his knowledge, the activity of his faculties, and the depth or quickness of his feelings. Every man's language has, first, its individual peculiarities; secondly, the properties common to his class; and thirdly, words and phrases of universal use.'

84 Woolf, 'Craftsmanship', p. 140

85 Ibid.

86 Woolf, 'The Man at the Gate', pp. 104, 110, and 106.

Reference to Greek represents a powerful conjunction between Woolf's and Coleridge's conceptions of language, for these conceptions both focus on that original power of words that both writers meant to reactivate. More importantly, and crucial to our topic, is the fact that the *fragmented* nature of our reappropriation of that original state appears to be the element that renders ancient Greek a language capable of reactivating the potentialities of words:

> we cannot pick up infallibly one by one all those minute signals by which a phrase is made to hint, to turn, to live. Nevertheless, it is the language that has us most in bondage; the desire for that which perpetually lures us back.[87]

It is thus the separateness, the lack, the perpetual desire for what we fail to appropriate that may reignite 'sunken' potentialities by leading us far from the comfort and the confidence provided us by the language we feel we possess — our native language. Significantly, it is precisely this power that equates, for Woolf, to poetry:

> to understand him [Aeschylus] it is not so necessary to understand Greek as to understand poetry. It is necessary to take that dangerous leap through the air without the support of words which Shakespeare also asks of us. For words, when opposed to such a blast of meaning, must give out, must be blown astray, and only by collecting in companies convey the meaning which each one separately is too weak to express. Connecting them in a rapid flight of the mind we know instantly and instinctively what they mean, but could not decant that meaning afresh into any other words. There is an ambiguity which is the mark of the highest poetry; we cannot know exactly what it means. [...] The meaning is just on the far side of language. It is the meaning which in moments of astonishing excitement and stress we perceive in our minds without words.[88]

As meaning is, for Woolf, 'on the far side of language' it is there, to unknown lands, that one needs to travel to experience the perpetual deferral of meaning that reactivates the endless potentialities of words: 'Chief among these sources of glamour and perhaps misunderstanding

87 Woolf, 'On Not Knowing Greek', p. 11.

88 Ibid., p. 7.

is the language. We can never hope to get the whole fling of a sentence in Greek as we do in English.'[89]

Yet Greek is obviously for Woolf, as it was for Coleridge, not just *a* foreign language, but one of the distant mothers of their mother tongue — a point of origin to which the English language is connected via the indirect lineage of Latin and the Romance languages. It is perhaps in this sense that for Woolf Greek represents what her (direct) mother tongue lacks: 'the compactness of the expression' ('Shelley takes twenty-one words in English to translate thirteen words of Greek'),[90] offering words that are 'so clear, so hard, so intense, that to speak plainly yet fittingly without blurring the outline or clouding the depths, Greek is the only expression'.[91]

In this sense, Woolf's notion of mother tongue does speak of that sense of identity discussed at the beginning of this essay: the building of our individualities on the maternal/linguistic lineage that defines us. Nonetheless, instead of being a datum, that heritage is placed by Woolf into a dynamic process that recombines native and non-native language, real/individual and imagined/universal identities. Woolf's quest seems to be pointed towards debunking all the elements that constrain language into homogeneity: habits, as we have seen, but also the falsifying idea of a culturally homogeneous language:

> royal words mate with commoners. English words marry French words, German words, Indian words, negro words, if they have a fancy. Indeed, the less we inquire into the dear Mother English the better it will be for that lady's reputation.[92]

Such emphasis on the mixed nature of languages allows Woolf to question a monolithic and codified conception of language and to embark instead on the search for a *different* universal, all-encompassing, form of expression. The common ground is, for Woolf, not a common culture or language — one providing us with the false belief that we are able to understand each other as speakers of the same mother tongue — but rather a system of communication cutting across differences —

89 Ibid., p. 11.

90 Ibid.

91 Ibid.

92 Woolf, 'Craftsmanship', p. 142.

of culture, language, class, gender — to reach and express the shared experience of the encounter between the world and the mind. Woolf's perpetual quest for a universal, fictive, and ideal language of the mind entails constant tension between, on the one hand, her awareness of the essentially private, subjective, culture-bound, and I-centred quality of language, and, on the other, the challenge to overcome these boundaries to reach a universal, I-less form of expression. The language of the mind thus becomes a dreamed language, an ideal whose origins may be reinvented via a reappropriation of the past where the foreign, rather than the familiar, becomes the matrix:

> In spite of the labour and the difficulty it is this that draws us back and back to the Greeks; the stable, the permanent, the original human being is to be found there. These are the originals, Chaucer's the varieties of the human species.[93]

Significantly, to go back to the connection between mother and tongue, a similar process seems to apply for Woolf to her own origins, in the way her parents and her childhood are transfigured and reinvented in the 'elegy' of *To the Lighthouse*:[94]

> I used to think of him & mother daily; but writing The Lighthouse, laid them in my mind. And now he comes back sometimes, but differently. (I believe this is true — that I was obsessed by them both, unhealthy; & writing of them was a necessary act).[95]

The figures of her parents and the memory of her childhood had to become unreal, to lose the reality of what was familiar, so as to acquire a different, universal, even impersonal reality[96] — similar to how, according to Woolf, in Greek poetry 'we are drawn to steep ourselves

93 Woolf, 'On Not Knowing Greek', p. 4.

94 *The Diary of Virginia Woolf*, III, p. 34: 'I have an idea that I will invent a new name for my books to supplant "novel." [...] But what? Elegy?'.

95 Ibid., III, p. 208. See also Woolf, 'A Sketch of the Past', pp. 80–81: 'Until I was in the forties — I could settle the date by seeing when I wrote *To the Lighthouse* [...] the presence of my mother obsessed me. [...] I wrote the book very quickly; and when it was written, I ceased to be obsessed by my mother.'

96 See also, on the composition of *The Waves*, *The Diary of Virginia Woolf*, III, p. 236: 'this shall be Childhood; but it must not be *my* childhood; & boats and the pond; the sense of children; unreality; things oddly proportioned.'

in what, perhaps, is only an image of the reality, not the reality itself, a summer's day imagined in the heart of a northern winter'.[97]

The image of reality resulting from the transfiguration implied in the artistic process reveals how for Woolf the true common language, the one attempting to express the core of our shared human experience, is actually the language of imagination: literary language, or, more widely, the language of artistic forms. The shared literary/artistic heritage can provide us with the sense of an alternative collective identity cutting across transcultural and translinguistic differences, although, as I have shown with reference to the character of Louis, this idea may again lead to dangerous consequences, in terms not only of levelling individualities but also of establishing sociocultural hegemonic classes. The shared heritage of literary imagination can in its turn become a discriminating tool dividing societies, this time not in terms of national identities but rather on the basis of socio-economic (and, in Woolf's times, also gendered) power.[98] In this sense, as it happens in *The Waves*, even the 'well-laid sentences [...] never obscure or formless' of the classical past may need to lose their too solid, monolithic, explicit configuration: 'how tired I am of stories, how tired I am of phrases that come down beautifully with all their feet on the ground!'.[99] In Woolf the quest for a universal language of the mind seems never to be disjoint from a constant emphasis on preserving differences so as to avoid a mystifying homogeneity. As mentioned, the stress is on the sense of lack and distance revealed by differences and by impossible appropriations, as Woolf underlines also in her point regarding the impossible equivalence in translation.[100] Furthermore, the dreamed and ideal universal language of imagination constantly needs to undergo processes of refinement so as to become light, quick, dynamic, as in Coleridge's idea of words as wheels: 'we must shape our words till they

97 Woolf, 'On Not Knowing Greek', p. 11.

98 It is worth recalling Woolf's own experience of not accessing the college education that her brothers benefitted from. On Woolf's self-education to the Latin and Greek classics see Hermione Lee, *Virginia Woolf* (London: Vintage, 1997), pp. 142–44.

99 Woolf, *The Waves*, pp. 23 and 199.

100 Besides 'On Not Knowing Greek' see Virginia Woolf, 'The Russian Point of View', in *Collected Essays*, I, pp. 238–46. On Woolf and translation, see Emily Dalgarno, *Virginia Woolf and the Migrations of Language* (Cambridge: Cambridge University Press, 2012).

are the thinnest integuments of our thoughts.'[101] Ancient Greek thus becomes for Woolf the ideal language, in the fashion of an alternative, reinvented, and forever-lost mother tongue: 'spare and bare as it is no language can move more quickly, dancing, shaking, all alive, but controlled.'[102] In this sense, Woolf's reinvention of the idea of mother tongue connects to Lepschy's point that 'no one is a native speaker of the language of poetry': it is a language to which we are bound to remain forever separated, and that we simultaneously feel as familiar and foreign, in those dynamics between real and ideal, between the exactness and the perpetual deferral of meaning, that I have singled out in *The Waves*.

101 Virginia Woolf, *Orlando* (London: Vintage, 1992), p. 111.
102 Woolf, 'On Not Knowing Greek', p. 11.

'I know you can cant'

Slips of the Mother Tongue in Fred Moten's *B Jenkins*

JEFFREY CHAMPLIN

The poetry of Fred Moten has a way of putting you in your place while also calling to a better world. Fusing the Black Arts tradition with high theory, its appeal to freedom often operates with utopian tones, but rather than seeking transcendence it takes to the rhythms and breaks of language. In his collection *B Jenkins,* Moten literalizes the poetic appeal to the mother tongue in a way that opens it to an awareness of its mediated essence. Reading the volume in terms of Friedrich Kittler's techno-psychological history of the family allows us to cast Moten's detuning of natural language in terms of a cultural mastery streaked with affirmative disfluency. With the cant, slang slides towards a broader awareness of the limits of knowledge. There, language may emerge for perceiving the role of the technological mother tongue in our post-national age.

Framing my inquiry in a tradition of critical hermeneutics pressures metaphysical narratives in their political and technological form. This article, hedging closely to its source as a talk at the 'Untying the Mother Tongue' conference, can only begin to articulate a broader theory of rogue pedagogy that I am currently developing from a number of different directions. The specifics of this close reading of Moten, however, emerged from a seminar students and I referred to as 'Occupy

Poetics' that I taught at Bard College's campus in Palestine in 2015. Reading within a terrain of contested nationality, we began with the prophetic force of Shelley's 'A Defence of Poetry's. We then turned to literary resistance in Moten, Mahmoud Darwish, and texts from the Arab Spring (including Amina Saïd and Nawal El Saadawi).[1] In each case, we asked how poetry casts bodies through specific spaces and in so doing recodes landscapes of power.

Who did we think we were, to try to read Moten under these conditions? The Palestinian, American, and European students of the seminar were multilingual and spoke English with varying degrees of fluency. One could object that we were not appropriately versed in African American culture and literature, especially in its most difficult, twenty-first century cast. But on the other hand, the students were not content to leave American Studies to itself. For them, African American literature offered an extraordinary lexicon of resistance, a library of freedom but also of continued bondage. Indeed, they often linked such writers as Frederick Douglass, Malcolm X, Frantz Fanon, and Edward Said to create hybrid canons of postcolonialism. With Moten though, we faced a challenge known to all teachers, indeed, all advocates, of the avant-garde. Who is really ever ready for what Charles Bernstein praises as 'the difficult poem', much less what Friedrich Schlegel affirms as the 'incomprehensibility' of literature?[2]

At the heart of *B Jenkins*, we heard a line that affirmed a poetics of deficiency: 'I know you can cant.' The secret code of the drifter may

---

1 For a foundational text on the relation between American Studies and postcolonial studies, see Bill Ashcroft, Gareth Griffiths, and Helen Tiffin, *The Empire Writes Back: Theory and Practice in Post-Colonial Literatures* (London: Routledge, 2003 [1989]).

2 Note that Bernstein's text moves directly from textual difficulty to a plural injunction: '[T]he first step in dealing with the difficult poem is to recognize that this is a common problem that many other readers confront on a daily basis. You are not alone!'. See Charles Bernstein, 'The Difficult Poem', *Harper's Magazine*, 306.1837 (June 2003), available at Electric Poetry Center <http://writing.upenn.edu/epc/authors/bernstein/essays/difficult-poem.html> [accessed 21 June 2017]. Friedrich Schlegel also manages to keep the focus in connection, even while circling around its possible failure: 'Of all things that have to do with communicating ideas, what could be more fascinating than the question of whether such communication is actually possible?' ('On Incomprehensibility', in *Friedrich Schlegel's 'Lucinde' and the Fragments*, trans. and intro. by Peter Firchow (Minneapolis: University of Minnesota Press, 1971), pp. 259–71 (p. 259)).

not go so far as untying the mother tongue, but it promises ever more exquisite bindings.

The title of Fred Moten's collection refers to his mother and pictures her prominently on the cover. Moten has described the book with a deceptively simple poetics that, while emotionally compelling in its own right, also implies a narrative of cultural fluency. He says that he composed the individual poems based on references to the work of writers and artists he came to know directly or indirectly through his mother. Scanning the table of contents one sees, for example, James Baldwin, Bessie Smith, and Walter Benjamin. The poems sketch many small portraits that lead to a multidimensional image of the mother in language that would replace the actual cover photo.[3]

So it is easy to understand the collection as a moving elegy to B Jenkins, who died in the year 2000. On a broader level of cultural history though, Moten also engages the epochal relationship between poetry and the mother. The work of Friedrich Kittler can help us articulate this connection. In his study *Poet, Mother, Child,* Kittler elaborates the role that the mother played around 1800 in establishing a new regime of education in which reading with the mother initiates the desire to learn by speaking words aloud spontaneously rather than merely repeating present models.[4] Learning in this way linked the child from the family through the body of the mother to the national language, German, which replaced the earlier emphasis on the international language of Latin.

Scholars most commonly go to Kittler for his work on the role of technology in discourse formation. Like Foucault, he sees history in terms of epochs, and here he emphasizes the shift from the extended family (*Sippe*) to the nuclear family that took place at the turn of

3 Here I draw on a discussion that Moten kindly held with my students in Palestine, beaming in from midnight in California, bearer of generosity and intellectual light. I by no means intend to minimize this statement of authorial poetics, which, combined with the artistic strength of the poems, made a lasting impression on myself and all the students in attendance. Instead, this article seeks to add an additional frame and scale of analysis.

4 Friedrich Kittler, *Dichter, Mutter, Kind* (Munich: Wilhelm Fink, 1991). A selection of this text is available in English: Friedrich Kittler, 'Poet, Mother, Child: On the Romantic Invention of Sexuality', in *The Truth of the Technological World: Essays on the Genealogy of Presence*, trans. by Erik Butler (Stanford, CA: Stanford University Press, 2014), pp. 1–16.

the nineteenth century. Importantly though, Kittler describes both the poet and the mother in terms of their mediating role. Within this historical narrative, he focuses on the move from the nurse, who merely teaches children to repeat the signs of an external system, to the mother, who encourages the child to talk to itself, and thus produce its interiority by talking to her. I quote:

> the coupling of orality and poetry stems from a psycho-pedagogy that, since Locke and Rousseau, has prescribed that mothers themselves should nurse and speak to the being without language (*infans*) in their charge.[5]

Poetry became the operative technology for the creation of the child-subject.

From this point of view we can see *B Jenkins* as affirming a particular kind of identity. Though running counter to state power, the Black Arts movement so important to Moten did, in some of its modalities, call on cultural black nationalism. Moten writes to the mother as one who inspired him to become a poet — a poet as the epitome of the reflective, creative person. Right away though, we see that *B Jenkins* affirms identity only through an edit, or a scratch. Starting with the title of the book, Moten literalizes the question of the mother tongue by asking how to address not just what Kittler calls 'the mother imago': the metaphysical mother who naturalizes language. Going further, he employs his mother's proper name. And more than that, he de-names her from the start, abbreviating with the 'B', and later de-capitalizing to 'b'.

The collection begin with a poem titled 'b jenkins' and then ends with a different poem with the same title. The first one formally models the entire volume in three stanzas. Now these kinds of texts require that one speculate a bit even to get started. So I will suggest that the first stanza speaks of the mother, the second of culture, the third of the son. In addition to thorough readings of the poems, I strongly recommend the Moten's own recordings of the poems that are accessible in the

5 Kittler, 'Poet, Mother, Child', p. 6.

University of Pennsylvania online collection.[6] The poem starts with a happy memory, perhaps of growing up in the mother's house, and with a reference to a flower and the blues singer Bertha Lee. The 'territory sunflower' names a single plant, which I see as taken out of its own field to create a domestic centre.[7]

After the domestic set-up, the poem goes underground. The second stanza falls into a six-word pattern that matches the six sentences of the whole poem. The rhythm falters just once, with the line: 'between break and secret | vaulted'. The pair 'break'/'secret' holds together through the rhythm, then 'vaulted' marks a turn. We go down to where a secret might be held. Once there, the basement functions as a utopia, a liberatory space that overcomes racial divisions, as indicated by the hairstyles of the 'long-haired hippies and afro-blacks'.[8] Moten brings us down to a light place of popular culture, to a hidden song. Certain readers will recognize the quote from James Brown's 'Get on the Good Foot'; this quote is later referenced in the Digable Planets song 'Jimmi Diggin Cats'. Without citation though, this all weaves into one sonic fabric.[9]

Let us keep going. When reading the third verse with my students, one held up on the phrase 'born way before you was born'.[10] Is the grammar correct? Is this a typo? In short: 'am I getting this right?' The difficult poem assumes the fluency of the reader to reconstruct, or at least to contrast, artistic speech with normal speech. Familiar since modernism, yet still trying our wits, and our patience, this type of poem defers our quest for meaning. Here, the poem seems to connect, to speak from the heart, at least if one knows the code. In the instance of 'dialect', also sometimes called an 'ethnolect', Moten generalizes the use of 'was' to the second person singular ('you'). He makes an art of

6 Fred Moten, *B Jenkins* (Durham, NC: Duke University Press, 2009). Readings can be accessed at PennSound <http://writing.upenn.edu/pennsound/x/Moten.php> [accessed 21 June 2017].

7 Ibid., p. 1.

8 Ibid., p. 1.

9 James Brown, 'Get on the Good Foot (Parts 1 & 2)', *Get on the Good Foot* (Polydor Records, 1972); Digable Planets, 'Jimmi Diggin Cats', *Reachin' (A New Refutation of Time and Space)* (Capitol Records, 1993).

10 Moten, *B Jenkins*, p. 1.

code switching, exaggerating from vernacular to the near-idiolect, the completely personal language, of the poem.

Down and down. With the reference to a 'slip' of the tongue in my title I am veering off into the unconscious. But for the reader this registers more as a skip than a slip, a mini break of a jump on the record. As Moten's first theoretical study reveals, the jazz break stops time in time, while also rolling towards what comes next.[11] In terms of the reading with Kittler that I proposed above, this line would mark the integration of the mother tongue with the language of the poet. The poet slips fluently into his native speech. Yet in the next poem we will see a declaration that critiques this idea of unity.

When he assigns the final poem of the collection the same proper name, 'b jenkins', Moten further disassembles the propriety of the mother tongue. This poem shifts technological scenes, transporting us from the phonograph to the telephone. This phone also repeats though, skipping and wearing into old tracks. I envision a conversation, with the poet older in life. To me, it sounds like the poet begins and his mother responds.

It is as if there is a sort of homecoming, though one marked by loss and distance. On the phone there is always an absence to be mourned, as Avital Ronell teaches us in *The Telephone Book*. Ronell emphasizes the disconnect instead of the identity-forming mediation, though in another sense she and Kittler engage in a common task of critiquing metaphysics through technology.[12] Moten's poem engages both of these dimensions.

On the line, a single line stands out as both encouragement and awareness of deficiency: 'I know you can cant.'[13] In the recording of the poem, Moten reads the line with a rhythmic run that then lands with emphasis on the last word.[14] I initially read *cant* in terms of 'slang', in

---

11 Fred Moten, *In the Break: The Aesthetics of the Black Radical Tradition* (Minneapolis: University of Minnesota Press, 2003).

12 Avital Ronell, *The Telephone Book: Technology, Schizophrenia, Electric Speech* (Lincoln: University of Nebraska Press, 1989). Drawing on another dimension of Ronell's work, we can also think how the call of the mother in Heidegger is set up so you cannot get out of it. See Martin Heidegger, *What Is Called Thinking?*, trans. by J. Glenn Gray (New York: Perennial Library, 2004).

13 Moten, *B Jenkins*, p. 95.

14 This can be heard in the University of Pennsylvania recording recommended above.

terms of the *Oxford English Dictionary*'s entry 'to speak in the peculiar jargon or "cant" of vagabonds, thieves, and the like'. In relation to theory, another valence is: 'to use the special phraseology or jargon of a particular class or subject'.[15] Canting relates the thief to the theorist.

Now, according to the lens that Kittler offers, this could be the mother affirming the poet-child's fluency in the dialect. As if to allay a fear: 'I know you understand our minor language.' At the same time though, we can also hear *cant* as 'cannot', as negating what Derrida calls the monolingualism of the other. It brings down the self-assumed speech of power. Something shifts in the originary occupation of the mother tongue. In a sense, all culture colonizes, but we still must describe its specific enunciations. An imperative to speak the one, non-native language of the other emerges from Moten's poem and Derrida's text, precisely to dispossess the master of his claim of a monopoly on meaning.[16]

Who can approve the cant, who would claim to regulate it? The other Kant, Immanuel, though pushing imagination far in an experience of the sublime, would land us safely back at the shores of reason. But we know by now to be wary of poetry that claims to speak its limit. Perhaps, as rogue language, the cant even affirms the error. But can one really go on with language gone wrong? Can we successfully perform it?

I have been thinking about these questions in terms of a pedagogical exploration of the concept of the 'rogue reader' that I originally elaborated in response to the terrorism depicted in works of Goethe, Schiller, and Kleist. Drawing on the figure of the fortune teller in *Michael Kohlhaas*, I sighted a uniquely transformative role for minoritized figures in periods when standard protocols of political representation fail. In the classroom, I have found that generative writing in response

15 'Cant, n.3.', in *OED Online* (Oxford: Oxford University Press, 2020) <https://www.oed.com/view/Entry/27198> [accessed 24 February 2023].

16 Perhaps surprisingly, for a thinker so associated with a courageous defence of difference, he tells of how he felt compelled to speak French with a perfect Parisian accent. Instead of meaning to harm the language he wanted to 'make it do something'. In this regard one might say that deconstruction works like poetry, in that it does to concepts what poetry does to language more broadly. Jacques Derrida, *Monolingualism of the Other; or, The Prosthesis of Origin*, trans. by Patrick Mensah (Stanford, CA: Stanford University Press, 1998).

to traumatic texts of literature and political theory can affirm hybrid crossings between students' intellectual analyses and their personal experience.[17]

Barbara Cassin's critique of 'globish' has become something of a touchstone for those that fear that English may just pave the way for assimilation into global markets.[18] I recognize that in our current era, learning English means speaking-for-and-to capitalist power. Standards of language acquisition do police work. However, in the face of instrumentalization, I suggest not backing away, but pushing forward. Students who engage culture broadly and critically open the possibility of creating new approaches to the dominant code. The comparative perspective developed in language classes, when placed in a much wider context, may well lead to language both *more* useful and *more questioning* of definitions of use.[19]

As a noun, *cant* also means 'border', 'side', 'brink', 'edge', and 'corner'. Attacks on 'globish' can obscure actual new linkages between cultures. Instead of a vague total English, we have varieties of hybrid speech that create new ties of resistance. 'Cantish', then, if one must, but not 'Globish'.[20] Technology plays a key role in this process. As we read through the entire volume of Moten's poems, we sometimes began class with small groups that collectively investigated texts. Cellphones out, the classroom buzzed in a symphony of proper names, hip

17 See Jeffrey Champlin, *The Making of a Terrorist: On Classic German Rogues* (Northwestern, IL: Northwestern University Press, 2015) and Jeffrey Champlin, 'Rights, Revolution, Representation: Thinking Through the Language of the French Revolution', in *Teaching Representations of the French Revolution*, ed. by Julia Douthwaite, Catriona Seth, and Antoinette Sol (New York: Modern Language Association of America, 2019), pp. 69–77.

18 See the conversation with Cassin in 'The Power of Bilingualism: Interview with Barbara Cassin, French Philosopher and Philologist', e-flux conversations (March 2017) <https://conversations.e-flux.com/t/the-power-of-bilingualism-interview-with-barbara-cassin-french-philosopher-and-philologist/6252> [accessed 21 June 2017]. Note that 'globish', for all its faults, at least indicates an alternative to 'broken English'. The real question though, would be how to combine these formulations in a way that fuses brokenness with the global.

19 See Emily Apter, *Against World Literature: On the Politics of Untranslatability* (New York: Verso, 2013). In my view, Apter's justified concerns about untranslatability offer an opportunity to articulate an embodied planetary literature.

20 We can also recall that the verb 'cant' comes from *cantāre*, 'to sing, chant'. The word can also mean 'to slant' something, such as a board. See the *OED* for the fascinating full range of meanings for 'cant' as both a noun and a verb.

hop music, the blues, and the particular Arabic-English that the students call 'gharra-bezee'.[21] Screens large and small displayed paintings and portraits.

In terms of Kittler's historical projection, such a scene suggests a move away from the nurse/mother opposition and in the direction of a technological mother tongue. For a generation 'raised by the Internet', the stakes are no longer romantic subjectivity (which was allied for a time with Cold War individualism). And we are also not going back to rote repetition, but onward to a practice of citationality that rewrites language in specific confines and establishes new cultures.

Finally, one could once also say: 'to become "cant" as meaning "become well" or "recover your strength"'. Moten writes: 'I know you can cant. I know you can make it if you try.'[22] As I hear Moten, through Sly and the Family Stone, '*it*' is language.[23] And language is power.

---

21 A portmanteau that fuses the words *Arabic* and *Inglizi* (for 'English' in Arabic); Arablish (also known in Palestine as 'Arabezy').

22 Moten, *B Jenkins*, p. 95.

23 Sly and the Family Stone, *Stand* (Epic/Sony, 1969).

The Mother Tongue of Love and Loss

Albert Cohen's *Le Livre de ma mère*

CAROLINE SAUTER

In loving memory of my mother

Irmgard Leo-Grunwald

Losing one's mother. No human expression will ever be able to capture the crude brutality of this experience. The pain of loss and the intensity of love coming together in the instant of my mother's death surpass my language capacity. Crying, whining, groaning, mourning — speech acts or speechless acts in the face of the most invincible, most undeniable human reality: death. My mother's death.

In his 1954 narrative *Le Livre de ma mère*, translated into English under the title *Book of my Mother* by his wife Bella Cohen, Albert Cohen, the French-Swiss-Greek-Jewish writer, attempts to come to terms with the reality of losing his mother, in occupied France, in 1943, while he is safely in London. (Incidentally, it is one of the last books I gave my mother before her death.) It is a book of love and loss: a book about his mother's love for him, and his love for his mother, for her who is now dead and lost forever. Yet this story of love and loss is as much about the life and death of the narrator's adored mother as it is about the process of writing the very book entitled *Le Livre de ma mère*, or *Book of my Mother*. In what follows, I will read Albert Cohen's work as a poetics of love and loss. It is, however, a poetics that disavows the claim to expression and selfhood, a poetics of otherness. The mother, in Cohen's book, is the paradigmatic figure of otherness: she is an outcast of society, a Jewish woman in Vichy France, a foreigner in Switzerland, originating from Corfu, and the only woman in a household of men. Not least, her speech is marked by otherness — by a foreign accent, by funny phrases. She says things differently than others. The same is true for literature, a form of language that is characterized by figurality, that is, by saying things differently. Literature, I will argue, is a motherly space in the sense that it (m)others the language of the self. It is in this sense that I will read literature as a 'mother tongue' of love and loss.

My reading will proceed in three steps: First, I will trace the peculiar kinship of love and death, *l'amour et la mort*, in *Le Livre de ma mère*. Second, my close readings will analyse the mother as the other, the other literally inscribed in the 'm-other' of *Book of my Mother*. Third, and in conclusion, I will describe the notion of reading and writing literature as *filio-logy*, as a logic of filiation, of 'son-ship'.

LOVE AND DEATH

The power of love has always been described in terms of death. This is true, for instance, in *shir ha-shirim*, the Song of Songs — a collection of biblical love poetry that Albert Cohen extensively draws on in all his works. The only definition of love in the Song of Songs describes the power of love and passion with images of death: 'set me as a seal upon your heart, a seal upon your arm', it says, 'for love is strong as death, passion is cruel as the grave (*she'ol*). Its flashes are flashes of fire, a blazing flame' (Song of Songs 8. 6; Revised Standard Version (RSV)).

The only image that seems to be a possible expression of the intense experience of love is the ultimate, universal, and inescapable liminal experience, the utter unknown — death. Death can never be put into words that are *not* figures of speech, since one can express neither one's own nor another's experience of death. Similarly, the experience of love is often conceived as going beyond the clear-cut limits of referential speech. Death, therefore, just like love, must be expressed in figures of speech — in literature. As Julia Kristeva remarked so insightfully in her *Tales of Love*, 'the language of love' — and the same is true for the expression of death — 'is impossible, inadequate, immediately allusive when one would like it to be most straightforward; it is a flight of metaphors — it is literature.'[1] The 'flight of metaphors', the literary images that connect *love* and *death* here, in the biblical Song of Songs, are flash, flame, and fire: they refer to an all-consuming, potentially dangerous, and powerfully violent element that easily gets out of control and is enormously destructive.[2] This threatening potential is what connects love and death metaphorically.

Extending the metaphor, one could say: the strength, the force, the violence of both love and death set our language on fire. Fire, flash, and flame are images for the threatening potential that love and death have for language. In other words, language will be confronted with the threatening fact of its own limitations whenever it tries to put love or death into words. Therefore, writing a book of love and death, as Cohen does, is operating in a dangerous realm, on the verge of linguistic and literary expression.

The narrator in Albert Cohen's *Le Livre de ma mère* is very much aware of this liminal position vis-à-vis language. Consider, for instance, the last sentence in episode XII. After a psalm-like, hymnic repetition and reverberation of the phrase 'Amour de ma mère, à nul autre pareil', translated into English by Bella Cohen as 'my mother's incomparable love',[3] the narrator comes to a halt at the hymn's culminating point, and writes, in the French original: 'Je te dis gravement: ma Maman';[4] in English: 'I say to you gravely, "my Maman".'[5] And here, at this point,

1 Julia Kristeva, *Tales of Love*, trans. by Leon Roudiez (New York: Columbia University Press, 1987), p. 1. See also Julia Kristeva, *Histoires d'amour* (Paris: Denoël, 1983), p. 9: 'Impossible, inadéquat, immédiatement allusive quand on le voudrait le plus direct, le langage amoureux est envol de metaphors: il est de la littérature.'

2 Michael Fishbane, in his *The JPS Bible Commentary: Song of Songs* (Philadelphia, PA: The Jewish Publication Society, 2015), p. 209, states: 'Pounding in the maiden's heart, love is all-consuming—vanquishing its victims like death.'

3 Albert Cohen, *Le Livre de ma mère* (Paris: Gallimard, 1954), pp. 88–106; Albert Cohen, *Book of my Mother*, trans. by Bella Cohen (New York: First Archipelago Books, 1997), pp. 79–92.

4 Cohen, *Le Livre de ma mère*, p. 106.

5 Cohen, *Book of my Mother*, p. 92; translation modified. The unmodified translation reads: 'I say to you gravely, "Maman".' It is quite telling that the translation by Cohen's wife chooses to omit or suppress the possessive pronoun '*ma* Maman', '*my* mother', here. In the translator's bio on the book jacket, Bella Cohen describes her translation

the text is cut off, and the episode is — *finie*. 'Je te dis gravement: ma Maman.'[6]

There is a substantial difference between the adverb *gravement*, 'gravely', and the childish expression, almost indistinguishable from a baby's playful babble, that this gravity is ascribed to: 'ma Maman'. '[M]a Maman' is the most eloquent, the gravest, in fact, the only possible utterance that an eminent, ageing poet can always and only and still find to address his long-deceased mother. Like a small child, enchanted and delighted with each new string of syllables learned, the narrator pronounces a string of resounding syllables, babbling: *mamaman*. In the instance of this repetition, their semantic quality becomes doubtful — are those two words? One word? Any word or words at all? Is it babble? Does it have meaning? Does it matter if it does or does not? Is the narrator imagining going back to what is lost, namely the pre-linguistic babble of a child that has just learned to master some first words? Is he attempting to refind his mother tongue in those grave words? The tongue that was there before there was meaning? Possibly the first meaning-filled, meaningful words he ever uttered?

'[M]a Maman': this grave babble, gravest of all acts of babbling, those joyful yet painful syllables — *mamaman*, 'ma Maman' is what all attempts at creating a language of love for the dead mother can amount to. And tellingly, Cohen's narrator pronounces those words 'gravement', as he says in French. In English, a language that was not Cohen's mother tongue, nor his mother's tongue (nor, for that matter, the mother tongue of his wife, who is his translator), the English 'grave' in the French *gravement* connects love and death. Those words spoken gravely, those grave words: 'ma Maman', they could be the inscription on her tombstone. '[M]a Maman' reposes, gravely, in her grave. Words that are coming from far away, from the first stages of language acquisition, have always already been spoken with the gravity of the grave. First words, last words. The chapter must end here.

Or consider this section of episode XVIII. I am quoting part of it both in the French original and in Bella Cohen's English version:

---

as a 'labor of love', thereby occupying the mother's position in 'birthing' her love ('labor').

6 Cohen, Le Livre de ma mère, p. 106.

> Je me regarde dans la glace, mais c'est ma mère qui est dans la glace. J'ai un chagrin qui devient ce corps, je suis blanc et tout moite. Sur ma joue, ce ne sont pas des larmes, ce privilège des peu malheureux, mais des gouttes qui coulent du front. Ces sueurs de la mort de ma mère sont glacées. [...] Il me reste une glace et mon égarement que j'y regarde, que je regarde en souriant pour avoir envie de faire semblant de vivre, tout en murmurant avec un petit rire un peu fou que tout va très bien, Madame la Marquise, et que je suis perdu. Perdu, perdi, perdo, perda.
>
> (I stare in the mirror, but it is my mother who is in the mirror. My grief becomes physical, and I am pale and clammy. My cheeks are wet not with tears — the privilege of those who suffer little — but with drops trickling down from my forehead. The sweat of the death of my mother is ice-cold. [...] What is left to me is a mirror and the bewilderment which I contemplate in it, which I contemplate with a smile so as to want to simulate living, while I murmur with a slightly mad little laugh that everything in the garden is lovely and that I am sunk. Sunk, sank, sink, sonk.)[7]

The mirror gives way to an uncanny reflection, one that destabilizes the notion of selfhood and identity: 'Je *me* regarde [...] mais c'est *ma mère*.' I look at myself in the mirror, but what I see is not myself, even though I look at me, but her. 'Ma mère', not 'ma Maman', but my mother, the other, whom I am and am not a part of. Identities are as loosely connected to words as bodies are to life: 'J'ai un chagrin qui devient ce corps.' My grief, my sorrow, my affliction become *this* body (*ce* corps), the narrator says; grief does not simply 'become physical', as the translator has it. Rather, in the French original, the narrator's grief, his sorrow, his affliction become the very body that stares at him in the mirror — his mother's body, another body, the body of an other, a body that is not his own, a body that gave birth to his body, a body that protected, that nourished and cherished his tiny body. His mother's body: a body that is now a corpse.

In looking at himself and seeing his mother in the mirror, the narrator's own living body merges into his mother's cold, lifeless body:

7 Cohen, *Le Livre de ma mère*, pp. 129–30; Cohen, *Book of my Mother*, pp. 117–18.

> Sur ma joue, ce ne sont pas des larmes, ce privilège des peu malheureux, mais des gouttes qui coulent du front.
>
> (My cheeks are wet not with tears — the privilege of those who suffer little — but with drops trickling down from my forehead.)[8]

The sweat drops on the narrator's forehead that have or have not wetted his cheeks are reminiscent of Christ's agony on the Mount of Olives in the New Testament, immediately before his arrest and crucifixion. As the gospel of Luke has it: 'And being in an agony Jesus prayed more earnestly: and his sweat was, as it were, great drops of blood falling down to the ground' (Luke 22. 44; King James Version (KJV)). Cohen's narrator alludes to this image yet distorts it into what one could read as an inverted — mirrored — *pietà*. While the intensity of agony surpasses the possibility of tears ('the privilege of those who suffer little'), the body of his dead mother and his own living body merge, and death and life — her death and his life — fall together in the mirror image. He says: 'Ces sueurs de la mort de ma mère sont glacées.' The demonstrative *ces* refers to the sweat drops flowing from his forehead that he has described before as 'gouttes qui coulent du front' (drops trickling down from my forehead). The sweat drops on his cheek are the sweat drops of 'ce corps' (this body), his mother's body that merges into his own: '*those* [not, as Bella Cohen has it, *the*] sweat drops of my mother's death'.

When Christ is sweating blood on the Mount of Olives, he is sweating the very liquid that the Hebrew Bible associates with life:

> for the life of the flesh is in the blood, and I [the Lord] have given it to you upon the altar to make an atonement for your souls; for it is the blood that maketh an atonement for the soul (Leviticus 17. 11; KJV).

Cohen's narrator, however, sweats not life, but death. He prefigures his own impending death in identifying with his mother's. In the Hebrew Bible, sweat and death are closely linked: 'in the sweat of thy face shalt thou eat bread', says God in cursing Adam after the Fall, 'till thou return unto the ground; for out of it wast thou taken: for dust thou art,

8 Ibid.

and unto dust shalt thou return' (Genesis 3. 19; KJV). The narrator is acutely aware of this connection between sweat and death. He is, paradoxically, imagining dying his mother's death and sweating her last, icy drops, but unlike her icy sweat of death, his sweat is of life, and this is what makes (or does not make) him cry.

'Ces sueurs de la mort de ma mère sont glacées', the narrator says. But he continues: 'Il me reste une glace' (What is left to me is a mirror). '[G]lacées' (ice-cold) and 'glace' (mirror) are almost the same word in French, the language that the narrator chooses to mourn his mother. Life and death come together in the mirror-image. As ice-cold as her death drops is the mirror whose reflection is mirroring not his own body, but hers. His drops are not the hot, life-filled blood drops of Christ, but the ice-cold sweat drops of Adam's death — a death that stares at him in the mirror through his mother's eyes. What is left to the narrator is the 'glace', the mirror, that displays his mother's 'glacée' agony. He is suffering her death in beholding himself as being her, in becoming her likeness.

Therefore, his greatest suffering is the necessity to stay alive. Being alive after his mother's passing is described as sin, the 'sin of living' (péché de vie). 'Let's face it', reads a passage from episode xx, 'I too am but one of the living, a sinner like all the living [...]. My mother is dead but I am hungry, and soon, despite my grief, I shall eat. Sin of living.'[9] In the same episode, the narrator links poetic creation to the sin of living:

> ... et ma main bouge égoïstement en ce moment. Et si ma main dessine des mots qui disent ma douleur, c'est un mouvement de vie, c'est-à-dire de joie, en fin de compte, qui la fait bouger, cette main. Et ces feuilles, demain je les relirai, et j'ajouterai d'autres mots, et j'en aurai une sorte de plaisir. Péché de vie. Je corrigerai les épreuves, et ce sera un autre péché de vie.
>
> (... my hand is moving selfishly now. And if my hand traces words which tell of my grief, it is a movement of life, that is of joy after all, which stirs that hand. And tomorrow I shall reread these words and that will give me a kind of pleasure. Sin of living. I shall correct the proofs, and that too will be sin of living.)[10]

9 Cohen, *Book of my Mother*, pp. 127–29.

10 Cohen, *Le Livre de ma mère*, p. 139; Cohen, *Book of my Mother*, p. 127.

The shame and guilt, the sin of living (péché de vie), which is at the heart of poetic creation, is exactly the 'égarement' he describes in the mirror scene discussed above: 'Il me reste une glace et mon égarement que j'y regarde' (what is left to me is a mirror and the bewilderment which I contemplate in it). What he sees when he beholds the mirror, after all, is himself — but he sees himself as an 'égarement', an aberrance, an aberration, or obliquity (and not only a 'bewilderment', as Bella Cohen has it), and it is this aberrance that he beholds ('*mon* égarement que j'y regarde'). In this sense, the notion of identity and selfhood is othered: he sees himself as other by seeing another than himself, namely his mother, in the mirror, instead of himself. And once the notion of identity, of selfhood and stability, is disavowed, disabled, and destroyed, language is let loose, and linguistic meaning becomes meaningless. This is exemplified in the continuation of this passage, which I am therefore quoting again, to comment on in more detail:

> Il me reste une glace et mon égarement que j'y regarde, que je regarde en souriant pour avoir envie de faire semblant de vivre, tout en murmurant avec un petit rire un peu fou que tout va très bien, Madame la Marquise, et que je suis perdu. Perdu, perdi, perdo, perda.[11]

In Bella Cohen's English version, this passage reads:

> what is left to me is a mirror and the bewilderment which I contemplate in it, which I contemplate with a smile so as to want to simulate living, while I murmur with a slightly mad little laugh that everything in the garden is lovely and that I am sunk. Sunk, sank, sink, sonk.[12]

The phrase 'avoir envie de…' bristles with life: it literally entails the words *en vie*, 'in life', alive, yet this liveliness is distorted by contrasting it with '*faire semblant* de vivre', 'to *simulate* living'. To be *en vie*, literally to be 'in life', is only a semblance of life after his mother's loss. There is no sense in living after and beyond her death, no meaning.

---

11 Cohen, *Le Livre de ma mère*, pp. 129–30. This passage from *Le Livre de ma mère* (1954) is repeated almost verbatim in Albert Cohen's later masterpiece, the novel *Belle du Seigneur* (Paris: Gallimard, 1968), p. 592, which incidentally was written in very close collaboration with Bella Cohen: 'Perdu, perdi, perda, perdo, murmurait-il…'.

12 Cohen, *Book of my Mother*, p. 118.

This meaninglessness is expressed by a seemingly nonsensical murmur: 'tout va très bien, Madame la Marquise', or, in English: 'everything in the garden is lovely.' The narrators in both the French original and the English version choose to include a song line from popular culture here. The French is a quote from a 1935 *chanson* by Paul Misraki. Misraki's song is a silly musical phone conversation in which a noblewoman calls her butler at home and learns about all the calamities that have befallen her household during her absence, from her favourite mare's death to her castle's complete destruction in fire and finally her husband's suicide, each of them being a direct consequence of the previous one. This series of deaths and catastrophes is sung cheerfully, and repeatedly interrupted by the butler's line: 'tout va très bien, Madame la Marquise' (all is very well, my lady, dear countess).[13]

This foolish and not-at-all-reassuring harmlessness, together with the music's cheerfulness, stands in sharp contrast with the horrible, in fact gruesome, facts that are being recounted. Quoting this *chanson* line, Cohen's narrative thus introduces an element of instability, in which form and content are at odds. Therefore, the closing phrase ('je suis perdu. Perdu, perdi, perdo, perda', or, in Bella Cohen's English: 'I am sunk. Sunk, sank, sink, sonk') takes the meaning of a verb (a word of doing, a *Tu-Wort*, as a childish schoolboy German would have it) apart and literally *un-does* it.[14] The meaning of *perdre*, 'losing', is lost, *perdu*.

(M)OTHER

But there is another *clin d'œil*, another allusion, here. (And I am very conscious of the echo of *deuil*, 'mourning' and 'sorrow', in *clin d'œil.*) The silly telephone conversation of popular culture that Cohen's narrator quotes, with the line 'tout va très bien, Madame la Marquise', also refers to an actual telephone conversation with a noblewoman that the narrative obsessively comes back to. It is a scene that literally haunts

13 Bella Cohen's English version chooses a line from a popular song by the music hall artist Marie Lloyd: 'Everything in the garden is lovely.'

14 While Albert Cohen's French echoes the father (*père*) in the insistence on loss (*perte*), within the repeated, broken line 'perdu [*père*-du], perdi [*père*-di], perdo [*père*-do], perda' (is a *père da*? Or might he be, to reference Freud, *fort*?), Bella Cohen's English translation literally inscribes the son: 'Sunk, sank, sink, *sonk*.'

the entire *Book of my Mother* and that is deeply entangled with feelings of guilt and shame and regret. I would even venture to say that it is being mourned throughout Cohen's narrative, since it is at the heart of the mother-son relationship. It is described in episode x, earlier in the book:

> Je fus méchant avec elle, une fois, et elle ne le méritait pas. Cruauté des fils. Cruauté de cette absurde scène que je fis. Et pourquoi? Parce que, inquiète de ne pas me voir rentrer [...], elle avait téléphoné, à quatre heures du matin, à mes mondains inviteurs qui ne la valaient certes pas. Elle avait téléphoné pour être rassurée, pour être sûre que rien de mal ne m'était arrivé. De retour chez moi, je lui avais fait cette affreuse scène. Elle est tatouée dans mon cœur, cette scène. [...] Et pourquoi cette indigne colère? Peut-être parce que son accent étranger et ses fautes de français en téléphonant à ces crétins cultivés m'avaient gêné. Je ne les entendrai plus, ses fautes de français et son accent étranger.
>
> (I was spiteful to her once, and she did not deserve it. Oh, the cruelty of sons! Oh, the cruelty of the absurd scene which I made! And for what reason? Because at four in the morning, worried that I had not yet come home [...], she had phoned the smart set who had invited me and who were certainly her inferiors. She had phoned to be reassured, to be sure I had come to no harm. On my return I made an abominable scene. That scene is tattooed on my heart. [...] And why was I so shamefully angry? Perhaps because her foreign accent (*son accent étranger*) and her incorrect French (*ses fautes de français*) when she phoned those cultured cretins had embarrassed me. Nevermore will I hear her incorrect French and her foreign accent.)[15]

In this telephone scene, the mother — the worried, caring, loving mother — is the incarnation of the other. The otherness of the narrator's mother is a leitmotif that runs as a red thread through the narrative, on the plot level as well as on a poetological level. This has, I think, a specific reason: In Cohen's *Le Livre de ma mère*, the search for a linguistic or more specifically literary expression of love and loss is inseparable from questions of origin. As a foreigner, as a Jew, as an author in Vichy France and Switzerland, the narrator is struggling with

15 Cohen, *Le Livre de ma mère*, pp. 73–74; Cohen, *Book of my Mother*, pp. 65–66.

questions of origin and belonging, and the emblematic figure of origin is the mother. The mother, however, is also the figure of being different, being-other. In English — a language that is not my mother tongue, nor Cohen's — the 'other' is uncannily inscribed into the very word *m-other*. In highlighting the literal 'other-ness' of the mother figure, Cohen's *Book of my Mother* gradually disavows the notion of origin and belonging and substitutes it with estrangement. *Le Livre de ma mère* is very much about the process of its own creation. But its poetics runs counter to what we think of as poetic. It is not about finding a language or a literary form of expression for the seemingly inexpressible, intense experiences of love and loss. It is, rather, about coming to terms with otherness — one's own otherness, one's mother's otherness, and the utter otherness, the cruel and unimaginable otherness of her death.

This otherness is displayed not only on the plot level, but also in the language Cohen's narrator chooses to employ. In one episode, the narrator fabricates a seemingly nonsensical text by taking bits and pieces of childhood ditties (supposedly songs that he learned from his mother) and arranging them anew.[16] This strategy gives way to surprising — and possibly untranslatable — constellations:

> Une vache éprise Chante dans l'église D'un air lascif. [...] Une vache blanche Danse sur la branche D'un air significatif. Une vache juive S'évente sur la rive D'un air craintif. [...] Voilà. La douleur, ca ne s'exprime pas toujours avec des mots nobles.
>
> (A cow in night attire Sings in the church choir With a suggestive air. [...] A lily-white cow Prances on a bough With an expressive air. A small Jewish cow Fans her sweating brow With a fugitive air. [...] There. Grief is not always expressed in noble words.)[17]

---

16 Tellingly, this 'little pastime' (as Bella Cohen has translated it in *Book of my Mother*, p. 122) that the narrator desperately seeks in order to escape his obsession with death ('aujourd'hui, je suis fou de mort', p. 134) stands under the sign of untranslatability: 'M'amuser neurasthéniquement tout seul en inventant des vaches qui font des choses étranges et d'un air qui finit toujours en if' (Cohen, *Le Livre de ma mère*, p. 135). What if this *if* would be pointing to a potentiality of meaning? Bella Cohen's attempt at translating this more or less untranslatable series of wordplays reads: 'I shall amuse myself listlessly all alone by inventing cows which do strange things with a "something" air, the "something" has to and in -ive' (Cohen, *Book of my Mother*, p. 123).

17 Cohen, *Le Livre de ma mère*, p. 135; Cohen, *Book of my Mother*, pp. 123.

The non-noble words of grief and pain are laughable, estranged, out-of-place, othered words, and yet they are part of his book, and hence of literature. Literature *itself* becomes, for the narrator, a space of otherness, of estrangement and distortion. Literature is an act of othering language, othering speech. As such, it is perhaps a motherly space: the space of the other-as-the-mother (my own deceased mother was a woman of the word, an author and translator). In episode XIII, the narrator remarks in passing:

> Étrange que je ne m'aperçoive que maintenant que ma mère était un être humain, un autre être que moi [...].
>
> (Strange that only now do I realize that my mother was a human being, someone apart from myself [...].)[18]

The whole sentence stands under the sign of strangeness, estrangement, or foreignness: '[é]trange que...', '[s]trange that....' Unlike the English, the French has a striking, sensual, uncanny similarity between 'autre' (other) and 'être' (being). It is as if being was always already an *other* being, being as another, being 'an other', being other. A strange kind of being, being as estrangement: *Autre être. Être autre.*

French is the language that Cohen uses as his mother tongue, even though it never was his mother's tongue. It is the language the narrator in Cohen's book chooses to sing the *chant de mort*, the 'song of death',[19] in remembrance of his mother. Yet it was never really a language that mother and son shared. She spoke French strangely, estranged, *étranger*, with a strong 'foreign accent' (un accent étranger).[20] Perhaps she, with her accent, the foreign accent of the stranger — perhaps she pronounced *la mère* (mother), *l'amour* (love), and *la mort* (death) exactly the same. Perhaps not. In any case, the more attentively one listens, the more they are not different. There is an episode in the famous *Derrida* film by Amy Kofman, supposedly a documentary, in which the director asks Derrida if he has anything to say about love (*l'amour*). Tellingly, Derrida 'mishears' her at first, and he asks back: 'la mort',

18 Ibid., p. 108; p. 94.

19 Ibid., p. 169; p. 157.

20 Ibid., pp. 73–74; pp. 65–66.

death?[21] *La mère, l'amour, la mort* — words that become distorted and estranged from what one could call their meaning, if one is willing to listen to their reverberations in a foreign language, an other language, in a strange accent, the accent of a stranger, 'my mother's incorrect French'.[22]

The telephone scene that evokes and reveals the mother as the other is one that reiterates throughout the narrative — and it haunts not only the narrator, but also the narrator's dreams. Consider episode XIV:

> Dans mon sommeil, qui est la musique des tombes, je viens de la voire encore, belle comme en sa jeunesse, mortellement belle et lasse, si tranquille et muette. [...] Elle m'a expliqué que ce n'était de sa faute si elle était morte et qu'elle tâcherait de venir me voire quelquefois. Puis elle m'a assuré qu'elle ne téléphonerait plus à la Comtesse. 'Je ne le ferai plus, je demande pardon', m'a-t-elle dit en regardant ses petites mains où des taches bleues étaient apparues. Je me suis réveillé et toute la nuit j'ai lu des livres pour qu'elle ne revienne pas. Mais je la rencontre dans tous les livres. Va-t'en, tu n'es pas vivante, va-t'en, tu es trop vivante.
>
> (In my sleep, which is the music of tombs, I have just now seen her again, beautiful as in her youth, mortally beautiful and weary, so placid and mute. [...] She explained that it was not her fault that she was dead, and that she would try to come and see me sometimes. Then she assured me she would never again phone the countess. 'I'll never do it again. Please forgive me', she said, looking at her little hand on which blue marks had appeared. I woke and read books all night so that she would not come back. But I find her in all the books. Go away, you are not alive. Go away, you are too alive.)[23]

The dreamer, in his dream, encounters an apparition, a spectre, a ghost. Unlike Hamlet, he encounters his mother's ghost, not his father's. And

21 This exchange is reported and commented on in Michal Ben-Naftali, '"I Have an Empty Head on Love": The Theme of Love in Derrida, or Derrida and the Literary Space', *Oxford Literary Review*, 40.2 (2018), pp. 221–37. In fact, *la mort* and *l'amour* have an uncanny kinship in Derrida's philosophy. It is, for instance, not surprising that he devoted an aphoristic commentary to Shakespeare's tragedy of the 'star-cross'd lovers', *Romeo and Juliet*. See Jacques Derrida, 'Aphorism Countertime', trans. by Nicholas Royle, in *Acts of Literature*, ed. by Derek Attridge (London: Routledge, 1992), pp. 414–33.

22 Cohen, *Book of my Mother*, p. 66.

23 Cohen, *Le Livre de ma mère*, pp. 113–14; Cohen, *Book of my Mother*, pp. 99–100.

unlike Hamlet's father, this ghost does not ask for revenge, but for forgiveness. A spectre is an *autre être*, a strange being (if it is one), in-between life and death.[24] The 'hauntology' of this indistinct state of being of an *autre être* is paradoxical: The narrator highlights that his mother's ghost is 'silent and mute' (si tranquille et muette) even as she speaks and has a voice. When she speaks, she asks for forgiveness for the telephone call to 'the countess' that haunts the narrator, and that never ceases to haunt him throughout the narrative: a haunted scene of haunting, or a scene of 'haunted writing'.[25]

And tellingly, this dream scenario is then transferred or transformed into literature: The mother's hands have 'blue marks' (taches bleues) — blue like ink, the very ink that the narrator is spreading over his paper, the very ink that is conjuring up the haunted dream image of his dead mother that is in the process of being narrated. In a later episode, his own hands are stained with blue ink from his pen: 'I came back to my table and took up my pen. It leaked, and I have blue marks on my hands.'[26] Her hands, like his, have *stigmata*. Ink-stigmata. They are stigmatized as being made of ink, as being literature. Literature is not an escape from death, quite on the contrary. Literature is the residue of the dead. Thus, the scene of haunted writing continues and becomes a scene of haunted reading: 'I woke and read books all night so that she would not come back. But I find her in all the books. Go away, you are not alive. Go away, you are too alive.'[27] Literature is a haunted space. It is the space of the mother, 'not alive' and 'too alive' at once. Literature is the space of the mother and therefore of the other.

FILIO-LOGY

For the narrator in Cohen's *Le Livre de ma mère*, 'doing literature' is an act of son-ship . Writing, for him, is a *filio-logy*: the words of a son, *filius*. His

24 Jacques Derrida, *Specters of Marx: The State of the Debt, the Work of Mourning and the New International*, trans. by Peggy Kamuf (London: Routledge, 1994).

25 Avital Ronell, *Dictations: On Haunted Writing* (Champaign: University of Illinois Press, 2006).

26 Cohen, *Book of my Mother*, p. 155. The French original, in Cohen, *Le Livre de ma mère*, p. 168, reads: 'Je suis revenu à ma table, et j'ai repris mon stylo. Il a coulé et j'ai des taches bleues sur la main.'

27 Cohen, *Book of my Mother*, p. 100.

words are words of filiation. 'Fils des mères encore vivantes', the narrator implores towards the end of his book, 'n'oubliez pas que vos mères sont mortelles.'[28] In Bella Cohen's English version, this passage reads:

> Sons of mothers who are still alive [*fils des mères encore vivantes*], never again forget that your mothers are mortal. I shall not have written in vain if one of you, after reading my song of death, is one evening gentler with his mother [...]. These words addressed to you, sons of mothers who are still alive, are the only condolences I can offer myself.[29]

The son, *le fils*, is addressing his fellow sons, *les fils*. The narrator is inscribing himself and his work into a line of tradition, of filiation. In French, *les fils*, the plural form of *le fils*, the son, is a homology: *les fils* can also mean 'the threads': the threads that make up a texture, a *textum*, a text; the threads that weave a story, as Walter Benjamin would have it[30] — a story that is being told, and retold, and re-retold, and gains a life of its own. 'Fils des mères encore vivantes' could also be the threads of living mothers: the threads that weave the lives of those mothers who are still alive and still have stories to tell. Words spoken to *les fils* who have living mothers make his 'song of death' the narrator's only comfort, because he knows that *les fils* —both the sons and the threads — will produce the afterlife of his own deceased mother. The weaving will continue.

Philology, like *filio-logy*, is an intense and intimate relation that reveals language's (motherly) otherness. As Werner Hamacher — whose absent voice I am weaving into this text of mine — said so beautifully in his *95 Theses on Philology*: 'Philology is inclination not only for another empirical or potentially empirical language but for the otherness of language, for linguisticity as otherness, for language itself as perpetual alteration.'[31] Perhaps it is here, in the revelation of language's utter otherness, in the mothering and othering of language, that we truly encounter our mother tongue.

28 Cohen, *Le Livre de ma mère*, p. 169.

29 Cohen, *Book of my Mother*, p. 157.

30 Walter Benjamin, 'Der Erzähler. Betrachtungen zum Werk Nikolai Lesskows', in Benjamin, *Gesammelte Schriften*, ed. by Rolf Tiedemann and Hermann Schweppenhäuser, 7 vols (Frankfurt a.M.: Suhrkamp, 1972–91), II.2 (1977), pp. 438–65.

31 Werner Hamacher, '95 Theses on Philology', trans. by Catharine Diehl, *diacritics*, 39.1 (2009), pp. 25–44 (p. 26).

The Staircase Wit

or, The Poetic Idiomaticity of Herta Müller's Prose

ANTONIO CASTORE

Herta Müller was awarded the Nobel Prize in literature in 2009 for depicting, 'with the concentration of poetry and the frankness of prose, [...] the landscape of the dispossessed'.[1] In response to the Prize motivation thus worded by the Swedish Academy, on 7 December of the same year she gave a lecture, entitled 'Every Word Knows Something of a Vicious Circle',[2] in which she reflects upon the role of language — and especially the language of literature — in a context of human deprivation. The speech lends itself to be read as both a general reflection on language ('*Every Word* Knows Something') and a personal statement of poetics, as it also stages a primal scene of writing ('But the writing began in silence, there on the stairs, where I had to come

1 The Nobel Foundation, *Les Prix Nobel: 2009* (Stockholm: The Nobel Foundation, 2010), pp. 361–73. Nobel Prize Outreach AB 2021, 'Herta Müller — Facts' <https://www.nobelprize.org/prizes/literature/2009/muller/facts/> [accessed 10 February 2021].

2 Herta Müller, 'Jedes Wort weiß etwas vom Teufelskreis', Nobel Lecture, online video recording, NobelPrize.org, 7 December 2009 <https://www.nobelprize.org/prizes/literature/2009/muller/lecture/> [accessed 10 February 2021]; in English as 'Every Word Knows Something of a Vicious Circle', trans. by Philip Boehm <https://www.nobelprize.org/uploads/2018/06/muller-lecture_en.pdf> [accessed 20 February 2023]; in print as 'Jedes Wort weiß etwas vom Teufelskreis', in Müller, *Immer derselbe Schnee und immer derselbe Onkel* (Munich: Hanser, 2011), pp. 7–21.

to terms with more than could be said.').[3] In line with most of her essayistic production, Müller combines narrative with meta-narrative strategies. The autobiographical account — or the 'auto-fiction', as she prefers to call it — naturally gives rise to the linguistic annotations that are central to her argumentation, as well as to comment and broader analysis. Like a map used for orientation, the Nobel lecture connects a multitude of Müller's territories and can help find a way through them. The peculiar origin of this text allows for reading it as a compendium — and an *enactment* at the same time — of her meditations on the creative process and the very space of literature, resulting in a self-portrait of the artist in the making of her own work.

The Nobel Lecture was written and delivered before the Swedish Academy in German, Müller's mother tongue and the language of all her published works, with the original title: 'Jedes Wort weiß etwas vom Teufelskreis.' Although elsewhere in her *oeuvre* Müller discusses more directly and extensively her relationship with her mother tongue, this text provides valuable hints to frame the issue in a broader context and, eventually, to open up new perspectives on it — even beyond her own words. Beyond her own words, indeed, for the Nobel lecture *shows* more than it says, or to put it more precisely, it reveals Müller's attitude to her native language less in specific assertions than in her word choice and use.

IDIOMS AND *SPRACHBILDER*; OR, THE MOTHER TONGUE SEEN THROUGH THE LENS OF POETRY

An interesting case is represented by idioms that occur in relevant positions of the text. A closer look at them is solicited by Müller's frequent mentioning of idioms in her essays and lectures, as well as by her use of them in the titles of her novels. The way in which she employs them, though, is never trivial, nor is it simply a way of reproducing everyday or colloquial speech. Rather, as I would like to claim here, it is symptomatic of a more general attitude of hers towards language and the mother tongue. In the Nobel lecture as elsewhere, idioms perform a twofold, and partly contradictory, function. On the one hand, they stand for the specificity of a language and evoke familiar constellations

3 Müller, 'Every Word', p. 7.

of meanings and images; on the other, they undergo a process of *displacement*, which eventually leads to a redefinition of the original terms and, as a consequence, of the way they structure experience.

Defined by the *OED* as 'form[s] of expression [...] used in a distinctive way in a particular language', idioms are indeed a hallmark of the mother tongue(s).[4] Categorized as formulaic expressions, they encode a mostly figurative and non-compositional meaning, i.e., a meaning that is 'not deducible from the meanings of the individual words', although in some cases, as some scholars contend, the literal meaning may play a role in the comprehension process. Whereas 'idiom' is a fuzzy category, it is possible to identify some properties that contribute to defining prototypical examples of idioms. Among them, Nunberg, Sag, and Wasow mention: conventionality, inflexibility, figuration, proverbiality, informality, and affect. ('[I]dioms are typically used to imply a certain evaluation or affective stance toward the things they denote.') They explain 'Conventionality' as follows:

> a relation among a linguistic regularity, a situation of use, and a population that has implicitly agreed to conform to that regularity in that situation out of a preference for general uniformity.[5]

This feature is strictly connected to the 'proverbiality' that is supposed to characterize prototypical idioms: 'Idioms are typically used to describe — and, implicitly, to explain — a recurrent situation of particular social interest.'[6] Newmark, who considers idiom as an 'extended metaphor', identifies two main functions of idioms: the pragmatic and the referential. Although controversial in its definition, the latter is more interesting in relation to the concerns of this essay, as it pertains to the aesthetic domain and invokes the concentration of form, a concept that is also mentioned as a feature of Müller's writing in the statement of the Nobel committee. Indeed, as Newmark puts it, the referential function is used 'to describe a mental process or state,

4 'Idiom, n.', in *OED Online* (Oxford: Oxford University Press, 2020) <https://www.oed.com/view/Entry/91031> [accessed 15 December 2021].

5 Geoffrey Nunberg, Ivan A. Sag, and Thomas Wasow, 'Idioms', *Language*, 3 (1994), pp. 491–538 (p. 492).

6 Ibid., p. 493.

a concept, a person, an object, a quality or an action more *comprehensively and concisely* than is possible in literal or physical language'.[7] Idioms have also attracted considerable interest among cognitive linguists, who have made a significant contribution to our understanding of idioms, beginning with the seminal works of George Lakoff and Mark Johnson on conceptual metaphors and continuing with more recent studies, which extend into several directions.[8] In particular, it has been shown that many elements of idioms are tied to productive grammatical patterns and schemes of human thought.[9] Raymond Gibbs, among others, mentions this aspect in order to emphasize the role of idioms as instances of the creativity of natural language. On this point the linguist's gaze coincides with that of the poet.

Asked to what extent the language acquired as a child in her native village of the Banat had affected her as a writer, Müller replied that every language is rich with metaphors and that literariness itself (*das Literarische*), far from being a unique quality of the works of writers and poets, is a quality inherent in many cultural artefacts, such as folklore, proverbs, idioms, and images of superstition.[10] Although she does not provide further explanation, Müller seems less interested in the narratives that these forms potentially entail than in the proliferation of images that are produced by popular culture by the means — and through the mediation — of language. Thus, the mother tongue is not only a medium for everyday communication or writing, it is also a collective archive in which the products of linguistic creativity of many anonymous speakers are recorded. At the same time, Müller is aware that in the common perception the poetic quality of many 'verbal images' (Sprachbilder) is concealed by habit.[11] To let this quality

---

7 Peter Newmark, *A Textbook of Translation* (New York: Prentice Hall, 1988), p. 104; my emphasis.

8 George Lakoff and Mark Johnson, 'Conceptual Metaphor in Everyday Language', *The Journal of Philosophy*, 8 (1980), pp. 453–86.

9 Raymond W. Gibbs, Jr., 'Idioms and Formulaic Language', in *The Oxford Handbook of Cognitive Linguistics*, ed. by Dirk Geeraerts and Hubert Cuyckens (Oxford: Oxford University Press, 2007), pp. 697–725.

10 Herta Müller, *Mein Vaterland war ein Apfelkern. Ein Gespräch mit Angelika Klammer* (Munich: Hanser, 2014), pp. 89–90.

11 Ibid., p. 90: 'Tausende Sprachbilder, die wir aus Gewohnheit benutzen, ohne darauf zu achten, dass sie poetisch sind' (Thousands of verbal images that we use out of habit, without paying attention to the fact that they are poetic).

emerge, a different gaze upon language is necessary. In this light, the sentence with which Müller, almost incidentally, switches her focus and reconstructs a hypothetical origin of idioms becomes particularly meaningful:

> I imagine that at some point each of our verbal images was uttered by someone, by accident or on purpose. Someone else has then adopted it countless times and it has prevailed.[12]

This move is important exactly because it allows for a return to a point of absolute singularity, where idioms are *not yet* conventionalized but can instead be seen in their originality, as individual creations, utterances capable, by a singular twist of language, to disclose new ways of perceiving, and consequently naming or addressing, objects, experiences, and emotions. Such a gaze on language, which temporarily brackets usage conventions, is similar to the naive gaze of a child. Indeed, in Müller's recollection, proper idioms do not differ from pregnant expressions that she heard as a child from her grandparents and that caught her imagination. No matter if her grandpa drew the maxim 'When flags flutter, reason slips into the trumpet' from somewhere else or if it was a product of his mind: it is greeted by the child as if coined in that very moment. The same effect is produced by the familiar warning of her grandmother: 'Don't think there, where you must not.'[13] It stuck in her mind because it was 'poetic' (poetisch). And she could recognize it as such, though still unaware of the very existence of literature, because it 'stirred something' inside her ('Dieser Satz hatte mich aufgewühlt.'). The verb *aufwühlen* — similarly to the English 'to stir' — belongs indeed to the same semantic field of terms that Müller used to refer to the effects of true art, and especially of any 'rigorous' piece of literature, be it in prose or in poetry. For her, it is indeed a prerogative of such works to give rise to an 'invented perception' (erfundene Wahrnehmung), as she calls it, that induces a state

12 Ibid.: 'Ich stelle mir vor, jedes unserer Sprachbilder hat irgendwann mal jemand zufällig oder absichtlich gesagt. Und jemand anders hat es unzählige Male übernommen und es hat sich durchgesetzt' (my translation; if not declared otherwise, all translations from Müller's texts, with the exception of the Nobel lecture, 'Every Word', are mine.)

13 Müller, *Mein Vaterland*, p. 90.

of disturbance, perturbation, 'errancy' (Irrlauf), 'unrest' (Unruhe).[14] I shall come back later again to this. For now, it may be enough to single out some additional points.

First, Müller envisions an affinity between idiomatic expressions and poetry. Second, it is possible to start outlining a sort of chiastic relationship between the two of them: on the one hand, idioms — and by extension the mother tongue — are looked at and judged from the angle of poetry; on the other, every poetic expression is seen as inherently having the potential to become idiomatic.[15] A third point is worth mentioning, yet it requires some specification. I am referring to my previous claim: Müller looks at idioms and verbal images with a gaze that is specifically aimed at capturing singularity in the linguistic event and presupposes a momentary abstraction from conventionality. This does not entail denying the role played by these forms of expression in the system of language as a whole, nor does it mean considering the semantic stratification brought in by collective usage as irrelevant. On the contrary, the poetic reading and use of idioms is in most cases implicitly played against the expectations produced in readers and listeners by habit and conventions. A similar dialectics involving singularity and collectiveness is at work in Müller's lecture on poetry 'In jeder Sprache sitzen andere Augen.'[16] As the title suggests, in this text Müller explores the thesis that different languages embody quite different ways of experiencing reality. She does so by means of examples taken from everyday Banat Swabian as well as from standard

---

14 All these terms occur many times throughout Müller's essays and lectures. For a more comprehensive view on their interrelations, see Herta Müller, *Der Teufel sitzt im Spiegel* (Berlin: Rotbuch, 1991), and especially Herta Müller, 'Wie Wahrnehmung sich erfindet', in Ibid., pp. 9–32, and 'Wie Erfundenes sich im Rückblick wahrnimmt', in Ibid., pp. 33–56.

15 Müller elaborates on this more thoroughly in her essay 'So ein großer Körper und so ein kleiner Motor', in *Immer derselbe Schnee*, pp. 84–95. In this text, written on the occasion of Müller's being awarded the Walter Hasenclever Literature Prize, she actually does not mention idioms. Instead, she uses the expression 'erring' or 'wandering comment' (wandernder Kommentar) to refer to phrases such as that in the title of her speech: 'Such a big body and such a small motor'. Phrases like that, once used literally to denote a physical state or object (in this case, her father's truck), can by virtue of their evocative quality serve, if used metaphorically, or 'idiomatically', to both evaluate and describe different situations.

16 Herta Müller, 'In jeder Sprache sitzen andere Augen', in *Der König verneigt sich und tötet* (Munich: Hanser, 2003), pp. 7–39.

German and Romanian. Müller personifies language by saying that each language has different eyes. Her standpoint is a poetic one; her aim is clearly not to engage in a theoretical discussion. Yet the underlying thesis has a long history and is still debated by philosophers and linguists. Known as the 'Sapir-Whorf hypothesis' or more generically as the 'linguistic relativity hypothesis', it has found differing formulations, which agree at least on the basic assumption that 'different languages carve the world up in different ways, and that as a result their speakers think about it differently'.[17] After affirming a strong connection between the distinctive forms of a language and the patterns of conceptualization and perception, though, Müller restrains from proposing an overall and unifying view. Rather, in the same lecture, she insists that language 'lives in singular instances [im Einzelfall]',[18] and concludes that 'you have to learn *every time anew* what it has in mind by carefully listening to it [ablauschen]'.[19] In this case, her insistence on an approach to linguistic events freed from former prejudices and assumptions is geared less towards unveiling the hidden poetic quality of certain expressions than interpreting them properly. The verb *ablauschen*, which is used by Müller, deserves a brief annotation. While it might be translated as 'to learn by listening carefully', it more properly means 'to learn by eavesdropping'. This second connotation evokes the detestable surveillance practices of the secret police of authoritarian states. If this holds true, then by embracing the term as a key point in the process of understanding Müller applies to it the same process that she tries to explain: she assigns a new value to the term and asks the reader to acknowledge it *as if* it were coined anew.

THE NOBEL LECTURE: CIRCLING AROUND IDIOMS

Like many other titles of Müller's works, the title of the Nobel lecture is quite enigmatic and opaque. One would expect the reading of the text to make its meaning more transparent, but that is the case only

17 Chris Swoyer, 'The Linguistic Relativity Hypothesis: Supplement to "Relativism"', *Stanford Encyclopedia of Philosophy* (Spring 2003) <https://stanford.library.sydney.edu.au/archives/spr2015/entries/relativism/supplement2.html> [accessed 17 July 2020].

18 Müller, 'In jeder Sprache', p. 39.

19 Ibid.; my emphasis.

to a certain extent. Before analysing the structure and content of the lecture, it might be worth reflecting on the expectations raised by the title in the reader/listener. As studies in semiology and reception theory have widely demonstrated, titles, along with para-textual and textual elements such as the opening words, contribute in large part to orienting the reading process. In this case, the title 'Every Word Knows Something of a Vicious Circle' evokes a somewhat mysterious atmosphere surrounding the life and functioning of words, implicitly promising to reveal the secret that is alluded to by the expression 'every word *knows something*'. The implicit personification of 'word' suggests that, in what follows, language will be treated not as an inert object of study, but rather as something living or inherently entangled with life. The main focus of the title, though, is on its last part, with the 'vicious circle' directly predicating a property of words. In light of what I discussed above, it might be interesting to note that 'vicious circle' is itself an idiomatic expression. It derives from the Latin *circulus vitiosus* and would probably be classified among the cross-cultural idioms, since it is common among speakers of different languages and cultures, with only slight variation. In German, the concept is expressed by a partially different form, which retains the idea of circularity but is neither a mere calque nor a literal transposition from the equivalent Latin expression. The characterization changes: where the Latin-based forms have a 'vicious', i.e., a 'faulty' circularity, the German *Teufelskreis* has a devilish one: 'a circle (*Kreis*) of the Devil (*Teufel*)'.

The issue of translation, especially in relation to idioms, will resurface later. Yet the brief notes above already suggest that here resides another point of affinity between idioms and poetry. In the case of both poetry and idioms, translation is a hard task, sometimes verging on the extreme of impossibility. As we have seen, even when it is possible to identify a close match between idioms belonging to different languages, a small difference of form may be sufficient to produce different chains of metaphorical and culturally bound associations, which translation would necessarily leave behind.[20] In any case, many

20 See, among others, Mona Baker, *In Other Words: A Coursebook on Translation* (London: Routledge, 2011), p. 72: 'An idiom [...] may have a similar counterpart in the target language, but its context of use may be different; the two expressions may have different connotations, for instance, or they may not be pragmatically transferable.'

scholars maintain that idioms are stored in memory and processed by the brain as phrases and that many of them are no longer perceived as metaphorical or containing other kinds of figuration. If this is true, both the German *Teufelskreis* and the English 'vicious circle' in the title, at this point, are likely to be intended in almost the same way, as referring to the realm of logic or rhetoric, and as leading to some kind of paradox. According to the dictionaries, they denote a 'fallacious mode of reasoning' or arguing in which premises and conclusions refer to one another, and are supposed to be each other's cause;[21] or, by extension, they denote a dead end brought about by a never-ending series of unpleasant, interdependent events or factors.[22] It remains to verify whether and to what extent these expectations will be fulfilled, contradicted, or modified by the text itself.

'DO YOU HAVE A HANDKERCHIEF': TOWARD A POETIC IDIOMATICITY

The Nobel lecture can be roughly divided into three parts. The first, and the longest one, is in turn composed of a series of independent tableaus or scenes, describing different situations (or 'stations') in

---

Baker mentions four strategies to translate idioms: finding an idiom of similar meaning and similar form in the target language; finding an idiom of similar meaning and different form; paraphrasing; literally transposing. While the last of these strategies is the one that presents the highest coefficient of foreignization and is, according to Larson, the most dangerous, paraphrasing is the extreme attempt to convey a content at the expense of form, in the absence of an expression with an equivalent function.

21 The *OED* registers 'vicious circle' under both the entries 'vicious, adj. 9' and 'circle, n. 19'. The latter entry gives the following definition: 'A fallacious mode of reasoning, wherein a proposition is used to establish a conclusion, and afterwards proved by means of the conclusion which it has been employed to establish; so that, as in a circle, there is really no starting-point.' See *OED Online* <https://www.oed.com/view/Entry/33187> [accessed 20 July 2021]). At 'vicious, adj. 9a', 'vicious circle' is mentioned as pertaining to both logic and pathology. For the latter sense, the *OED* provides (9b) the following definition: 'A morbid process consisting in the reciprocal continuation and aggravation of one disorder by another'. Also mentioned (9c) is a generic meaning that keeps similar negative connotations: 'A situation in which action and reaction intensify each other; a self-perpetuating process of aggravation' (*OED Online* <https://www.oed.com/view/Entry/223179> [accessed 20 July 2021]).

22 The German Dictionary *Duden* defines 'Teufelskreis' as follows: 'ausweglos scheinende Lage, die durch eine nicht endende Folge unangenehmer, einander bedingender Geschehnisse, Faktoren herbeigeführt wird'. See 'Teufelskreis', *Duden Online* (Berlin: Bibliographisches Institut, 2021) <https://www.duden.de/rechtschreibung/Teufelskreis> [accessed 20 July 2021].

the author's life and connected only by the recurrence of the same expression. The second part is more reflective in tone and leads to a meditation on language and writing. It also contains what I have called a 'primal scene of writing'. The third part is the conclusive one. It is introduced by another autobiographical scene of writing, which prompts a final thought on the salvific potential of words for 'those whom dictatorships deprive of dignity every day' and, more generally, for 'the acute solitude of a human being'.[23]

> DO YOU HAVE A HANDKERCHIEF was the question my mother asked me every morning, standing by the gate to our house, before I went out onto the street. I didn't have a handkerchief. And because I didn't, I would go back inside and get one. I never had a handkerchief because I would always wait for her question. The handkerchief was proof that my mother was looking after me in the morning. [...] The question DO YOU HAVE A HANDKERCHIEF was an indirect display of affection.[24]

This is the opening paragraph of the lecture, with the question 'Do you have a handkerchief' marking its very beginning. The same question will recur many times afterwards throughout the text. The use of capital letters, in which it is written, makes its repetition stand out graphically in the pages of the lecture text, thus preparing the reader to receive it as something more than a mere rhetorical motif. By pointing at the 'circularity' announced by the title, repetition will prove to be in itself a constitutive part of the meaning of the text. While the phrase is repeated in identical form, it nevertheless needs to be situated — and carefully listened to, or 'eavesdropped on' — every time anew, in order to fully reveal its meaning. From the very beginning, in fact, in excess of its literal meaning, the question is charged with a lateral meaning that addresses what cannot be expressed in speech. If it is not (yet) a matter of figurality in any strict sense, it is certainly a case of a signification process that counts 'indirectness' and 'disguise' among its most salient features.

---

23 Müller, 'Every Word', p. 10.

24 Ibid. p. 1.

> Anything more direct would have been embarrassing and not something the farmers practiced. Love disguised itself as a question. That was the only way it could be spoken: matter-of-factly, in the tone of a command, or the deft maneuvers used for work. The brusqueness of the voice even emphasized the tenderness.[25]

If every word needs a context to be correctly interpreted, in this case the context is to be understood in a broader sense than the restricted conversational setting. The phrase 'Do you have a handkerchief' (the absence of the question mark mimics the ambiguous status of a question 'in the tone of a command') is so deeply rooted in the language and culture in which it is produced that outside of them it would probably be intended in its literal sense only. The language and culture at issue are those of a small village of farmers belonging to the German-speaking community settled in the Romanian region called Banat. It does not matter that much, at this point, to specify that the language is a variant of the Swabian dialect or to emphasize that it is the language of a minority. What is more important to note is that it is — to put it in Wittgenstein's terms — a 'form of life' (Lebensform), with its own rules, its own 'language-games', and its own interdicts.[26] In Müller's recollection, the question 'Do you have a handkerchief', produced within that specific form of life, actually behaves in the same way as an idiom, as a 'form of expression [...] used in a distinctive way in a particular language'.

But what does it mean 'to have a handkerchief' in *that* particular language, which is a form of life and a world (Wittgenstein)? And what is the meaning of the handkerchief within the compass of the lecture? 'No other object in the house, including ourselves, was ever as important to us as the handkerchief.' The importance of the object is also conveyed by the fact that 'we had a handkerchief drawer at home' and that its organization complied with strict criteria: it 'was always partitioned into two rows, with three stacks apiece'.[27] Position, size,

25 Ibid.

26 Ludwig Wittgenstein, *Philosophical Investigations*, trans. by G. E. M. Anscome, P. M. S. Hacker, and Joachim Schulte, ed. by Hacker and Schulte (Oxford: Wiley-Blackwell, 2009), p. 15 (§ 23).

27 Müller, 'Every Word', pp. 3–4.

and ornamentation of the handkerchiefs turn the drawer into 'a family portrait in handkerchief format', with its power hierarchies and gender differences objectified and reproduced in smaller scale: the men's handkerchiefs, for father and grandfather, positioned on the left, 'were the biggest, with dark stripes along the edges in brown, grey or Bordeaux'. The women's handkerchiefs were on the right, had light blue, red, or green edges, and were smaller. The children's handkerchiefs 'were the smallest: borderless white squares painted with flowers or animals'. They lie in the middle, between the men's and women's stacks. The further partition of each of the three types into two rows followed the calendar division between weekdays and Sundays.

'Objects [Gegenstände] have always been important to me.' Thus Müller declares in her essay 'In jeder Sprache sitzen andere Augen'.[28] Indeed, they have a prominent role in her aesthetics. In a 2007 lecture on poetics presented at the University of Zurich, she describes the act of writing as a process that involves two conversations. The first one is precisely a conversation of the 'linguistic gaze' (sprachlicher Blick) with 'the real objects of life', while the second one occurs between 'the conditions negotiated in that first conversation and the paper, that is, their turning into sentences'.[29] In a shattered image of the world such as Müller's, fragments and fractures, under the pressure of fear and trauma, prevail over any totalizing, unitary, all-embracing view, while details are enlarged at the expense of the whole. In this world, objects are the ultimate bearer of meaning. Yet, their meaning is neither stable nor transparent. They are proof not that the world is as it is, but rather that it reveals itself insofar as it undergoes transformations. Objects do not even seem to have a meaning on their own, for themselves. Like linguistic signs, they point beyond themselves in quite an arbitrary way. They are signifiers of something unknown or to come. On the one hand, objects are linked with identity, namely the identity of those who own them:

> Their appearance was part of the image of the persons who owned them, like the persons themselves. They were always

28 Müller, 'In jeder Sprache', p. 15.

29 Herta Müller, 'Gelber Mais und keine Zeit', in *Immer derselbe Schnee*, pp. 125–45 (p. 135).

> inseparable from what and how a person was. They are the outermost part of the person, lifted off the skin.[30]

On the other hand, the purport of that linkage is opaque, just as that of the object itself. Handkerchiefs act like other objects of real life that travel through Müller's texts. In these instances, an object is charged with a meaning that often remains hidden and reveals itself only after the same — or almost the same — object has occurred in different contexts. The presence of a handkerchief punctuates the entire lecture, sewing together different events of the author's life as well as the narrative that retells them. In fact, each of the auto-fictional tableaus of the first part revolves around a different use of the handkerchief in a particular situation of life. Which is tantamount to saying that each revolves around a different meaning of 'handkerchief', if — to put it with Wittgenstein — 'the meaning of a word is its use'.[31] Station after station, from one occurrence to the next, what actually remains unchanged is the word designating the object: this word guarantees the possibility for an object to be both the same and to differ from itself; it also triggers, along with the wandering of the object throughout the text, the wandering of meanings in unpredictable directions towards unpredictable aims.[32]

Compared with other objects, the handkerchief has a peculiarity, which lies at the basis of the handkerchief's utmost importance in everyday life: 'Its uses were *universal*.' Müller singles some of them out: 'sniffles; nosebleeds; hurt hand, elbow or knee; crying, or biting into it to suppress the crying'.[33] The list goes on at length, including examples in which the handkerchief, properly used or adapted to a specific aim, may work as relief against headache, pain, heat, or rain, or may help remember things, and may even help take care of the dead.

30 Müller, 'In jeder Sprache', p. 15: 'Ihr Aussehen gehörte zum Bild der Menschen, die sie besaßen, wie die Menschen selbst. Sie gehörten immer zu dem, was und wie ein Mensch war, untrennbar dazu. Sie sind der äußerste von der Haut weggehobene Teil der Person.'

31 Wittgenstein, *Philosophical Investigations*, § 43.

32 Müller, 'In jeder Sprache', p. 18: 'The objects recur time and again. Alexandru Vona writes: "There is a pressing presence of things, whose aim is unknown to me."' (Die Gegenstände wiederholen sich immer wieder. Alexandru Vona schreibt: 'Es gibt eine bedrängende Gegenwart der Dinge, deren Zweck ich nicht kenne.')

33 Müller, 'Every Word', p. 4.

If poverty and deprivations are the material ground where people's resourcefulness breeds and the manifold uses of the handkerchief are rooted, on a narrative and linguistic level the *universality* of its uses transforms the handkerchief into a kind of universal signifier, ready to receive the seeds of figurality and make them bear fruit. This is what happens in one of the Nobel lecture's first auto-fictional scenes, which tells of the harassment Müller had to endure in the workplace for refusing to collaborate with the Romanian secret police. After finding all doors closed, having no other place to stay and yet not being willing to resign or indulge her persecutors, she sits on a handkerchief in the stairway, with the handkerchief *becoming* her office. 'I was a staircase wit and my office was a handkerchief', she writes in a central and densely meaningful passage.[34] At the same time real and metaphorical, the handkerchief *is* indeed the only place — a free place, a place of her own, not subjected to the authority of others — where she can keep doing her work, namely her technical translations, for the factory. Yet, it also stands for a space of resistance and dignity, a shelter against abuse of power and oppression. In another auto-fictional story told in the lecture, the handkerchief is not a real object but features only as a mental image, working as a vehicle within a metaphor. The story is that of Uncle Matz, who in the 1930s had first become a fanatic Nazi and then an SS-officer, to the consternation of his father, Müller's grandfather, who 'owed his entire fortune to the credit advanced by Jewish business friends'. Uncle Matz had asked to be sent to the front and soon afterwards had found his death on a mine. A picture of his remains was sent back to his family.

> The death photo is hand-sized: in the middle of a black field a little grey heap of human remains can be seen resting on a white cloth. Against the black, the white cloth lies as small as a children's handkerchief, a white square with a strange design painted in the middle.[35]

The comparison between the white 'cloth' (Tuch) with the uncle's remains and the children's 'handkerchief' (Taschentuch), prompted by the word assonance along with the visual resemblance, exceeds the

34 Ibid., p. 3.
35 Ibid., p. 6.

merely denotative dimension to which the sentence, if taken alone, would confine it. The ghostly apparition of the handkerchief, as a return after many other appearances, conjures up a crowd of associated meanings and heterogeneous reverberations. In particular, it recalls scenes of the lecture that are linked to the narrator's childhood, such as the description of the 'handkerchief's drawer', or that are centred around the concept of 'care', whether it be the care for the dead (Müller tells how handkerchiefs were used to keep the dead person's mouth closed, before composing the corpse, or to cover their face, in the case of someone collapsing out in the street) or the care of a mother for her child, such as in the opening scene of the text. The comparison, as if picturing the object at the threshold of its metamorphosis, introduces a change of perception in the scene, which alters the plain neutrality of description. This is an instance of the process Müller calls 'invented perception', by which writing, insofar as it alters reality, seizes its truth more deeply. In this case, the altered perception of the death cloth as a child handkerchief objectifies the careful gaze of the mother:

> For my grandmother this photo was a combination [...]: on the white handkerchief was a dead Nazi, in her memory was a living son. [...] She prayed every day, and her prayers almost certainly had double meanings as well. Acknowledging the break from beloved son to fanatic Nazi, they probably beseeched God to perform the balancing act of loving the son and forgiving the Nazi.[36]

New layers of significance open up when the 'handkerchief' (both the object and the word designating it) is read within the pattern of repetitions that started at the very beginning of the text with the question: 'Do you have a handkerchief.' This very question, intended in its idiomatic sense of an 'indirect display of affection', provides the keystone for both the structure of the lecture as a whole and the interpretation of the single occurrences (reincarnations) of the 'handkerchief'.

This is a key point and needs to be understood correctly. The phrase 'Do you have a handkerchief' is not registered as an idiom in any dictionary, and yet it behaves as such, after being defined as such

36 Ibid.

in the opening paragraph of the text. As seen above, its meaning — not being literal — is 'figurative' in a peculiar way and is strictly dependent on the language (intended as a 'form of life') within the limits and borders of which it is originally produced. The other features proper to 'prototypical idioms' — inflexibility, informality, and affect — can also be attached to this phrase, as it implies an evaluation and an affective stance toward the thing it denotes.[37] 'Do you have a handkerchief' also has the characteristic of 'proverbiality' insofar as it 'describe[s] — and, implicitly, [...] explain[s] — a recurrent situation', although in our case the process is somehow reversed.[38] It is the reference to the idiom (the phrase 'Do you have a handkerchief'), via the repetition of the same expression ('the handkerchief'), that sheds light on the different — and apparently unrelated — scenes of life and connotes them as having hidden, deep, common roots and traits. But the point that I find crucial here is that the recurrent reference to the idiomatic phrase 'Do you have a handkerchief' establishes a new conventionality, not among the population of speakers of a specific language, as is the case with proper idioms, but among the readers of the lecture within the confined space of the text. This is what I suggest calling 'poetic idiomaticity': a feature of Müller's prose by which certain expressions are redefined with regard to their meaning and use according to a dynamic set of rules and internal relations that the text negotiates with its addressee in the very process of its own constitution as a text. Within this frame, Müller's peculiar attitude towards her mother tongue becomes evident. The mother tongue is necessary, but only in order to be overcome and superseded. It is the first and 'most familiar' (vertrauteste) access point to the world of signification and yet it is useful insofar as it allows a new language, the language of the work, the language of poetry, to take place.[39] In this regard, the mother tongue is not unlike Wittgenstein's 'ladder', which must be thrown away after having climbed up on it. One must surmount it; then one sees the world correctly. This could be claimed of the mother tongue

37 Nunberg, Sag, and Wasow, 'Idioms', p. 492.

38 Ibid., p. 493.

39 Müller, 'In jeder Sprache', p. 26.

by applying to it what the philosopher claims at the end of his *Tractatus* about the very propositions that have led the reader up to that point.[40]

THE DEVIL'S CIRCLE OF THE MOTHER TONGUE

The poetic idiomaticity of the phrase 'Do you have a handkerchief', established by the lecture, is just an example of a more general quality of words: namely, their power to connect things, to establish relations among disparate situations and experiential domains, and, in so doing, to make new sense of them. This additional state of comprehension of life and reality, to which language gives access, can only be brought about by writing, as Müller suggests in a passage of the lecture that makes the first explicit reference to the title:

> Can we say that it is precisely the smallest objects — be they trumpets, accordions, or handkerchiefs — which connect the most disparate things in life? That the objects are in orbit and that their deviations reveal a pattern of repetition — a vicious circle [Teufelskreis], or what we call in German a devil's circle. We can believe this, but not say it. Still, what can't be said can be written. Because writing is a silent act, a labor from the head to the hand.[41]

Defined in direct opposition to speech, writing represents the space or the medium in which 'the real objects of life' and the words designating them arrange themselves in such a way as to signify differently than they ordinarily do and consequently to open up new paths of sense-making. This move not only subverts the Platonic view according to which the spoken word would inherently be more apt to address truth, but, as I shall show in the next section, also undermines the myth of the mother tongue in one of its pillars, namely immediacy. What starts to be outlined here is the picture of a mother tongue governed by a different temporality and a different logic, a mother tongue 'as writing' and 'labour' that contradicts the principle of a language providing an immediate access to meaning thanks to its closeness to the speaking subject, its constant being 'at hand' (parat stehen).[42]

---

40 Ludwig Wittgenstein, *Tractatus Logico-Philosophicus*, trans. by F. P. Ramsey and C. K. Ogden, intro. by Bertrand Russell (London: Kegan Paul, 1922), p. 90 (§ 6.54).

41 Müller, 'Every Word', p. 7.

42 Müller, 'In jeder Sprache', p. 28.

The different logic of words that writing makes possible is represented in the Nobel lecture by the figure of the 'vicious circle'. Remarkably, the German term *Teufelskreis* from the source text is rendered with an expanded translation that provides both the corresponding English idiom — 'vicious circle', in fact — and the literal meaning, 'what we call in German a devil's circle'. The translator's choice is motivated by the intrinsic ambiguity of the expression, which, as any idiom, may signify differently according to whether it is understood as a stock unit (i.e., a phrase) or is analysed compositionally, i.e., by taking into account the meanings of the single words composing the idiom. Both possibilities are latently active here, and Müller clearly plays on the oscillation between these two options. She presupposes the conventional meaning of the idiom as a unit but at the same time, by (mis)placing the expression into a context that makes it sound inappropriate, she obliterates it. Indeed, at the point of the lecture where it occurs first, the compound word *Teufelskreis* sounds odd and forces the reader to revise her/his own expectations as well as to question its meaning. None of the meanings assigned by dictionaries, listed above, to the idiom 'vicious circle' easily applies to the narrative of the Nobel lecture.[43] Neither a fallacious, circular argument nor a pathological and 'self-perpetuating process of aggravation' is an apt descriptor of the 'pattern of repetition' of the objects or words connecting the different life-scenes in the Nobel lecture. Nor is a wholly negative, claustrophobic situation with no way out. No relation of cause and effect, nor any of action and reaction link these events. Above all, their circularity exceeds a simplistic, negative characterization. On the contrary, the unforeseen connections that repetition establishes among the unpleasant events narrated (the harassment suffered in the workplace, the uncle's death, Oskar Pastior's deportation, and others) contribute to a new understanding of them.

> Nothing but the whirl of words [Wortwirbel] could grasp my condition. It spelled out what the mouth could not pronounce. I chased after the events [Gelebten], caught up in the words

43 See notes 21 and 22.

> and their devilish circling [im Teufelskreis], until something emerged I had never known before.[44]

The mis/dis-placement of the expression *Teufelskreis* suggests a redefinition from 'vicious' to 'devil's circle'. As if it had never been used before, the expression calls for a (re)interpretation that starts from the words that compose it and recombines them into a new figuration, halfway between an event of magic, which involves the evocation of spirits, and a psychoanalytic session. The image of the *Teufelskreis* gives tangible shape to the immaterial and chaotic process of literary creation, especially with regard to auto-fictional or autobiographical accounts, with its combination of control and dispossession, abandonment to the unconscious paths of memory, as well as to the impersonal power of language. In the scene depicted above, the creative subject is almost completely passive, with her role being only that of a scene-setter and a conjurer who is herself possessed by the summoned spirits, while all agency resides in words and language.

> Parallel to the reality, the pantomime of words stepped into action, without respect for any real dimensions, shrinking what was most important and stretching the minor matters. As it *rushes madly* ahead, this *devilish* circle [Teufelskreis] of words imposes a kind of *bewitched* [verwunschene] logic on what has been lived.[45]

Carried by the whirlwind of words, the writing subject cannot help but attend passively the mute show by which language alters reality and reinterprets — and even reinvents — past experiences. As if they were under a spell, words animate themselves and enact a 'representation' that mirrors back a deformed image of the past. A couple of lines below, the passage reads as follows: 'The words are what takes possession of me.' By subtly weaving the threads of the metaphors of 'bewitchment' and 'magic' in this passage, Müller unfolds a meditation on auto-fictionality that develops throughout all of her work. Traces of it are already found in 1991, in a book tellingly called *Der Teufel sitzt im Spiegel* (The Devil Sits in the Mirror),[46] and later in her 1996 book *In*

44 Müller, 'Every Word', p. 7.

45 Ibid.; translation modified, my emphasis.

46 Müller, *Der Teufel*.

der Falle. In the latter text, a reference to Jorge Semprún becomes crucial, as she cites him to assert that literary invention is indispensable for the truth of memory to be conveyed: 'The truth of written memories must be invented.'[47] The importance of the reference lies in the context from which it is taken, since Semprún's meditation concerns the experience of the Nazi concentration camps as well as the possibility of capturing the 'substance' of such a dense event and, by extension, of 'all great historical experiences'. To 'shape [one's] evidence into an artistic object, a space of creation. Or of re-creation.'[48] For Semprún, this is the only way 'of conveying some of the truth of such testimony'. On one hand, Müller's citation of Semprún implicitly compares the experience of the *Lager* with that of the Romanian authoritarian state (or perhaps with the density of any traumatic event?). On the other hand, it reverses Semprún's call for a gesture of — I dare say, masculine — authorial resolve (the 'artifice of a masterly narrative') into an articulated process that is governed by the autonomy of language as well as by a kind of wisdom or intelligence of words:

> The words dictate what has to happen, you follow their sound, an exact mathematics up to the surprise attack brought to the real objects by the metaphor. The invented words take a deep breath, you don't know what they allow, you try. They grab what they need. And what they do not allow, they reject. For them nothing is indifferent. Words are keen-eared, intuition makes them clever.[49]

This passage from her 2007 lecture on poetics well describes the creative process as a process of dispossession or, at least, of tentative negotiation, in which the author, far from being in control of her subject and means, finds in language both a dictator and an ultimate judge. This process, triggered by the devil's circle of words, is even radicalized in the Nobel lecture. Here, the loss of control over the way lived experiences are reshaped by language is embodied in the pantomime, since this is the place where a complete reversal of roles is performed between the writing I and the personified words, with the latter taking

47 Herta Müller, *In der Falle* (Göttingen: Wallstein, 1996), pp. 21–22.

48 Jorge Semprún, *Literature or Life*, trans. by Linda Coverdale (London: Viking, 1997), p. 13.

49 Müller, 'Gelber Mais', p. 136.

on human affects, actions, and volition, and the former being subjected to them. This can lead to extreme consequences when it comes to the treatment of sensitive arguments or, to put it in Semprún's terms, of particularly dense experiences, such as dictatorship is for Müller. Not unlike what happens in the case of trauma, dictatorship, being (one of) the main source(s) of her anguish and cares, as well as what she often mentions as lying at the origin of her need to write, cannot be deliberately thematized. Rather, even if present, it remains hidden, while language chooses its own way to show without saying, in the essential deferment of fiction.

> Their pantomime is ruthless and restive [rabiat und bleibt ängstlich], always craving more but instantly jaded. The subject of dictatorship is necessarily present, because nothing can ever again be a matter of course once we have been robbed of nearly all ability to take anything for granted. The subject is there implicitly, but the words are what take possession of me. They coax the subject anywhere they want. Nothing corresponds anymore [nichts mehr stimmt] and everything is true [wahr].[50]

Another reversal is at work here. In a general sense, in fact, one could maintain that dictatorship is what triggers the vicious, devil's circle of words, insofar as every word can be intentionally misinterpreted and thus leads to 'excruciating consequences', while silence can become tantamount to connivance with the authoritarian power. Yet, at this point, it should be definitely clear that *Teufelskreis* does not attain to words as a logical or a rhetorical attribute, but that it rather denotes a symbolic space as well as a peculiar condition of possibility in which words fully unfold their power to reshape experience. It is an inherently ambiguous condition, both perturbing and enlightening, at the same time powerful and full of pain, which takes on the character of magic insofar as it addresses the nexus linking (literary) creation and perception by evoking a sort of external and impersonal faculty, which works according to its own laws, independent of reason or will.

In this sense, the expression *Teufelskreis* (devil's circle) seems to recall the image of the 'magic circle', *Zauberkreis*, as preserved in medieval iconography as well as in superstition or in exoteric praxis. The

50 Müller, 'Every Word', p. 7; translation modified.

entry for *Zauberkreis* in the German dictionary of Jakob and Wilhelm Grimm renders all the ambivalence of the term, which designates both a spatial domain and a magic power confined into 'a circle that is mostly visibly drawn on the earth'.[51] While the circle protects against evil and is a space inside of which the magician can 'conjure up the spirits' or even 'banish the devil' (as well as 'the evil spirit'), it is also a space in which the magician can 'fall under the spell of magical beings'. This very ambiguity is, I suppose, the deep essence of the *Teufelskreis* in its attribution to words.

If one moves a step further and, in line with what Müller herself authorizes elsewhere, uses this expression as an 'errant comment',[52] abstracting it from the specific meaning assigned to it in the Nobel lecture, the figure of the *Teufelskreis* can moreover help reconcile her apparently contradictory statements concerning the mother tongue and language in general. Müller oscillates between the two poles of a complete distrust of language and an acknowledgement of its boundless power.

Indeed, in a conversation with Michael Lentz, Müller admits that words have something like a 'magic quality' because 'they potentially have and can do everything', they are 'latently capable of anything'.[53] Yet elsewhere she maintains that 'it is not true that there are words for everything', and, in particular, that no language has words capable of reproducing either thought in its non-verbal manifestations or what moves inside us, in our 'inner districts' (inneren Bereiche). In general, says Müller, language fails precisely when it comes to expressing what

51 'Zauberkreis, m.', in *Deutsches Wörterbuch von Jacob und Wilhelm Grimm*, digital version, part of the *Wörterbuchnetz of the Trier Center for the Digital Humanities* <http://www.woerterbuchnetz.de/DWB?lemid=Z01853/> [accessed 11 February 2021]. In the dictionary of the Brothers Grimm, the 'magic circle' or *Zauberkreis* is defined as a magic 'Bann'. In the same dictionary, the German term *Bann* is only marginally attested with reference to magic. In fact, sense (1) records the meaning of 'the power and jurisdiction of a spiritual or secular judge' while, according to sense (2), *Bann* is the region upon which that power is exerted, often in relation with obligations or prohibitions. Sense (3) is that of a *dictum* or *interdictum* ('Bann, m.', in *Deutsches Wörterbuch* <https://www.woerterbuchnetz.de/DWB?lemid=B00667> [accessed 11 February 2021]).

52 See note 15 above.

53 Herta Müller, *Lebensangst und Worthunger: im Gespräch mit Michael Lentz: Leipziger Poetikvorlesung 2009* (Berlin: Suhrkamp, 2010), p. 51.

is 'crucial' (das Entscheidende), vital, or essential.[54] She is also sceptical of the Western faith in talking and discourse to unravel 'confusion' (Wirrnis).[55] In addition, while she is fascinated by the power of words, she is afraid of it. 'I don't trust language' (Ich traue der Sprache nicht), she restates, because falsification, disguise, and deceit are inherent in its way of signifying.[56] And yet, nothing else but 'trust' (Vertrauen) literally lies at the roots of her intimacy (Vertrautheit), her 'effortless love' (unangestrengte Liebe) for her mother tongue: 'I have never loved my mother tongue because it is the better language, but because it is the most intimate' (die vertrauteste).[57]

TREPPENWITZ; OR, THE MOTHER TONGUE AS WRITING

In the *Teufelskreis*, that is, in the in-between time-space of creation, of the 'labor from the head to the hand' preluding to writing, words abstracted from their ordinary context of use enter into new relations with other words and with new contexts. In the same way as in poetry, these connections are mainly governed by form, especially sound, as well as by the images evoked by the combinations of words and sounds. In doing so, words, in their unexpected connections, modify — or reinvent — perception and produce a renewed understanding of reality.

It is in this light that one should read young Herta's attempts to rename flowers according to their qualities so as to enter into communication with them, or later, after being banned from her office, her consultations of the dictionary for the words (and the metaphorics) pertinent to her new 'environment' in the factory, namely the 'stairs' (Treppen).[58] She runs through and collects the terms *Antritt*

54 Müller, 'In jeder Sprache', p. 14: 'Es ist nicht wahr, daß es für alles Worte gibt. Auch daß man immer in Worten denkt, ist nicht wahr. Bis heute denke ich vieles nicht in Worten, habe keine gefunden, nicht im Dorfdeutschen, nicht im Stadtdeutschen, nicht im Rumänischen, nicht im Ost- oder Westdeutschen. Und in keinem Buch. Die inneren Bereiche decken sich nicht mit der Sprache, sie zerren einen dorthin, wo sich Wörter nicht aufhalten können. Oft ist es das Entscheidende, über das nichts mehr gesagt werden kann.'

55 Ibid., p. 15.

56 Herta Müller, 'Immer derselbe Schnee und immer derselbe Onkel', in *Immer derselbe Schnee*, pp. 96–109 (p. 98).

57 Müller, 'In jeder Sprache', p. 26: 'Ich habe meine Muttersprache nie geliebt, weil sie die bessere ist, sondern die vertrauteste.'

58 Müller, 'Jedes Wort', p. 11.

(literally, entrance) and *Austritt* (exit) for the first and the last step of a staircase, and *Treppenwangen* (stairs' cheeks) and *Treppenaugen* (stairs' eyes) for the lateral support structure of the staircase and the free rooms between the steps;[59] she also collects *Treppenzins* (literally, stair interests), which comes from economical jargon, and *Treppenwitz* (staircase wit), which flows from literature into ordinary language.[60] All this is clearly possible only within the system of a specific language, in this case German, and thanks to the 'intimacy' the writer has with respect to her own mother tongue.

Indeed, in the case mentioned above, the compass of the 'devilish circle of words' coincides with the perimeter of the mother tongue, with both its power and limits, both of them eventually converging into the extreme horizon line of untranslatability. 'The limits of my language mean the limits of my world.'[61] Paraphrasing Wittgenstein's well-known assertion, one could affirm that there are two kinds of limits of the mother tongue. The first limit concerns the way each language carves up the world or structures both perception and conceptualization. The second limit, which is common to every language or to language *per se*, concerns the confrontation with the 'inexpressible' (das Unaussprechliche), with that 'whereof one cannot speak'.[62] While formally keeping itself within the system of her mother tongue, Müller's language reveals itself as constantly striving to strain both types of limits. Müller pursues this aim precisely by seizing on the peculiarities of writing as a medium or, one could also say, by reshaping her mother tongue as writing.

In the Nobel lecture, as in other essays of hers that do not claim theoretical coherence, Müller's argumentation proceeds less in a strictly structured sequence of assertions than by images colliding with one

59 In the English version of this passage (Müller, 'Every Word', p. 3), the translator has introduced some changes in order to keep the correspondence between technical terms denoting parts of the staircase and names of body parts. 'Treppenwangen' (stair stringers) and 'Treppenaugen' have not been translated. Instead of them, two other terms, namely 'hand' and 'nosing', have been introduced. These changes affect the sentence that follows in the same page: 'HAND and NOSING — so the stair has a body', where the German original, instead of 'a body', has 'ein Gesicht' (a face).

60 Müller, 'Every Word', pp. 3 and 8.

61 Wittgenstein, *Tractatus*, § 5.6.

62 Ibid., § 6.522 and § 7.

another. 'Verbal images' (Sprachbilder) that arise from metaphors, idioms, or unusual combinations of words take it upon themselves to transpose into the linearity of prose the simultaneous presence of several planes of perception inherent in author's non-verbal thought ('it is not true that one always thinks in words').[63] That was the case first with the *Taschentuch*, the handkerchief, and then with the *Teufelskreis*, the vicious/devil's circle of invention, which in turn comes along as part of a broader scene — 'a primal scene of writing' — that has its figurative centre in the 'stairs' (Treppen). Indeed, in the Nobel lecture Müller links the very origin of her writing to the period in which she, after refusing to collaborate as an informer for the *Securitate*, the Romanian secret police, was excluded from her office. After this expulsion she would take refuge on a handkerchief smoothed down on a step in the staircase.[64] '[T]he writing began in silence, there on the stairs.'[65] Yet these stairs, I would claim, are not a mere denotative element in a realistic autobiographical account, but rather an image that, as if in a dream, must be metaphorically explored to fully disclose its meaning in relation to writing. First and foremost, stairs are a space of transit: they refer to the actual precariousness of the author's situation, but also to a more essential quality of writing, or of a language that would conform with writing, namely its being off-place, homeless and Heimat-less, stateless. 'Basically, my *Heimat* is not my mother tongue [...] but that which is spoken', she writes — once again in the wake of Jorge Semprún — in *Heimat ist das, was gesprochen wird*.[66]

Central to the primal scene of writing described in the Nobel lecture is the verbal image 'staircase wit' (Treppenwitz), which anaphorically punctuates the entire scene by occurring four times in the space of just a few pages, always in the same semi-formulaic sequence: 'When I was a staircase wit.'[67] Apparently unfitting for the context of the pages that host it, the expression stands out also because of its opaqueness, or rather its ambivalence. As with *Teufelskreis*, in fact,

63 Müller, 'In jeder Sprache', p. 14.

64 In other places in her *oeuvre*, Müller links it with her father's death.

65 Müller, 'Every Word', p. 7.

66 Herta Müller, *Heimat ist das, was gesprochen wird. Rede an die Abiturienten des Jahrgangs 2001* (Blieskastel: Gollenstein, 2001).

67 Müller, 'Every Word', pp. 3, 7, and 8.

Treppenwitz also corresponds to an idiom that oscillates between a literal and a figurative meaning. Indeed, a literal interpretation makes sense of it as an epithet for the author herself, who is subject to both sarcastic comments about her situation and malicious rumours (she is believed to be exactly what she refused to become, i.e., an informant). Yet, another interpretation, which would restore the figurative meaning of the idiom, would be not only possible but much more revealing, especially if considered in relation to writing. *Treppenwitz*, in fact, just like the English 'staircase wit', is originally a translation from the French *esprit d'escalier*. This expression was used for the first time by Denis Diderot around 1770–80, in his *Paradoxe sur le comédien*, to describe a situation in which the right reply to a remark received comes to his mind only too late, 'at the bottom of stairs', that is, after having left the gathering.[68] Rather than fitting the author herself, 'staircase wit' seems to be a proper attribute of writing's 'afterwardness', a way of depicting its peculiar epiphany, its mode of belated understanding or its tendency to retroactively attribute meaning to lived experiences. Hence emerges the peculiar temporality of a mother tongue that is forged on the model of writing and in the duration of labour. In fact, stairs are a space not of a full and stable presence, but rather of transience and deferral — an interstitial domain connecting past and future, experience and virtualities.

> Since *now* I really had to make sure I came to work, but *no longer had an office*, [...] *I stood in the stairwell, unable to decide* what to do. I *climbed up and down the stairs* a few times and suddenly I was again my mother's child, because I HAD A HANDKERCHIEF. I placed it on one of the stairs *between the second and third floor*, carefully smoothed it out and sat down. I rested my thick dictionaries on my knee and translated the descriptions of hydraulic machines.[69]

It is no coincidence that the stairs are also the space of translation, a metaphorical space in between languages. Indeed, the language of Müller's writing dwells in that intermediate space. Müller makes the

68 Denis Diderot, *Paradoxe sur le comédien*, in Diderot, *Œuvres complètes de Diderot*, ed. by Jules Assézat and Maurice Tourneux, 20 vols (Paris: Garnier, 1875–77), VIII (1875), pp. 361–423, (p. 383).

69 Müller, 'Every Word', p. 3; my emphasis.

mother tongue strain against its limits precisely insofar as she does not claim for it either purity or a unique and absolute access to the world of meanings. The mother tongue does not define itself in an exclusive opposition to other languages. Rather, being — as Müller acknowledges — 'momentary and unconditional like one's own skin', and 'vulnerable just like this',[70] it is exposed to the other languages' gaze and relativized by it.

> From one language to another there occur metamorphoses. The view of the mother tongue confronts what is seen differently in the foreign language. One has one's mother tongue without doing anything. It is a dowry that arises unnoticed. It is judged by a language that, in addition, comes later and comes along differently. The mother tongue is no longer the only station of things. Yes, of course, the mother tongue remains immovably what it is. On the whole, one believes its measure, even if this is relativized by the gaze of the language that comes later.[71]

Müller's observation is not an abstract or merely theoretical one. It relies on her experience of being born in a multilingual and multi-ethnic region, the German-speaking Banat in Romania. There, the Swabian dialect, spoken in her home village (*Dorfsprache*), was confronted first with 'standard German' (*Hochdeutsch*), learned at school, and later with the Romanian spoken in the city, which was for her not only the beloved language of folk songs and popular culture, but also the hated bureaucratic language of party meetings and propaganda, as well as of the secret questionings by the *Securitate*. What Müller conceives with her writing is a language that acknowledges the otherness of the other language and hosts it without either assimilating it or completely yielding to its fascination. That is the case with Romanian, which she feels — in ways similar to Kafka's experience with regard to Czech — is closer to the senses and more akin to her sensitivity than German is. In 2003 she wrote about this: 'I haven't written a single sentence in Romanian in my books yet. But of course Romanian always writes with me [mitschreibt] because it grew into my gaze.'[72] And indeed, the

70 Müller, 'In jeder Sprache', p. 28.

71 Ibid., pp. 25–26.

72 Ibid., p. 27.

alien gaze of the foreign language, which is embodied and yet not fully domesticated, stirs the mother tongue from the inside and forces it to run against its limits, to question them and to enter into unexplored domains of perception. This is what happens, for instance, with the literal translation of idioms that have no correspondence in the target language, as in the case of the title of her novel *Der Mensch ist ein großer Fasan auf der Welt* (Humans are a big pheasant in the world),[73] which reproduces a Romanian saying into German and plays on the different connotations that the bird metaphorically assumes in the two languages, namely a boastful person in German and an awkward one in Romanian. A similar process is also induced by the confrontation between words that denote the same object in the two languages yet have different genders, as is the case with 'lily' or 'rose', which are feminine in German and masculine in Romanian. In each case, the confrontation resolves itself into the establishing of both a new hybrid linguistic space and a corresponding queer or androgynous figure.[74]

One last point needs mentioning. As already seen with the passage on the *Teufelskreis* and the pantomime of words, one of the main features Müller ascribes to writing is its being a silent act. This, for her, is such an important characteristic that she makes the very possibility of a writing that deals with 'the inexpressible' dependent on it: 'But the writing began in silence, there on the stairs, where I had to come to terms with more than could be said. What was happening could no longer be expressed in speech.' Also, a few lines before, she had affirmed: 'Still, what can't be said can be written. Because writing is a silent act.'[75] This seems to be an annotation to the famous final proposition of Wittgenstein's *Tractatus*: 'Whereof one cannot speak, thereof one must be silent.'[76] If this indeed is a possible subtext, Müller takes it both seriously and literally, and adds a postil that paradoxically contradicts it by confirming it. A language that would conform with writing (as a silent act) — a language *as* writing — can indeed aspire to addressing 'the inexpressible' (das Unsagbare), 'what is crucial' (das

73 Herta Müller, *Der Mensch ist ein großer Fasan auf der Welt* (Frankfurt a.M.: Fischer Verlag, 2009).

74 Müller, *Heimat ist das*, pp. 16–17.

75 Müller, 'Every Word', p. 7.

76 Wittgenstein, Tractatus, §7.

Entscheidende), or, to put it with Wittgenstein again, the 'problems of life' that would not be touched at all 'even if all possible scientific questions [were] answered'.[77] It would not be a language purified by formal logic, but rather a language that knows something of vicious circles, i.e., of the alternative, bewitched logic of poetry. Silence does not mean that language has become unnecessary, as she experienced with the 'language of the village' (Dorfsprache), where the perfect correspondence between words and things as well as the fatigue of fieldwork set the rule: 'What you do doesn't need to be doubled in words.'[78] In the case of writing, silence is tantamount not to the absence of language, but rather to the possibility for it to be, and especially to be forged anew in such a way as to run against the walls of its own cage.[79] It is a space of possibility and 'gestation', free from the constraints of use, in which language may experience a new relation to reality, which rests no longer on the denomination of things and states of being but rather on the reinvention of perception (erfundene Wahrnehmung) and destabilization of thought (what she calls 'Irrlauf im Kopf'). Unusual metaphors, unexpected combinations of words, new verbal images can take reality by surprise, says Müller, and thus reveal unknown aspects of it. They in fact contribute to that 'density' — or pregnancy, as one could say — of language that allows for a state of 'errancy of thought' (Irrlauf) that leads it beyond words, towards the inexpressible, 'where no words can dwell' (wo sich keine Worte aufhalten können).[80]

Finally, silence also has a political meaning. Unlike 'talking', which 'led to excruciating consequences',[81] it eludes control and surveillance, it cannot be eavesdropped on. The unspoken language that begins in silence, the mother tongue as writing, is a space of freedom and resistance. Müller was aware of both the 'vulnerability' of one's mother tongue and the violence perpetrated in the name of any ethnocentrism.[82] She

77 Ibid., § 6.52.

78 Müller, 'In jeder Sprache', p. 8: 'Was man tut, muss im Wort nicht verdoppelt werden.'

79 This expression paraphrases the concluding sentence of Ludwig Wittgenstein, 'A Lecture on Ethics', in Wittgenstein, *Philosophical Occasions: 1912–1951*, ed. by James Klagge and Alfred Normann (Cambridge: Hackett, 1992), pp. 37–44.

80 Müller, 'In jeder Sprache', p. 14.

81 Müller, 'Every Word', p. 7.

82 Müller reflects on this point in many essays and interviews, but see especially Müller, *Mein Vaterland*, and Müller, 'In jeder Sprache'.

recognizes the former, for instance, in the brutalization of German inherent in war songs sung by her father as well as in the dull Romanian of dictatorship, and the latter, ethnocentric violence, in the deportation of her mother to a Soviet detention camp simply for being German or, conversely, in the obtuse defence of a purity of tradition on the part of the German community of the Banat. Strongly believing in the inseparability of language from the use one makes of it, Müller downsizes the role of the mother tongue in defining one's belonging when she privileges a common agreement about contents over a commonality of language: '*Heimat* is not language, but rather what is said.'[83] Yet, the Nobel lecture — as I have tried to show in this essay — seems to suggest a more complex relation. Far from being unique or irreplaceable, or even the closest language to one's way of feeling, for Müller the mother tongue is the more trusted key to establish a new conventionality, a poetic idiomaticity of a language to come.

83 Müller, 'In jeder Sprache', p. 36. See also Müller, *Heimat ist das*.

Wandering Words

Translation against the Myth of Origin in Fritz Mauthner's Philosophy

LIBERA PISANO

> Vaterlandsliebe ist nur Liebe zur Muttersprache
>
> Fritz Mauthner

A DIASPORIC PHILOSOPHY OF LANGUAGE

At the beginning of the last century, the crisis of a whole series of values that started with Nietzschean philosophy led to the collapse of classical reason, the failure of the teleological understanding of history, and a radical scepticism towards tradition. It was in this context that the so-called *Sprachkrise* (crisis of language) emerged.[1] This was an intense debate in the years leading up to World War I in which poets and intellectuals — such as Hugo von Hofmannsthal, Arthur Schnitzler,

* This article was funded by the European Union's Horizon 2020 research and innovation programme under Marie Skłodowska-Curie grant agreement N° 101027857.

1 See Katherine M. Arens, 'Linguistic Scepticism: Towards a Productive Definition', Monatshefte, 74.2 (1982), pp. 145–55; Franco Rella, *Il silenzio e le parole* (Milan: Feltrinelli, 1984); Allan Janik and Stephen Toulmin, *Wittgenstein's Vienna* (New York: Touchstone, 1973); Libera Pisano, 'Silence, Translation and Grammatical Therapy: Some Features of Linguistic Scepticism in the Thought of Rosenzweig and Wittgenstein', in *Yearbook of the Maimonides Centre for Advanced Studies 2017*, ed. by Giuseppe Veltri and Bill Rebiger (Berlin: De Gruyter, 2017), pp. 121–43.

Karl Kraus, and others — discussed language and its limits. In this context, language became a constitutive and insurmountable obstacle to the grasp of reality. The phenomenon of the *Sprachkrise* has not yet received the attention it deserves, and it has been interpreted as a purely literary movement rather than as a philosophical and cultural turning point. In my opinion, the linguistic turn that philosophy took later in the twentieth century would have been inconceivable without the *Sprachkrise,* which preceded it and made it possible. Interest in the limits of language was the common denominator of the thinkers of those years and constitutes a kind of philosophical *koiné.*

It is no coincidence that this phenomenon received special attention among German-Jewish thinkers. First of all, in response to a philosophical urgency, thinkers like Fritz Mauthner, Gustav Landauer, Martin Buber, Walter Benjamin, Margarete Susman, and Franz Rosenzweig resorted to considering Judaism as a heterodox element with respect to the German tradition, an alternative that can offer new paths for interpreting the world through a new philosophical and historical filter. Although these thinkers held different positions, Judaism offered them a hermeneutical horizon and a counter-image during the incubation period of the end of German-Jewish history. They can therefore be described as the last witnesses of a German-Jewish tradition who, in the first decades around 1900, more or less consciously reflected their double philosophical and political identities in a linguistic spectrum. In fact, all of these authors have a dual affiliation with both the Jewish tradition and German philosophy, and their sceptical attitude or critical distance from language is also autobiographical. Linguistically speaking, they were 'bifurcated souls'.[2]

At a time when völkisch ideology and nationalist thought were gaining strength in the German-speaking world and even entering the Zionist movement, this constellation of German-Jewish thinkers reflected on uprooting, exile, community, and language in a very different way, which I would like to call a 'diasporic philosophy of language'. By this, I mean a reflection on language that problematizes the traditional identification between language, nation-state, and territory. By

2 The expression 'bifurcated souls' is used in Paul Mendes-Flohr, *German Jews: A Dual Identity* (New Haven, CT: Yale University Press, 1999), pp. 1–24.

rejecting the exclusivity of nationalism, this approach takes exile as a pivotal element in thinking about language and belonging. In this context, translation epitomizes a diasporic philosophy of language and assumes a central role with theological, political, and messianic value. It becomes a privileged prism through which to consider language, languages, identity, belonging, and the questioning of autochthony.

Fritz Mauthner, who was the linguistic sceptic *par excellence*, played a central — if somewhat forgotten — role in this constellation of authors, since his work can be considered the *trait d'union* between literature and critical thought which, thanks to the mediation of Gustav Landauer, became widespread among the German-Jewish milieu. In his works, Mauthner develops a critique of the origin, root, and ontological foundation of language that has anarchic echoes. Although his political positions were inclined towards conservatism, Mauthner's linguistic scepticism is one of the most radical examples of a critique of supposed linguistic autochthony.[3] Translation plays a fundamental role as a means of rejecting linguistic purity.

FRITZ MAUTHNER'S LINGUISTIC SCEPTICISM

Mauthner was a philosopher and linguistic sceptic, journalist, novelist, and playwright who lived on the fringes of academia. He was a German-speaking Jew born into an assimilated Bohemian Jewish family in 1849 and grew up in a Czechophone society. He studied law in Prague but did not graduate, as he wanted to devote himself to literature and journalism. In 1876, he moved to Berlin, where he started his career as a theatre critic, journalist, and writer.

3 Despite his long friendship with the anarchist Gustav Landauer, Mauthner did not share his political stance. However, Landauer's anarchism and Mauthner's conservatism never clashed, except during World War I. While Mauthner advocated active participation in war, Landauer defended the role of philosophy as 'the best means against madness and murder'. See Landauer's letter to Mauthner dated 29 September 1914 in Gustav Landauer and Fritz Mauthner, *Briefwechsel 1890–1919*, ed. by Hanna Delf (Munich: Beck, 1994), pp. 290–92. See also Fritz Mauthner, 'Zum Gedächtnis', *Masken: Halbmonatsschrift des Düsseldorfer Schauspielhauses*, 14.18/19 (1919), pp. 300–04 (p. 300); Carsten Schapkow, 'German Jews and the Great War: Gustav Landauer's and Fritz Mauthner's Friendship during Times of War', *Quest: Issues in Contemporary Jewish History*, 9 (October 2016), pp. 1–17 <https://www.doi.org/10.48248/issn.2037-741X/806>.

In response to the growing anti-Semitism of those years, Mauthner officially resigned from the Jewish religious community in 1891 without professing any other religion, including Christianity. In his *Erinnerungen* (Memoirs) he notes that as a Jew in a bilingual country, he had neither a mother tongue nor, as the son of a completely non-denominational Jewish family, a mother religion.[4]

Mauthner produced an enormous body of work: his three volumes masterpiece *Contributions to a Critique of Language*, a *Dictionary of Philosophy*, *Atheism and Its History in the Occident*, and numerous essays and novels.[5] In 1905, he moved from Berlin to Freiburg, and in 1909, he moved to Meersburg on Lake Constance, where he later died in 1923. As a modern Cratylus, who at the end of his life no longer spoke, Mauthner decided to spend the last years of his life in a glass house (*Gläserhäusle*) on Lake Constance, where he was able to find a kind of mystical rest, and he was therefore called the 'Buddha of the Bodensee'.

Mauthner's critique of language offers one of the most radical forms of linguistic scepticism in the history of philosophy. His work,

4 Fritz Mauthner, *Erinnerungen I: Prager Jugendjahre*, 3rd edn (Berlin: Holzinger, 2014), pp. 50–51: 'Wie ich keine rechte Muttersprache besaß als Jude in einem zweisprachigen Lande, so hatte ich auch keine Mutterreligion, als Sohn einer völlig konfessionslosen Judenfamilie.' See Carsten Schapkow, '"Ohne Sprache und ohne Religion?" Fritz Mauthners Sprachkritik und die zeitgenössischen Debatten über Deutschtum und Judentum', in *An den Grenzen der Sprachkritik. Fritz Mauthners Beiträge zur Sprach- und Kulturkritik*, ed. by Gerald Hartung (Würzburg: Königshausen & Neumann, 2013), pp. 19–49.

5 Fritz Mauthner, *Beiträge zu einer Kritik der Sprache*, 2nd edn, 3 vols (Stuttgart: Cotta, 1913); Mauthner, *Wörterbuch der Philosophie. Neue Beiträge zu einer Kritik der Sprache*, 2 vols (Zürich: Diogenes, 1980); Mauthner, *Der Atheismus und seine Geschichte im Abendlande*, vol. 4 (Stuttgart: DVA, 1923). For Mauthner's philosophy of language, see Gershon Weiler, *Mauthner's Critique of Language* (Cambridge: Cambridge University Press, 1970); Weiler, 'On Fritz Mauthner's Critique of Language', *Mind*, 67 (1958), pp. 80–87; Martin Kurzreiter, *Sprachkritik als Ideologiekritik bei Fritz Mauthner* (Frankfurt a.M.: Lang, 1993); Gerald Hartung, *Sprach-Kritik: Sprach- und kulturtheoretische Reflexionen im deutsch-jüdischen Kontext* (Weilerswist: Velbrück, 2012); Hartung, ed., *An den Grenzen der Sprachkritik: Fritz Mauthners Beiträge zur Sprache- und Kulturtheorie*; Joachim Kühn, *Gescheiterte Sprachkritik: Fritz Mauthners Leben und Werk* (Berlin: De Gruyter, 1975); Elizabeth Bredeck, *Metaphors of Knowledge: Language and Thought in Mauthner's Critique* (Detroit: Wayne State University Press, 1992); Bredeck, 'Crumbling Foundations: Fritz Mauthner and Philosophy after Philosophy', *Modern Austrian Literature*, 23 (1990), pp. 41–53; Libera Pisano, 'Misunderstanding Metaphors: Linguistic Scepticism in Mauthner's Philosophy', in *Yearbook of the Maimonides Centre for Advanced Studies 2016*, ed. by Giuseppe Veltri and Bill Rebiger (Berlin: De Gruyter, 2016), pp. 95–122.

which aims to show the limits of linguistic superstition, begins by pointing out the impossibility of a general definition of language beyond singular speech acts.[6] In fact, according to Mauthner, language is pure abstraction, a *Wesenloses Unding*,[7] an unessential no-thing, and a vain chimaera. This is mainly due to the fact that there is an immeasurable gulf between reality, which is understood as an unceasing flow,[8] and the immobility of language, which cannot grasp this flux and can only provide us with a deformed image of it. This gap is also the gap between the sensory experiences achieved through the senses — which for Mauthner are the 'accidental senses' (*Zufallssinne*), as an unintentional result of the evolution of human beings — and language as a collection of memory indices that offer only an approximation of experience.[9]

The distortion that language offers is due to its reifying mechanism, which crystallizes the movement of reality and gives reality to words and turns them into 'things'. Through this reification, words become fetishes and lead to the naive belief that nouns correspond to concrete objects and faithfully represent reality.

Language removes the uniqueness of our experience by turning it into a series of words and empty tautologies. However, although it can refer to reality only metaphorically, it is the sole means of human knowledge. Language's reference to reality is fundamentally metaphorical, and yet it is the only medium in which human knowledge, which is the result of a linguistic trap, can unfold. Even if language erases the unique-

6 Cf. Mauthner, *Beiträge*, I, p. 4: 'Was aber ist die Sprache, mit der ich es zu tun habe? Was ist das Wesen der Sprache? In welcher Beziehung steht die Sprache zu den Sprachen. Die einfachste Antwort wäre: die Sprache gibt es nicht; das Wort ist ein so blasses Abstraktum, daß ihm kaum mehr etwas Wirkliches entspricht.'

7 Cf. ibid., I, p. 181.

8 The ontological basis of this philosophy is the notion of reality as a constant flux, which reflects Ernst Mach's conception of it. Mauthner was greatly influenced by one of Mach's lectures delivered in Prague in 1872, because of the sceptical principles he presented as the theoretical basis of his physics. See Katherine M. Arens, *Functionalism and fin de siècle: Fritz Mauthner's Critique of Language* (New York: Lang, 1984).

9 According to Mauthner, the faculty of memory cannot be distinguished from its effects and there is only an illusory divergence between language, memory, ego, and consciousness. Memory is fundamentally unreliable because it can only approximate past sense experiences. Cf. Mauthner, *Beiträge*, I, p. 531: 'Aber das Gedächtnis ist auch wesentlich untreu. Das Gedächtnis wäre unerträglich, wenn wir nicht vergessen könnten. Und die Worte oder Begriffe, die erst durch das falsche Gedächtnis entstanden sind, wären für den Alltagsgebrauch ungeeignet ohne die Eigenschaft des Gedächtnisses: untreu zu sein.'

ness of human experience by turning it into a series of tautologies, and even if it refers to reality metaphorically, it provides us with knowledge. Therefore, a metaphor is not just a rhetorical figure, but instead reveals the functioning of language, or rather, language is a sum of metaphors: it can only refer to the world metaphorically, because words are images of images of images.[10]

All the supposed truths and sciences are a collection of metaphors.[11] For this very reason, Mauthner's scepticism is at the same time a radical attack on Western metaphysics. All metaphysical abstractions are false and the result of a linguistic deception that forces us to believe that every noun corresponds to a pre-existent substance. Since language is a series of abstractions, the entire history of philosophy, with some exceptions such as Hume and Kant, is nothing but a sum of meaningless problems and linguistic illusions. Therefore, Mauthner's *Beiträge* were written in an attempt to expose the tricks and lies of language, to show that it is useless as a means of perceiving reality, and to turn philosophy into a permanent critique of language.

Mauthner's linguistic scepticism can be conceived as a *pharmacon* of philosophy itself that should become a permanent critique of language, useful for revealing its fallacies, but also its inevitability. If the word is not representative of reality, the most important task of philosophy is to subject language to a profound critique — which is arguably 'paradoxical', since such a critique must be articulated in language — that exposes the superstition and tyranny that words exercise over human beings. In this sense, linguistic scepticism has a fundamentally liberating character. In fact, according to Mauthner, philosophy's most important and paradoxical task is liberation from the superstition and tyranny of words.

However, this liberation is in a way an impossible task. In fact, according to Mauthner, there is what we can call an inevitability of misunderstandings. 'We are', wrote Gustave Flaubert, 'all in a desert, no one understands anyone else.'[12] According to Mauthner, this lin-

10 See Fritz Mauthner, 'Die Sprache', in Mauthner and Gerald Hartung, *Die Sprache* (Marburg: Metropolis-Verlag, 2012), pp. 6–140 (p. 109).

11 On Mauthner's conception of metaphor, see Pisano, 'Misunderstanding Metaphors', pp. 110–14.

12 Mauthner quotes this verse by Flaubert; cf. Mauthner, *Beiträge*, I, p. 49.

guistic desert is unavoidable: 'There are no two men who speak the same tongue.'[13] In fact, it is impossible to say that the meaning and reference of a word are the same for everyone, because words precede us and do not correspond to our sensory experience. If reality is in flux and in incessant change, then words give us the illusion of immobility. Moreover, a word is not an adequate expression of inner processes, because it is a public product and an articulation in grammar, syntax, and semantics. As we have seen, the approximation of our random sense impressions and the ambiguity of words inevitably lead to metaphorical representations of reality. Nevertheless, memory — thanks to its preservation of traditions and habits — has a social role that coincides with the common use of language. The collection of words stored in one's memory is nothing but an exchange of linguistic habits that are supposed to be the same for everyone. This commonality proves the non-existence of a private language; in fact, if there is no correspondence between words and reality, then to speak of true communication would be utopian and meaning is determined only by use. By seriously doubting the possibility of true communication, Mauthner does away with the connection between signifier and signified and rejects the reference theory.[14] This revolutionary suspension of the teleology of signs could be interpreted, on the one hand, as an *epoché* of meaning, a stepping back from signification that unsurprisingly leads to silence;[15] on the other, Mauthner's critique of signification does not affect the social aspect of language; namely, the linguistic com-

13 Ibid., I, p. 56: 'Es gibt nicht zwei Menschen, die die gleiche Sprache reden. [...] Kein Mensch kennt den anderen. Geschwister, Eltern und Kinder kennen einander nicht. Ein Hauptmittel des Nichtverstehens ist die Sprache.'

14 Elisabeth Leinfellner, 'Fritz Mauthner', in *Sprachphilosophie, Philosophy of Language, La Philosophie du langage*, ed. by Marcelo Dascal, Dietfried Gerhardus, Kuno Lorenz, and George Meggle (Berlin: De Gruyter, 1992), pp. 495–509 (p. 499): 'Die Referenztheorie der Bedeutung hat Mauthner jedenfalls abgelehnt: wir geben Worte aus wie Banknoten und fragen nicht ob dem Wert der Note im Schatz etwas ein empirisches Referenzobjekt entspricht.'

15 Mauthner defines his silent resignation as a mystical apology, a godless mysticism that transcends the limits of language. He places himself in an apophatic tradition that doubts the reliability of words, starting from Plotinus, Cusanus, and Eckhart. Cf. Mauthner, *Beiträge*, I, p. 83. Mauthner never defines his silence as a Jewish silence. However, Judaism could be the religion of silence and silence could be a leitmotif of Judaism, as Franz Rosenzweig, André Neher, Paul Celan, and George Steiner would later testify.

munity.[16] In fact, despite the fact that every individual speaks their own language (*Individualsprache*), language functions only as a 'rule of the game' (*Spielregel*)[17] that acquires validity only when it is accepted by more than one speaker. Under this perspective, Mauthner's analysis concerns the interstitial space between individuals.[18] Language, according to him, 'has arisen and exists only between human beings; languages have arisen between peoples. There are no autochthonous languages.'[19]

AGAINST LINGUISTIC PURISM: MAUTHNER'S PHILOSOPHY OF TRANSLATION

In his introduction to the *Dictionary of Philosophy*, Mauthner develops a philosophy of translation in order to criticize linguistic purism. By 'linguistic purism', he means the defence of an original language that supposedly spontaneously arose without having any form of contact with other people. In this respect, he vehemently opposes the various descent theories (*Abstammungsthesen*) that assume that 'all Aryan languages are based on a common original language'.[20] Mauthner says that this supposed *Ursprache* cannot be described, since nobody can say anything about it, whether it was considered unique or whether it was articulated in dialects, whether there was a language even older than this one, and so on.[21] According to him, the original language is a phantom (*Gespenst*), just like the idea of an original people, nation,

16 According to Mauthner, the communist utopia can only be realized in language where there is no private property, but only common property (*Gemeinbesitz*). See Mauthner, *Beiträge*, I, pp. 24–27.

17 Cf. ibid., I, p. 25: 'Die Sprache ist nur ein Schein wert wie eine Spielregel, die auch umso zwingender wird, je mehr Mitspieler sich ihr unterwerfen, die aber die Wirklichkeitswelt weder ändern noch begreifen will.'

18 This also had an impact on Mauthner's conception of *Heimat*. See Thomas Hainscho, 'Fritz Mauthners Heimatbegriff: Zwischen Deutschnationalismus, jüdischem Selbsthass und Sprachkritik', *Colloquium: New Philologies*, 6.1 (2021), pp. 54–69 (p. 57): 'Er bezieht sich nicht rein auf Sprache, sondern umfasst auch eine soziale Gemeinschaft, die diese Sprache spricht.'

19 Fritz Mauthner, 'Einleitung', in Mauthner, *Wörterbuch der Philosophie*, p. lxi: 'Wie die Sprache nur *zwischen* den Menschen entstanden ist und besteht, so sind die Sprachen *zwischen* den Völkern entstanden. Es gibt keine autochthonen Sprachen.'

20 Ibid., p. xx.

21 Ibid., pp. xx–xxii; Mauthner, *Beiträge*, II, p. 389: 'Das Wort Ursprache bedeutet für die Gelehrten der indoeuropäischen Sprachwissenschaft ein Fabelwesen, die Sprache,

or homeland, which are nothing but abstractions and illusory concepts (*Scheinbegriffe*).[22] The destruction of these conjectures, the exposure of their falsity, is therefore 'not only a theoretical necessity of human knowledge, but also a practical advantage'[23] provided by the liberatory role of Mauthner's critique of language.

In contrast to Aryan chauvinism, which feels 'ashamed to have borrowed things or words from non-Aryan peoples, almost as if a contagion is first felt as a disgrace [*Ansteckung zunächst als Schande*]',[24] Mauthner argues that there is no initial possession, but rather borrowing and theft; no purity, but contagion, due to the wandering of words and the displacement of human beings.[25]

To dismantle this linguistic purism, Mauthner first points out that all cultures and languages are the result of *Entlehnung* and *Lehnübersetzung*,[26] of borrowings and loan translations. These key concepts have played a central role in all areas of culture. Borrowing, for example, is the basis of the entire *Völkerspsychologie*,[27] and through loan translations, ideas from all areas of thought, as well as names of diseases, numbers, plants, and nature — as Mauthner showed in several examples — have migrated from people to people. Even Christianity — and thus Latin as the universal language of the church — was nothing more than a loan translation of Hebrew and Greek.

Mauthner does not speak of translation in the classical sense, but as the paradigm of an encounter caused by the permanent wandering of human beings: imitations and borrowings constitute the history and formation of languages. He writes that 'countless useful terms have only become known through translation, so that each nation is

---

welche das Urvolk der Arier, dessen Existenz nicht bewiesen ist, zu einer Zeit, die wir nicht kennen, gesprochen haben soll.'

22 Mauthner, 'Einleitung', pp. xciii–xcv.

23 Ibid., p. xcv: 'Die Zerstörung von Scheinbegriffen, die Aufdeckung ihrer Falschheit ist also nicht nur ein theoretisches Bedürfnis für die menschliche Erkenntnis, sondern in sehr vielen Fällen auch ein praktischer Vorteil, weshalb der Sprachkritiker es sich gefallen lassen muss und mag, zu den Aufklärern gerechnet zu werden.'

24 Ibid., p. xxiii.

25 Ibid., p. xxvii: 'Die Wanderung von Sachen und von Namen für die Kulturgeschichte von ungleich größerer Bedeutung war als die Völkerwanderung.'

26 See ibid., p. xxvii.

27 Ibid., p. xvii: 'Ohne Nachahmung oder Entlehnung von Werten und Worten keine Völkerpsychologie, kein soziales Interesse in der Geschichte.'

deeply indebted to the other'.[28] Translation is a testimony of the limit of autochthony and a blatant sign of debt to other languages. Therefore, at the beginning, there cannot be an original possession, but rather an original debt to others.

Translations are obvious examples of linguistic exchanges and of word migration. Mauthner writes:

> None of our intellectual property is autochthonous, it is not national, it wanders through the centuries and millennia from people to people. Only a people's language, which is nothing but the *storehouse of wandering hereditary wisdom*, is supposed to be national, is supposed to be autochthonous. Only exceptionally, when it cannot be overlooked that it is a loan or a borrowed translation, is this fact admitted.[29]

In this perspective, Mauthner denounces the linguistic purism that results from a 'national self-deception' (*die nationale Selbsttäuschung*),[30] according to which there is a purity of the mother tongue. This self-deception leads to an absurd patriotism whose intention is to cleanse and free language from foreign words. With his formidable irony, he qualified this obsession with a pure language as an attitude of 'language sweepers' (*Sprachfegermeistern*), who were obsessed with cleansing and disinfecting their own language from foreign impurity.[31] Instead of the supposed cleanliness, Mauthner compares the wandering foreign words, as the lifeblood that makes languages dirty and fertile, to 'mud from the Nile'.[32]

This crusade against foreignness ignores the history of the words themselves. However, it is not always easy to find these foreign traces in one's own language, and sometimes scholars are 'blind and deaf'[33]

---

28 Ibid., p. lxiii.

29 Ibid., p. lv: 'Unser gesamtes geistiges Eigentum ist nicht autochthon, ist nicht national, wandert durch die Jahrhunderte und die Jahrtausende von Volk zu Volk. Nur die Sprache eines Volkes, die doch nichts weiter ist als die *Vorratskammer der wandernden Erbweisheit*, soll national, soll autochthon sein'; my emphasis.

30 Ibid., p. lxi.

31 See Fritz Mauthner, *Muttersprache und Vaterland* (Leipzig: Dürr & Weber, 1920), p. 13.

32 See ibid., p. 16: 'Stoßweise haben solche Kulturwanderungen ganze Mengen fremder Begriffe dem eigenen Boden zugeführt, schmutzig und ertragreich wie einen gesegneten Nilschlamm.'

33 Mauthner, *Einleitung*, p. lv.

to recognizing the provenance of the words. For example, purists do not recognize loan translations because there are words that wear the garb of 'our' language. Mauthner writes: 'Just as wandering people in foreign lands keep their native garments or put on foreign clothes, so it is with wandering words; they come in great numbers, sometimes as borrowings, sometimes as translations from one people to another.'[34]

There are three forms of borrowings: first, words that have passed into common usage and are difficult to recognize; second, words that retain a certain foreign sound; and third, technical terms that are not part of common usage, such as, for instance, the words of philosophy. One of Mauthner's main questions concerns the nature of the translation of philosophical expressions. He seeks to 'pursue the question of whether philosophical thought really gains as much from the translation of words into the native language as has been believed for several hundred years.'[35] The strategy adopted by Christian Wolff and Christian Thomasius, who began to establish philosophical writing in German, is harshly criticized. According to Mauthner, they offered a concrete example of purism, which he condemns with the help of illustrious examples such as Goethe, Jacob Grimm, and Leibniz.[36]

In the attempt to create a German philosophical terminology, Wolff wanted to write in pure German, excluding all foreign expressions. For Mauthner, this purist approach was not useful for at least two reasons: if the term to be translated does not exist in the destination language, then the new term is formed on the basis of the word to be translated and is explained by its *Modellwort* (model word);[37] if, on the other hand, an existing word in common use has been used for translation, then the philosopher who uses it technically needs to add the new figurative meaning to the old meanings of the word. In both cases, the transformation process that is at stake in the translation is antithetical to the idea of linguistic purism and its static aspect. Accord-

34 Ibid., p. lvi: 'Wie wandernde Menschen entweder ihr heimatliches Kleid in der Fremde beibehalten oder das fremde Kleid anlegen, so geht es auch den wandernden Worten; sie kommen in großen Scharen bald als Entlehnungen bald als Lehnübersetzungen von einem Volke zum andern.'

35 Ibid., p. lxxxix: 'Um die Frage zu untersuchen: worin besteht das Wesen der Übersetzung, insbesondere der Übersetzung philosophischer Ausdrücke?'

36 See ibid., p. lxii.

37 See ibid., p. xci.

ing to Mauthner, the introduction of foreign terms into a language is possible through the new formation of words or a change of meaning (*Bedeutungswandel*).[38]

Mauthner gives many examples of German philosophical words that bear the hidden traces of other languages. One blatant case is the German word for 'object,' which in the old version was not *Gegenstand* — a poor translation of the philosophical term *Objekt,* in Mauthner's opinion, as it still sounds wrong in German — but *Vorwurf,* which means 'reproach'. By following the etymological path, Mauthner argues that this must be the result of an incorrect translation, because it does not come from the Greek *hypokeimenon,* but from *antikeimenon,* a translation of 'objection' rather than 'object'.[39]

Mauthner not only gives philosophical explanations, but also examples taken from everyday languages. The sentence 'today is Friday 18 January 1907'[40] already includes loan translations, as is the case for everything that has to do with the calendar. He presents a huge list of loan translations of everyday words from Latin and German in order to show the extent of the exchange between the languages. His lists can be considered concrete examples of the dismantling of linguistic autochthony, almost an attempt at deconstruction *ante litteram*. In fact, according to Mauthner, an incalculable part of the vocabulary was and is created by translating the vocabulary of other languages.

Not only is most of 'our' vocabulary the result of translation, but the meaning of words will continue to change with future translations. In fact, a word that is already present in one's own language can be transformed in order to translate the foreign one.[41] Because of this constant change of meaning through translation, Mauthner says that 'words are even more unreliable than substances in an alembic still, words are always in *statu nascendi*'.[42] Every word is not only the result of previous wanderings, but also a promise of future ones. There is no

38 Concerning the changes of meaning, cf. Mauthner, 'Die Sprache', p. 109: 'Den Satz: dass aller Bedeutungswandel also endlich alle Wortbildung auf Metaphern oder auf Metaphern von Metaphern beruhe.'

39 Ibid., pp. 67–69.

40 Ibid., p. 74.

41 Ibid., p. 56.

42 Ibid., p. 109: 'Worte sind noch viel unzuverlässiger als Stoffe in der Retorte; Worte sind immer in statu nascendi.'

crystallized origin; rather, languages are in transit and are exposed to absolute translatability, which is the opposite of purity and fixedness. If there is no origin at the beginning, there remains only the absolute contamination. Therefore, translation is a necessary bastardization of languages.

The notion of a common root and of the self-contained purity of languages are abstractions, *Scheinbegriffe* (illusory concepts), that necessarily have political consequences. Mauthner writes:

> How can the individual continue to give away his property and his blood for love of the fatherland, which is only love of the mother tongue, when only the body of that language is the property of the people, only the sound; when the immeasurable sum of the ideas of art and science, of custom and law, is gathered from the ownerless property of foreign, barbaric, tyrannical, hated or despised peoples?[43]

However, this criticism of autochthony does not prevent him from thinking of a certain kind of linguistic patriotism.[44] In this critique of purism, the only possible patriotism is not a celebration of blood or a geographical bond with the soil, but what we can call a philological love for the mother tongue: 'Vaterlandsliebe ist nur Liebe zur Muttersprache' (Love of the fatherland is only love of the mother tongue).[45]

43 Ibid., p. 80: 'Wie kann der Einzelne noch Gut und Blut hingeben aus Vaterlandsliebe, die nur Liebe zur Muttersprache ist, wenn nur der Körper dieser Sprache Eigenbesitz des Volkes ist, wenn nur der Körper dieser Sprache Eigenbesitz des Volkes ist, nur der Laut, wenn die ungeheure Summe der Vorstellungen von Kunst und Wissenschaft, von Sitte und Recht zusammengeholt ist aus dem herrenlos gewordenen Eigenbesitz fremder, barbarischer, tyrannischer, gehaßter oder verachteter Völker?'

44 See Hainscho, 'Fritz Mauthners Heimatbegriff', p. 56: 'Patriotismus besteht also darin, die Heimat zu lieben, was wiederum bedeutet, die Mundart der Heimat zu lieben; das heißt, den Dialekt, der an dem Ort gesprochen wird, den man als Heimat bezeichnet.'

45 Mauthner, 'Die Sprache', p. 80. On this aspect, see Thomas Hainscho, 'A Homeless Patriot: Fritz Mauthner's Search for a Homeland in Language', in *Mother-Tongue and Father-Land: Jewish Perspectives on Language and Identity*, ed. by Libera Pisano, *Azimuth: Philosophical Coordinates in Modern and Contemporary Age*, 9.18 (2021), pp. 31–46 (p. 40): 'Mauthner indeed rejects the love of the father-land as misguided patriotism, but his ideas go well with nationalist positions that see language as an integral part of identity.'

LINGUISTIC *HEIMAT*: AN IMPURE LOVE

Mauthner lived in the antinomy of having a language assigned to him by fate and, at the same time, loving it very much. In *Die Sprache*, he writes:

> The love for one's own homeland, the love for one's own people, is essentially the love for one's own mother tongue, the learning of which is not difficult for us, the shortcomings of which we do not hear, do not feel. We love it much more passionately than we usually know. We love it with longing and jealousy.[46]

As a Jew born in a Slavic province of the Austro-Hungarian empire, he grew up in a multilingualism of three languages: the German of education, poetry, and kinship; the Czech of peasants and servants, but also the historical language of the Bohemian kingdom; and the Hebrew, the holy tongue, of the Old Testament, which also became the *Mauschel* German of Jewish peddlers and elegant businessmen alike.[47] Mauthner did not manage to master any of his three languages, and he therefore describes being deficient in his way of speaking them. He was born with no mother tongue and could not find his *Heimat* in any of these languages as a child. As he writes in his *Erinnerungen*, his Jewishness was, in a sense, a condition — a predestination — for being a sceptic of language.[48]

---

46 Mauthner, 'Die Sprache', p. 37: 'Die Liebe zur eigenen Heimat, die Liebe zum eigenen Volke ist aber wesentlich Liebe zur Muttersprache, deren Erlernen uns nicht schwer geworden ist, deren Mängel wir nicht hören, nicht fühlen. Wir lieben sie viel leidenschaftlicher, als wir gewöhnlich wissen. Wir lieben sie mit Sehnsucht und Eifersucht.'

47 Mauthner, *Erinnerungen*, 17.

48 Cf. ibid., p. 27: 'Ich habe darauf vorhin hingewiesen, dass ich als Jude im zweisprachigen Böhmen wie 'prädestiniert' war der Sprache meine Aufmerksamkeit zuzuwenden.' Even if on the one hand — as Thomas Hainscho stated — 'Mauthner's engagement with Judaism is more extensive on a biographical level than on a philosophical one' (see Hainscho, 'A Homeless Patriot', p. 33), the question of whether Judaism had more or less influence on his scepticism is a very important one to ask in theory. Indeed, Mauthner is one of the few authors to explicitly address the relationship between these two elements. With cunning of reason, Mauthner does so in a text published after his death in *The Menorah Journal* in 1924 under the title 'Scepticism and the Jews', which was published in English rather than German, his adopted linguistic language, as if he needed to speak about the connection between Judaism and scepticism in another language. Here, Mauthner addresses perhaps the biggest question of his life; namely, whether or not scepticism can be defined simply as a tendency or characteristic of Jewish thinkers or whether or not there is an affinity and correspondence between

> My linguistic conscience, my critique of language, was sharpened by the fact that I had to consider not only German but also Czech and Hebrew as the languages of my 'ancestors', that I had to carry around the cadavers of three languages in my own words. Yes, a philosopher of language could grow up under such psychological influences.[49]

In his essay 'Muttersprache und Vaterland', Mauthner tells how the German Jews of Bohemia discovered that Germany was their homeland when they were referred to as 'German' in 1968.[50] If the Czech people had a geographical homeland, Bohemian Germans had an artificial, linguistic one.[51] In particular, Mauthner lamented its lack of 'the fullness of dialectal forms',[52] since it was separated from the German soil. Therefore, his spoken German was untied from the *Boden* (soil); it was, in a way, a language in exile.

Mauthner's love for the German language, which he deliberately chose as his mother tongue, came only later. The act of choosing a mother tongue to love means that language cannot be inscribed in a natural determinism. It is not a real *Muttersprache*, but the result of

---

scepticism and Judaism. If on the one hand, Mauthner rejects an absolute coincidence between his Jewishness and scepticism precisely because there is no philosophical school of Jewish scepticism, on the other, he admits that linguistic scepticism has to do with a critique of religion as a liberation from its delusions. Mauthner himself wonders how it is possible to consider Jews sceptical when they believe in a God, the creator of the world. The relationship between scepticism and Judaism is the paradoxical relationship between religion and scepticism. See Fritz Mauthner, 'Skepticism and the Jews', *The Menorah Journal*, 1 (1924), pp. 1–14. The German version appeared many years later; cf. Mauthner, 'Skeptizismus und Judentum', *Studia Spinozana*, 5 (1989), pp. 275–307.

49 Mauthner, *Erinnerungen*, p. 28: 'Jawohl, mein Sprachgewissen, meine Sprachkritik wurde geschärft dadurch, dass ich nicht nur Deutsch, sondern auch Tschechisch und Hebräisch als die Sprachen meiner "Vorfahren" zu betrachten, dass ich also die Leichen dreier Sprachen in meinen eigenen Worten mit mir herumzutragen hatte. Jawohl, ein Sprachphilosoph konnte unter solchen psychologischen Einflüssen heranwachsen.'

50 Cf. Mauthner, *Muttersprache und Vaterland*, p. 8.

51 Cf. ibid., p. 7: 'So hatten die Tschechen ein natürliches Vaterland, die Deutschböhmen nur ein künstliches.'

52 Mauthner, *Erinnerungen*, p. 28: 'Der Deutsche im Innern von Böhmen, umgeben von einer tschechischen Landbevölkerung, spricht keine deutsche Mundart, spricht ein papierenes Deutsch [...]. Es mangelt an Fülle des erdgewachsenen Ausdrucks, es mangelt an Fülle der mundartlichen Formen.' On the difference between Mauthner's conception of *erdgewachsenes* and *papierenes Deutsch*, see Hainscho, 'Fritz Mauthners Heimatbegriff', pp. 59–60.

a precise choice.[53] One can say that his passion for German springs from his condition of uprootedness, as his multilingualism and Jewish deracination alike robbed him of the ability to feel at home. Mauthner uses this alienation from his roots as a starting point, but it is precisely this non-conformity with language that gives him the opportunity to articulate his scepticism and to recognize the sickness of language.

Even though Mauthner writes in his *Contributions* that 'the Jew becomes fully German (*Volldeutscher*) when the *Mauschel* expressions (*Mauschelausdrücke*) have become foreign to him or when he no longer understands them',[54] as a German speaker, he himself was corrupted by the hidden *Mauscheln* of the Jews he could understand, even if he did not use them. When he advocated for a radical linguistic assimilation, he was perfectly aware that he was contaminated.[55] Notwithstanding, he defended his love of the German language. Far from being an organism or a natural determinism,[56] for Mauthner, language is the fruit of a precise act of love.[57]

Despite his political conservatism, Mauthner elaborates a linguistic philosophy of uprooting. His radical thinking about translation is a paradoxical attempt to conceive a history of languages without a fixed point or origin, since they are in constant transformation and movement. If there was translation at the beginning, there is no loss of the original, but always a spurious process within which history unfolds.

---

53 On Mauthner's conception of *Muttersprache*, see Pascale Roure, 'La métaphore de la langue maternelle. Nationalisme linguistique et apories identitaires selon Fritz Mauthner', *Trajectoires*, 3 (2009) <https://doi.org/10.4000/trajectoires.245>.

54 Mauthner, *Beiträge*, I, p. 541.

55 See Sander L. Gilman, *Jewish Self-Hatred: Anti-Semitism and the Hidden Language of the Jews* (Baltimore: Johns Hopkins University Press, 1990), pp. 227–30. Gilman described Mauthner as an excellent example of an assimilated Jew whose idea of Jewish identity was nothing more than speaking with a Jewish accent.

56 On this aspect, cf. Gerald Hartung, 'Die Sprache', in Mauthner and Hartung, *Die Sprache*, pp. 141–224 (p. 183): 'Sprache ist, wie Mauthner betont, kein *Organismus*. Mit der Metapher von Organismus wurde in der Sprachphilosophie viel Missbrauch getrieben, denn sie suggeriert, dass Sprache eine Realität ist, die nicht des menschlichen Zutuns bedarf. Aber Sprache ist nach Mauthners Auffassung keine natürliche Einheit, sie existiert nicht für sich allein, sondern allein zwischen den Menschen.'

57 See Mauthner, *Muttersprache und Vaterland*, p. 52: 'Die Muttersprache und was drum und dran hängt, ist ein Gegenstand der Liebe; man empfindet die Einheit der Sprache, des Geistes und der Sitten wie ein enges verwandtschaftliches Band und liebt seine Sprachgenossen wie man seine Familie liebt [...]. Man liebt die Muttersprache sogar stärker als man seine Familie lebt.'

Translation is the precarious capture of a language in transit and the testimony of the wandering of words. Its transformative transit is constant, so that definition and possession are forbidden. The original debt that undermines one's autochthony is perfectly in line with a Jewish motif according to which land, language, and law do not belong to human beings.[58] This debt does not impede us from loving our mother tongue, which is considered not as the fruit of an immaculate womb, but as an illegitimate child; not the origin, but the Derridean prosthesis of the origin.[59]

In contrast to a metaphysics of origin that leads to an illusory autochthony, for Mauthner, translation is a way of radically thinking about uprooting, since language is a continuous product of borrowing, bastardization, stratification, and contingency. While on the one hand, he vehemently criticized the racial implications of ethnology and the Indo-Germanic theory of language, [60] on the other, he argues for a political conception of the mother tongue as a unique form of belonging to a community. At the centre of his diasporic philosophy of language is not possession, but borrowing; not purity, but contagion; not abstract crystallization, but transit. Words often err in a double sense: they make mistakes and they meander. The love of language, which is not a physical connection with the soil and the root, is a refuge that offers an always precarious *Heimat*. Mauthner's *Sprachliebe* is not a love of its purity. It is rather an impure love that requires word-refugees to live, which will infect the 'native' languages with an infinite translation.

58 Concerning this aspect, cf. Franz Rosenzweig, *The Star of Redemption*, trans. by Barbara E. Galli (Madison: Wisconsin Press 2005), pp. 317–24.

59 Derrida's maxim 'I only have one language; it is not mine' is already present in Mauthner's thought. See Jacques Derrida, *Monolingualism of the Other; or, The Prosthesis of Origin*, trans. by Patrick Mensah (Stanford, CA: Stanford University Press, 1998), p. 1.

60 See Mauthner, Beiträge, II, pp. 389–464 and pp. 603–71.

References

Abizadeh, Arash, 'On the Demos and its Kin: Nationalism, Democracy, and the Boundary Problem', *American Political Science Review*, 106.4 (2012), pp. 867–82 <https://doi.org/10.1017/S0003055412000421>

Abraham, Nicolas, and Maria Torok, 'Mourning *or* Melancholia: Introjection *versus* Incorporation', in *The Shell and the Kernel: Renewals of Psychoanalysis*, trans. by Nicholas T. Rand (Chicago: University of Chicago Press, 1972), pp. 27–128

—— *The Wolf Man's Magic Word: A Cryptonomy*, trans. by Nicolas T. Rand (Minneapolis: University of Minnesota Press, 1986)

Adelman, Rachel, *The Return of the Repressed: Pirqe De-Rabbi Eliezer and the Pseudepigrapha* (Leiden: Brill, 2005)

Agamben, Giorgio, *Homo sacer. Edizione integrale* (Macerata: Quolibet, 2018)

Aghion, Philippe, Torsten Persson, and Dorothee Rouzet, 'Education and Military Rivalry', National Bureau of Economic Research, Working Paper 18049 <http://www.nber.org/papers/w18049> [accessed 1 June 2017]

Alesina, Alberto, Bryony Reich, and Alessandro Riboni, 'Nation-Building, Nationalism and Wars', National Bureau of Economic Research, Working Paper 23435 <http://www.nber.org/papers/w23435.pdf> [accessed 1 June 2017]

Alighieri, Dante, *De vulgari eloquentia*, trans. by Steven Botterill (Cambridge: Cambridge University Press, 1996) <https://doi.org/10.1017/CBO9780511519444>

Amital, Rabbi Yehuda, *Jewish Values in a Changing World* (Jersey City, NJ: KTAV Publishing House, 2005)

—— 'Shabbat conversation' <http://etzion.gush.net/vbm/archive/5-sichot/48hazinu.php> [accessed 3 April 2022]

Apter, Emily, *Against World Literature: On the Politics of Untranslatability* (New York: Verso, 2013)

Arens, Katherine M., *Functionalism and Fin de Siècle: Fritz Mauthner's Critique of Language* (New York: Lang, 1984)

—— 'Linguistic Scepticism: Towards a Productive Definition', *Monatshefte*, 74.2 (1982), pp. 145–55

Arnove, Robert, and Harvey Graff, 'Introduction', in *National Literacy Campaigns*, pp. 1–28 <https://doi.org/10.1007/978-1-4899-0505-5_1>

—— eds, *National Literacy Campaigns: Historical and Comparative Perspectives* (New York: Plenum, 1987) <https://doi.org/10.1007/978-1-4899-0505-5>

Ashcroft, Bill, Gareth Griffiths, and Helen Tiffin, *The Empire Writes Back: Theory and Practice in Post-Colonial Literatures* (London: Routledge, 2003 [1989]) <https://doi.org/10.4324/9780203426081>

Attridge, Derek, 'Language, Sexuality, and the Remainder in *A Portrait of the Artist as a Young Man*', in *James Joyce and the Difference of Language*, ed. by Laurent Milesi (Cambridge: Cambridge University Press, 2003), pp. 128–41 <https://doi.org/10.1017/CBO9780511485206.008>

Auerbach, Erich, 'The Brown Stocking', in *Mimesis: The Representation of Reality in Western Literature*, trans. by Willard R. Trusk (Princeton, NJ: Princeton University Press, 2013)

—— 'Odysseus' Scar', in *Mimesis: The Representation of Reality in Western Literature*, trans. by Willard R. Trusk (Princeton, NJ: Princeton University Press, 2003), pp. 3–23

Baker, Mona, *In Other Words: A Coursebook on Translation* (London: Routledge, 2011)

Bakhtin, Mikhail, *Rabelais and his World*, trans. by Helene Iswolsky (Bloomington: Indiana University Press, 1984)

Banfield, Ann, *The Phantom Table: Woolf, Fry, Russell and the Epistemology of Modernism* (Cambridge: Cambridge University Press, 2000)

—— *Unspeakable Sentences: Narration and Representation in the Language of Fiction* (London: Routledge, 1982)

Barr, James, *Semantics of Biblical Language* (Oxford: Oxford University Press, 2004)

Beauvoir, Simone de, *The Second Sex*, trans. by Constance Borde and Sheila Malovany-Chevallier (New York: Vintage, 2011), pp. 159–63

Bell, Anne Olivier, ed., *The Diary of Virginia Woolf*, 5 vols (London: Penguin Books, 1980–85)

Benes, Tuska, *In Babel's Shadow: Language, Philology, and the Nation in Nineteenth-Century Germany* (Detroit, MI: Wayne State University Press, 2008)

Benjamin, Walter, 'Der Erzähler. Betrachtungen zum Werk Nikolai Lesskows', in Benjamin, *Gesammelte Schriften*, ed. by Rolf Tiedemann and Hermann Schweppenhäuser, 7 vols (Frankfurt a.M.: Suhrkamp, 1972–91), II.2 (1977), pp. 438–65

—— 'On Language as Such and on the Language of Man', in *Selected Writings*, ed. by Michael W. Jennings and others, 4 vols (Cambridge: Belknap, 2004–06), I (2004), pp. 62–74

Ben-Naftali, Michal, '"I Have an Empty Head on Love": The Theme of Love in Derrida, or Derrida and the Literary Space', *Oxford Literary Review*, 40.2 (2018), pp. 221–37

Berger, Anne, 'The Popularity of Language: Rousseau and the Mother-Tongue', in *The Politics of Deconstruction: Jacques Derrida and the Other of Philosophy*, ed. by Martin McQuillan (London: Pluto, 2007), pp. 98–115 <https://doi.org/10.2307/j.ctt18dztjp.11>

Berkhoff, Karel C., *Harvest of Despair: Death in Ukraine under Nazi Rule* (Cambridge, MA: The Belknap Press of Harvard University Press, 2004)

Bernstein, Charles, 'The Difficult Poem', *Harper's Magazine*, 306.1837 (June 2003)

Bielik-Robson, Agata, 'The Unfallen Silence: *Kinah* and the Other Origin of Language', in *Lament in Jewish Thought: Philosophical, Theological, and Literary Perspectives*, ed. by Ilit Ferber and Paula Schwebel (Berlin: De Gruyter, 2014), pp. 133–52 <https://doi.org/10.1515/9783110339963.133>

Blommaert, Jan, 'Superdiversity and the neoliberal conspiracy', Ctrl+Alt+Dem, 3 March 2006 <http://alternative-democracy-research.org/2016/03/03/superdiversity-and-the-neoliberal-conspiracy> [accessed 30 June 2017]

Bonfiglio, Thomas Paul, *Mother Tongues and Nations: The Invention of the Native Speaker* (New York: De Gruyter Mouton, 2010) <https://doi.org/10.1515/9781934078266>

Bosse, Heinrich, *Bildungsrevolution 1770–1830*, ed. by Nacim Ghanbari (Heidelberg: Winter, 2012)

—— 'Gelehrte und Gebildete – die Kinder des 1. Standes', *Das achtzehnte Jahrhundert*, 32.1 (2008), pp. 13–37

Bredeck, Elizabeth, 'Crumbling Foundations: Fritz Mauthner and Philosophy after Philosophy', *Modern Austrian Literature*, 23 (1990), pp. 41–53

—— *Metaphors of Knowledge: Language and Thought in Mauthner's Critique* (Detroit: Wayne State University Press, 1992)

Brown, James, 'Get on the Good Foot (Parts 1 & 2)', *Get on the Good Foot* (Polydor Records, 1972)

Burkhart, Dagmar, 'Narbe: Archäologie eines literarischen Motivs', *arcadia*, 40.1 (2005), pp. 30–60

Cahen, Didier, *Edmond Jabès* (Paris: Pierre Belfond, 1991)

Capelli, Piero, 'La parola creatrice secondo il giudaismo della tarda antichità', in *La parola creatrice in India e nel Medio Oriente. Atti del Seminario della Facoltà di Lettere dell'Università di Pisa, 29–31 maggio 1991*, ed. by Caterina Conio, 2 vols (Pisa: Giardini, 1994), I, pp. 155–72

Carroll, Robert, and Steven Prickett, eds, *The Bible: Authorized King James Version with Apocrypha* (Oxford: Oxford University Press, 1998) <https://doi.org/10.1093/actrade/9780199535941.book.1>

Caruth, Cathy, *Unclaimed Experience: Trauma, Narrative, and History* (Baltimore, MD: Johns Hopkins University Press, 1996) <https://doi.org/10.1353/book.20656>

Cassin, Barbara, 'The Power of Bilingualism: Interview with Barbara Cassin, French Philosopher and Philologist', e-flux conversations (March 2017) <https://conversations.e-flux.com/t/the-power-of-bilingualism-interview-with-barbara-cassin-french-philosopher-and-philologist/6252> [accessed 21 June 2017]

Cave, Terence, in *Recognitions: A Study in Poetics* (Oxford: Clarendon, 1988)

Celan, Paul, 'Und mit dem Buch aus Tarussa', in Celan, *Werke. Historisch-kritische Ausgabe. I. Abteilung: Lyrik und Prosa*, ed. by Beda Allemann and others, 16 vols (Frankfurt a.M.; Berlin: Suhrkamp, 1990–2017), VI: *Niemandsrose*, ed. by Axel Gellhaus, Holger Gehle, Andreas Lohr, and Rolf Bücher (Frankfurt a.M.: Suhrkamp, 2001), pp. 89–91

Champlin, Jeffrey, *The Making of a Terrorist: On Classic German Rogues* (Northwestern, IL: Northwestern University Press, 2015) <https://doi.org/10.2307/j.ctv47w3b6>

—— 'Rights, Revolution, Representation: Thinking Through the Language of the French Revolution', in *Teaching Representations of the French Revolution*, ed. by Julia Douthwaite, Catriona Seth, and Antoinette Sol (New York: Modern Language Association of America, 2019), pp. 69–77

Christ, Graciela, *Arabismen im Argot: ein Beitrag zur französischen Lexikographie ab der zweiten Hälfte des 19. Jahrhunderts* (Berlin: Peter Lang, 1991)

Cohen, Albert, *Belle du Seigneur* (Paris: Gallimard, 1968)

—— *Book of my Mother*, trans. by Bella Cohen (New York: First Archipelago Books, 1997)

—— *Le Livre de ma mère* (Paris: Gallimard, 1954)

Coleridge, Samuel T., *Aids to Reflection*, in *The Complete Works of Samuel Taylor Coleridge with an Introductory Essay upon his Philosophical and Theological Opinions*, ed. by William Greenough Thayer Shedd, 7 vols (New York: Harper & Brothers, 1853–54), I (1953)

—— *Biographia Literaria, or Biographical Sketches of My Literary Life and Opinions* (New York: Wiley & Putnam, 1847) <https://doi.org/10.1037/11970-000>

Condillac, Etienne Bonnot de, *Essai sur l'origine des connoissances humaines*, in *Œuvres philosophiques de Condillac*, ed. by Georges Le Roy, 3 vols (Paris: Presses universitaires de France, 1947–51), I (1947), pp. 1–118

Coogan, Michael, ed., *The New Oxford Annotated Bible: New Revised Standard Version with the Apocrypha*, 5th edn (Oxford: Oxford University Press, 2018)

Corey, Susan, 'Toward the Limits of Mystery: The Grotesque in Toni Morrison's Beloved', in *The Aesthetics of Toni Morrison: Speaking the Unspeakable*, ed. by Marc C. Conner (Jackson: University Press of Mississippi, 2000), pp. 31–48

D'ailleurs Derrida: Un film de Safaa Fathy (Derrida's Elsewhere: A Film by Safaa Fathy) (Gloria Films, 1999)

Dal Bo, Federico, *Deconstructing the Talmud: The Absolute Book* (Abingdon: Routledge, 2019) <https://doi.org/10.4324/9781315459899>

—— '"L'immediata intensità messianica del cuore". Paolinismo nel *Frammento teologico-politico* di Walter Benjamin', in *Felicità e tramonto*, ed. by Gabriele Guerra and Tamara Tagliacozzo (Macerata: Quodlibet, 2019), pp. 139–52 <https://doi.org/10.2307/j.ctvvb7n1j.13>

—— 'Legal and Transgressive Sex, Heresy, and Hermeneutics in the Talmud: The Cases of Bruriah, Rabbi Meir, Elisha ben Abuyah and the Prostitute', in *Jewish Law and Academic Discipline: Contributions from Europe*, ed. by Elisha Ancselovits and George Wilkes (Liverpool: Deborah Charles, 2016), pp. 128–51

—— *The Lexical Field of the Substantives of 'Word' in Ancient Hebrew: From the Bible to the Mishnah*, Abhandlungen für die Kunde des Morgenlandes, 124 (Wiesbaden: Harrassowitz, 2021)

—— *Il linguaggio della violenza. Estremismo e ideologia nella filosofia contemporanea* (Bologna: Biblioteca Clueb, 2021)

—— '"Paulinism" in the *Wissenschaft des Judentums*: On Scholem's Reception of Paul in his Interwar Hebrew Lectures on Sabbatianism', in *Grey Areas — Two Centuries of Wissenschaft des Judentums* (in preparation)

—— *Qabbalah e traduzione. Un saggio su Paul Celan traduttore* (Salerno: Orthotes, 2019)

Dalgarno, Emily, *Virginia Woolf and the Migrations of Language* (Cambridge: Cambridge University Press, 2012) <https://doi.org/10.1017/CBO9780511845642>

Darden, Keith, and Harris Mylonas, 'Threats to Territorial Integrity, National Mass Schooling, and Linguistic Commonality', *Comparative Political Studies*, 49.11 (2016), pp. 1446–79

Davies, Paul, 'A Fine Risk: Reading Blanchot Reading Levinas', in *Re-reading Levinas*, ed. by Robert Bernasconi and Simon Critchley (London: Athlone, 1991), pp. 201–26 <https://doi.org/10.5040/9781472547354.ch-012>

Derrida, Jacques, 'Abraham, l'autre', in *Le Dernier des Juifs* (Paris: Galileé, 2014), pp. 69–126

—— 'Abraham, the Other', in *Judeities, Questions for Jacques Derrida*, ed. by Bettina Bergo, Joseph Cohen, and Raphael Zagury-Orly, trans. by Gil Anidjar (New York: Fordham University Press, 2007)

—— 'Aphorism Countertime', trans. by Nicholas Royle, in *Acts of Literature*, ed. by Derek Attridge (London: Routledge, 1992), pp. 414–33

—— *Archive Fever: A Freudian Impression*, trans. by Eric Prenowitz (Chicago: University of Chicago Press, 1996) <https://doi.org/10.2307/465144>

—— 'Circonfession', in Jacques Derrida and Geoffrey Bennington, *Jacques Derrida* (Paris: Seuil, 1991), pp. 7–291

—— 'Circumfession', in Jacques Derrida and Geoffrey Bennington, *Jacques Derrida*, trans. by Geoffrey Bennington (Chicago: University of Chicago Press, 1993), pp. 3–315

—— *De l'hospitalité: Anne Dufourmontelle invite Jacques Derrida à répondre* (Paris: Calmann-Lévy, 1997)

—— *De la Grammatologie* (Paris: Éditions de Minuit, 1967)

—— 'Edmond Jabès and the Question of the Book', in *Writing and Difference*, trans. by Alan Bass (London: Routledge, 2002), pp. 77–96

—— *Monolingualism of the Other; or, The Prosthesis of Origin*, trans. by Patrick Mensah (Stanford, CA: Stanford University Press, 1998)

—— *Le Monolinguisme de l'autre ou la prosthèse d'origine* (Paris: Éditions Galilée, 1996)

—— *Of Grammatology*, trans. by Gayatri Chakravorty Spivak (Baltimore, MD: Johns Hopkins Press, 1976)

—— *Of Hospitality: Anne Dufourmontelle Invites Jacques Derrida to Respond*, trans. by Rachel Bowlby (Stanford, CA: Stanford University Press, 2000)

—— *Specters of Marx: The State of the Debt, the Work of Mourning and the New International*, trans. by Peggy Kamuf (London: Routledge, 1994)

—— 'A Testimony Given ...', in *Questioning Judaism: Interviews by Elisabeth Weber*, trans. by Rachel Bowlby (Stanford, CA: Stanford University Press, 2004), pp. 39–58

Diderot, Denis, *Paradoxe sur le comédien*, in Diderot, *Œuvres complètes de Diderot*, ed. by Jules Assézat and Maurice Tourneux, 20 vols (Paris: Garnier, 1875–77), VIII (1875), pp. 361–423

Digable Planets, 'Jimmi Diggin Cats', *Reachin' (A New Refutation of Time and Space)* (Capitol Records, 1993)

Docherty, Thomas, '"sound sense"; or "tralala"/"moocow": Joyce and the Anathema of Writing', in *James Joyce and the Difference of Language*, ed. by Laurent Milesi (Cambridge: Cambridge University Press, 2003), pp. 112–27 <https://doi.org/10.1017/CBO9780511485206.007>

Drob, Sanford L., *Kabbalistic Metaphors: Jewish Mystical Themes in Ancient and Modern Thought* (Jerusalem: J. Aronson, 2000)

Duden Online (Berlin: Bibliographisches Institut, 2021) <https://www.duden.de/rechtschreibung/Teufelskreis> [accessed 20 July 2021]

Duttlinger, Carolin, *The Cambridge Introduction to Franz Kafka* (Cambridge: Cambridge University Press, 2013) <https://doi.org/10.1017/CBO9781139049207>

Ellmann, Richard, *James Joyce*, new and rev. edn (Oxford: Oxford University Press, 1982)

Emmerich, Wolfgang, *Nahe Fremde: Paul Celan und die Deutschen* (Göttingen: Wallstein Verlag, 2020)

Eskin, Michael, *Poetic Affairs: Celan, Grünbein, Brodsky* (Stanford, CA: Stanford University Press, 2008) <https://doi.org/10.2307/j.ctvqsdtjn>

Feldmann, Roland, *Jacob Grimm und die Politik* (Kassel: Bärenreiter, 1970)

Fichte, Johann Gottlieb, *Reden an die deutsche Nation*, ed. by Alexander Aichele (Hamburg: Felix Meiner, 2008)

Fishbane, Michael, *The JPS Bible Commentary: Song of Songs* (Philadelphia, PA: The Jewish Publication Society, 2015)

Flores, Nelson, 'The Unexamined Relationship Between Neoliberalism and Plurilingualism: A Cautionary Tale', *TESOL Quarterly*, 47.3 (2013), pp. 500–20

Foucault, Michel, *The Archaeology of Knowledge and the Discourse on Knowledge*, trans. by A. M. Sheridan Smith (New York: Pantheon Books, 1972)

Frank, Tsivia Wygoda, *Edmond Jabès and the Archaeology of the Book: Text, Pre-Texts, Contexts* (Berlin: De Gruyter, 2022)

Freud, Sigmund, 'From the History of an Infantile Neurosis', in *The Standard Edition*, xvii (1973), pp. 1–124

—— 'Inhibitions, Symptoms and Anxiety', in *The Standard Edition*, xx (1973), pp. 75–176

—— *The Interpretation of Dreams*, in *The Standard Edition*, v (1973)

—— *The Standard Edition of the Complete Psychological Works*, trans. by James Strachey and others, 24 vols (London: Hogarth, 1953–1974)

Galston, David, *Archives and the Event of God: The Impact of Michel Foucault on Philosophical Theology* (Montreal: McGill-Queen's University Press, 2011) <https://doi.org/10.1515/9780773580589>

Gawthrop, Richard L., 'Literacy Drives in Preindustrial Germany', in *National Literacy Campaigns*, pp. 29–48 <https://doi.org/10.1007/978-1-4899-0505-5_2>

Gelbin, Cathy, and Sander Gilman, *Cosmopolitanisms and the Jews* (Ann Arbor: University of Michigan Press, 2017)

Gellner, Ernest, *Nations and Nationalism* (Ithaca, NY: Cornell University Press, 1983)

Gibbon, Edward, *The History of the Decline and Fall of the Roman Empire*, 1st edn, 6 vols (London: Strahan and T. Cadell, 1776–88), iii (1781)

Gibbs, Jr., Raymond W., 'Idioms and Formulaic Language', in *The Oxford Handbook of Cognitive Linguistics*, ed. by Dirk Geeraerts and Hubert Cuyckens (Oxford: Oxford University Press, 2007), pp. 697–725

Giller, Pinchas, *Reading the Zohar: The Sacred Text of the Kabbalah* (Oxford: Oxford University Press, 2001)

Gilman, Sander L., *Jewish Self-Hatred: Anti-Semitism and the Hidden Language of the Jews* (Baltimore: Johns Hopkins University Press, 1990)

Giusti, Francesco, 'The Hinge of Time: Mothers and Sons in Barthes and Augustine', *Exemplaria*, 33.3 (2021), pp. 280–95 <https://doi.org/10.1080/10412573.2021.1965731>

—— 'An Interminable Work? The Openness of Augustine's *Confessions*', in *Openness in Medieval Europe*, ed. by Manuele Gragnolati and Almut Suerbaum, Cultural Inquiry, 23 (Berlin: ICI Berlin Press, 2022), pp. 23–43 <https://doi.org/10.37050/ci-23_02>

Godo, Emmanuel, *La prière de l'écrivain* (Paris: Imago, 2000)

Grau, Conrad, *Die Preußische Akademie der Wissenschaften zu Berlin* (Heidelberg: Spektrum, 1993)

Grimm, Jacob, 'Aufforderung an die gesammten Freunde deutscher Poesie und Geschichte erlassen', in Reinhold Steig, *Clemens Brentano und die Brüder Grimm* (Bern: Lang, 1969), pp. 164–71

—— *Deutsche Grammatik*, ed. by Wilhelm Scherer and others, 4 vols (Berlin: Dümmler, 1870–98), i (1870), repr. in Jacob and Wilhelm Grimm, *Werke*, ed. by Ludwig Erich Schmitt and others, 47 vols (Hildesheim:

Olms, 1985–), x: *Deutsche Grammatik* ɪ, ed. by Elisabeth Feldbusch and Ludwig Erich Schmitt (1989)

—— *Kleinere Schriften: Reden und Abhandlungen*, 2 vols (Berlin: Dümmler, 1879), ɪ

Grimm, Jacob, and Wilhelm Grimm, *Briefe der Brüder Grimm an Savigny aus dem Savignyschen Nachlaß*, ed. by Wilhelm Schoof (Berlin: Erich Schmidt, 1953)

—— *Deutsches Wörterbuch von Jacob und Wilhelm Grimm*, digital version, part of the *Wörterbuchnetz of the Trier Center for the Digital Humanities* <http://www.woerterbuchnetz.de/DWB?lemid=Z01853/> [accessed 11 February 2021]

Grossberg, David M., *Heresy and the Formation of the Rabbinic Community* (Tübingen: Mohr Siebeck, 2017) <https://doi.org/10.1628/978-3-16-155334-9>

Groys, Boris, *Logik der Sammlung: Am Ende des musealen Zeitalters* (Munich: Hanser, 1997)

Hainscho, Thomas, 'Fritz Mauthners Heimatbegriff: Zwischen Deutschnationalismus, jüdischem Selbsthass und Sprachkritik', *Colloquium: New Philologies*, 6.1 (2021), pp. 54–69

—— 'A Homeless Patriot: Fritz Mauthner's Search for a Homeland in Language', in *Mother-Tongue and Father-Land: Jewish Perspectives on Language and Identity*, ed. by Libera Pisano, *Azimuth: Philosophical Coordinates in Modern and Contemporary Age*, 9.18 (2021), pp. 31–46

Hamacher, Werner, '95 Theses on Philology', trans. by Catharine Diehl, *diacritics*, 39.1 (2009), pp. 25–44

Hammerschlag, Sarah, *The Figural Jew: Politics and Identity in Postwar French Thought* (Chicago: University of Chicago Press, 2010) <https://doi.org/10.7208/chicago/9780226315133.001.0001>

Hartman, Geoffrey H., 'Wörter und Wunden, bei Wordsworth und Goethe', in *Grenzwerte des Ästhetischen*, ed. by Robert Stockhammer (Frankfurt a.M.: Suhrkamp, 2002), pp. 164–85

—— 'Words and Wounds', in *Saving the Text: Literature/Derrida/Philosophy* (Baltimore, MD: Johns Hopkins University Press 1981), pp. 118–67

Hartung, Gerald, *Sprach-Kritik: Sprach- und kulturtheoretische Reflexionen im deutsch-jüdischen Kontext* (Weilerswist: Velbrück, 2012)

—— ed., *An den Grenzen der Sprachkritik. Fritz Mauthners Beiträge zur Sprach- und Kulturkritik* (Würzburg: Königshausen & Neumann, 2013)

Hayard, Napoléon, *Dictionnaire Argot-Français* (Paris: Dentu, 1907)

Heidegger, Martin, *What Is Called Thinking?*, trans. by J. Glenn Gray (New York: Perennial Library, 2004)

Herder, Johann Gottfried, *Treatise on the Origin of Language*, in *Philosophical Writings*, trans. by Michael N. Forster (Cambridge: Cambridge University Press, 2002), pp. 65–164 <https://doi.org/10.1017/CBO9781139164634.007>

Hewitt, Lynne E., Judith F. Duchan, and Gail A. Bruder, eds, *Deixis in Narrative: A Cognitive Science Perspective* (Hillsdale, NJ: Lawrence Erlbaum Associates, 1995)

Hill, Alette Olin, *Mother Tongue, Father Time: A Decade of Linguistic Revolt* (Bloomington: Indiana University Press, 1986)

Hirsh, Elizabeth, and Gary A. Olson, '"Je — Luce Irigaray": A Meeting with Luce Irigaray', trans. by Elizabeth Hirsh and Gaëtan Brulotte, in *Women Writing Culture*, ed. by Elizabeth Hirsh and Gary A. Olson (Albany: SUNY Press, 1995), pp. 141–66

Homer, *The Odyssey with an English Translation by A. T. Murray*, 2 vols (Cambridge, MA: Harvard University Press, 1919), II

Horace, *Ars Poetica*, in *Epistles Book II and Epistle to the Pisones ('Ars Poetica')*, trans. by Niall Rudd (Cambridge: Cambridge University Press, 1989), pp. 58–74

Husserl, Edmund, *On the Phenomenology of the Consciousness of Internal Time (1893–1917)*, trans. by John Barnett Brough (Dordrecht: Kluwer Academic Publishers, 1991)

Irigaray, Luce, *I Love to You: Sketch for a Felicity Within History*, trans. by Alison Martin (New York: Routledge, 1996)

—— *Speculum of the Other Woman*, trans. by Gillian C. Gill (Ithaca, NY: Cornell University Press, 1985)

—— *This Sex Which Is Not One*, trans. by Catherine Porter with Carolyn Burke (Ithaca, NY: Cornell University Press, 1985)

Israel-Pelletier, Aimée, 'Edmond Jabès, Jacques Hassoun, and Melancholy: The Second Exodus in the Shadow of the Holocaust', *Modern Language Notes*, 123 (2008), pp. 797–818

Jabès, Edmond, *Aely*, in *Il libro delle interrogazioni*, pp. 1196–1473

—— *Elya*, in *Il libro delle interrogazioni*, pp. 1020–1195

—— *Un étranger avec, sous le bras, un livre de petit format* (Paris: Gallimard, 1989)

—— *A Foreigner Carrying in the Crook of his Arm a Tiny Book*, trans. by Rosmarie Waldrop (Middletown: Wesleyan University Press, 1993)

—— *Il libro delle interrogazioni. Testo francese a fronte*, ed. and trans. by Alberto Folin (Milan: Bompiani, 2015)

—— *Le Livre de Yukel*, in *Il libro delle interrogazioni*, pp. 327–590

—— *Le Livre des questions*, in *Il libro delle interrogazioni*, pp. 1–326

—— *Le Livre du dialogue* (Paris: Gallimard, 1984)

—— *Le Livre du partage* (Paris: Gallimard, 1987)

—— *El, ou le dernier livre*, in *Il libro delle interrogazioni*, pp. 1474–1685

Jakobson, Roman, *Child Language, Aphasia and Phonological Universals*, trans. by A. R. Keiler (The Hague: Mouton, 1968) <https://doi.org/10.1515/9783111353562>

Janik, Allan, and Stephen Toulmin, *Wittgenstein's Vienna* (New York: Touchstone, 1973)

Jaron, Steven, 'Le Remaniement', in *Edmond Jabès: l'éclosion des énigmes*, ed. by Daniel Lançon and Catherine Mayaux (Saint-Denis: Presses Universitaires de Vincennes, 2008), pp. 17–28 <https://doi.org/10.4000/books.puv.522>

Joyce, James, 'A Portrait of the Artist', in *The Workshop of Daedalus: James Joyce and the Raw Materials for 'A Portrait of the Artist as a Young Man'*, ed. by Robert E. Scholes and Richard M. Kain (Evanston, IL: Northwestern University Press, 1965), pp. 60–68

—— *A Portrait of the Artist as a Young Man*, ed. by Jeri Johnson (Oxford: Oxford University Press, 2008) <https://doi.org/10.1093/owc/9780199536443.001.0001>

Kafka, Franz, 'A Report to an Academy', trans. by Willa Muir and Edwin Muir, in *Complete Stories*, ed. by Nahum N. Glatzer (New York: Schocken, 1971), pp. 250–67

Karr, Don, *Collected Articles on the Kabbalah* (New York: Boleskine House, 1985)

—— 'Notes on the Study of Later Kabbalah in English: The Safed Period and Lurianic Kabbalah' <https://www.academia.edu/38974270/Notes_on_the_Study_of_Later_Kabbalah_in_English_The_Safed_Period_and_Lurianic_Kabbalah> [accessed 6 April 2022]

Keach, William, 'Romanticism and Language', in *The Cambridge Companion to British Romanticism*, ed. by Stuart Curran (Cambridge: Cambridge University Press, 2010), pp. 95–118 <https://doi.org/10.1017/CCOL0521333555.005>

Kittler, Friedrich, *Dichter, Mutter, Kind* (Munich: Wilhelm Fink, 1991)

—— *Discourse Networks 1800/1900*, trans. by Michael Metteer with Chris Cullens (Stanford, CA: Stanford University Press, 1990) <https://doi.org/10.1515/9781503621633>

—— 'Poet, Mother, Child: On the Romantic Invention of Sexuality', in *The Truth of the Technological World: Essays on the Genealogy of Presence*, trans. by Erik Butler (Stanford, CA: Stanford University Press, 2014), pp. 1–16

Klemperer, Victor, *The Language of the Third Reich: LTI — Lingua Tertii Imperii; A Philologist's Notebook*, trans. by Martin Brady (London: Continuum, 2007)

Kristeva, Julia, *Desire in Language: A Semiotic Approach to Literature and Art*, trans. by Leon Roudiez (New York: Columbia University Press, 1980)

—— *Histoires d'amour* (Paris: Denoël, 1983)

—— *Powers of Horror: An Essay on Abjection*, trans. by Leon Roudiez (New York: Columbia University Press, 1982)

—— 'Stabat Mater', trans. by Arthur Goldhammer, *Poetics Today*, 6.1/2 (1985), pp. 133–52

—— *Tales of Love*, trans. by Leon Roudiez (New York: Columbia University Press, 1987)

Kühn, Joachim, *Gescheiterte Sprachkritik: Fritz Mauthners Leben und Werk* (Berlin: De Gruyter, 1975) <https://doi.org/10.1515/9783110862515>

Kurzreiter, Martin, *Sprachkritik als Ideologiekritik bei Fritz Mauthner* (Frankfurt am Main: Lang, 1993)

La, Anthony, *Prussian Schoolteachers: Profession and Office, 1763–1848* (Chapel Hill: University of North Carolina Press, 1980)

Lacan, Jacques, 'Aggressiveness in Psychoanalysis', in *Écrits*, trans. by Bruce Fink (New York: W. W. Norton, 2006), pp. 82–101

Lacoue-Labarthe, Philippe, *Heidegger, Art and Politics: The Fiction of the Political*, trans. by Chris Turner (Oxford: Blackwell, 1990)

—— 'Typography', in Lacoue-Labarthe, *Typography: Mimesis, Philosophy, Politics*, ed. and trans. by Christopher Fynsk (Stanford, CA: Stanford University Press, 1998), pp. 43–138

Lacoue-Labarthe, Philippe, and Jean-Luc Nancy, *La Panique politique* suivi de *Le Peuple juif ne rêve pas* (Paris: Christian Bourgois, 2013)

—— 'La Panique politique', trans. by Céline Suprenant, in *Retreating the Political*, ed. by Simon Sparks (London: Routledge, 1997), pp. 1–31

—— 'The Nazi Myth', trans. by Brian Holmes, *Critical Inquiry*, 16.2 (1990), pp. 291–312

—— 'The Unconscious is Destructured Like an Affect (Part I of "The Jewish People Do Not Dream")', trans. by Brian Holmes, *Stanford Literary Review*, 6.2 (1989), pp. 191–209

Lakoff, George, and Mark Johnson, 'Conceptual Metaphor in Everyday Language', *The Journal of Philosophy*, 8 (1980), pp. 453–86

Lakoff, Robin, *Language and Woman's Place* (New York: Colophon Books, 1975)

Lamm, Kimberly, 'Getting Close to the Screen of Exile: Visualizing and Resisting the National Mother Tongue in Theresa Hak Kyung Cha's *Dictée*', in *National, Communal, and Personal Voices: New Perspectives in Asian American and Asian Diasporic Women Writers*, ed. by Begoña Simal and Elisabetta Marino (Münster: Lit Verlag, 2004), pp. 43–65

—— '"Mouth Work": Deconstructing the Voice of the Mother Tongue in Theresa Hak Kyung Cha's Video Art', in *Voice as Form in Contemporary Art*, ed. by Wenny Teo and Pamela Corey (= *Oxford Art Journal*, 43.2 (2020), pp. 171–83) <https://doi.org/10.1093/oxartj/kcaa011>

Landauer, Gustav, and Fritz Mauthner, *Briefwechsel 1890–1919*, ed. by Hanna Delf (Munich: Beck, 1994)

Lang, Berel, 'Writing-the-Holocaust: Jabès and the Measure of History', in *Writing and the Holocaust*, ed. by Lang (New York: Holmes & Meier, 1988), pp. 245–60

Lee, Hermione, *Virginia Woolf* (London: Vintage, 1997)

Lehman, Marjorie, *The En Yaaqov: Jacob ibn Habib's Search for Faith in the Talmudic Corpus* (Detroit, MI: Wayne State University Press, 2012)

Lehmann, Jürgen, and Christine Ivanovic, eds, *Kommentar zu Paul Celans 'Die Niemandsrose'* (Heidelberg: Winter, 1997)
Leinfellner, Elisabeth, 'Fritz Mauthner', in *Sprachphilosophie, Philosophy of Language, La Philosophie du langage*, ed. by Marcelo Dascal, Dietfried Gerhardus, Kuno Lorenz, and George Meggle (Berlin: De Gruyter, 1992), pp. 495–509
Lendevai, Paul, *Anti-Semitism Without Jews: Communist Eastern Europe* (New York: Doubleday, 1971)
Lepschy, Giulio, 'Mother Tongues and Literary Languages', *The Modern Language Review*, 96 (2001), pp. 33–49
Levinas, Emmanuel, 'La demeure', in *Totalité et Infini: Essai sur l'extériorité* (La Haye: Nijhoff, 1961), pp. 162–89
—— 'The Dwelling', in *Totality and Infinity: An Essay on Exteriority*, trans. by Alphonso Lingis (Pittsburgh, PA: Duquesne University Press, 1969)
—— *Otherwise than Being, or, Beyond Essence*, trans. by Alphonso Lingis (Pittsburgh, PA: Duquesne University Press, 2013)
Liddell, Henry G., and Robert Scott, eds, *A Greek-English Lexicon*, 9the edn (Oxford: Clarendon, 1961)
Lyons, John, *Semantics* (Cambridge: Cambridge University Press, 1977)
Man, Paul de, *Allegories of Reading* (New Haven, CT: Yale University Press, 1979), pp. 135–59
Mann, Michael, *The Sources of Social Power*, 2 vols (Cambridge: Cambridge University Press, 1986–93), II: *The Rise of Classes and Nation-States, 1760–1914* (1993)
Marcus, Jane, 'Thinking Back Through our Mothers', in *New Feminist Essays on Virginia Woolf*, ed. by Jane Marcus (London: MacMillan, 1981), pp. 1–30 <https://doi.org/10.1007/978-1-349-05486-2_1>
Mauthner, Fritz, *Der Atheismus und seine Geschichte im Abendlande*, vol. 4 (Stuttgart: DVA, 1923)
—— *Beiträge zu einer Kritik der Sprache*, 2nd edn, 3 vols (Stuttgart: Cotta, 1913)
—— *Erinnerungen I: Prager Jugendjahre*, 3rd edn (Berlin: Holzinger, 2014)
—— *Muttersprache und Vaterland* (Leipzig: Dürr & Weber, 1920)
—— 'Skepticism and the Jews', *The Menorah Journal*, 1 (1924), pp. 1–14; in German as 'Skeptizismus und Judentum', *Studia Spinozana*, 5 (1989), pp. 275–307
—— *Wörterbuch der Philosophie. Neue Beiträge zu einer Kritik der Sprache*, 2 vols (Zürich: Diogenes, 1980)
—— 'Zum Gedächtnis', *Masken: Halbmonatsschrift des Düsseldorfer Schauspielhauses*, 14.18/19 (1919), pp. 300–04
Mauthner, Fritz, and Gerald Hartung, *Die Sprache* (Marburg: Metropolis-Verlag, 2012)
McClelland, Charles, *State, Society, and University in Germany 1700–1914* (Cambridge: Cambridge University Press, 1980)

McCrea, Barry, *Languages of the Night: Minor Languages and the Literary Imagination in Twentieth-Century Ireland and Europe* (New Haven, CT: Yale University Press, 2015) <https://doi.org/10.12987/yale/9780300185157.001.0001>

Mendes-Flohr, Paul, *German Jews: A Dual Identity* (New Haven, CT: Yale University Press, 1999)

Mortensen, Ellen, *The Feminine and Nihilism: Luce Irigaray with Nietzsche and Heidegger* (Oslo: Scandinavian University Press, 1994)

Moten, Fred, *B Jenkins* (Durham, NC: Duke University Press, 2009)

—— *In the Break: The Aesthetics of the Black Radical Tradition* (Minneapolis: University of Minnesota Press, 2003)

Müller, Herta, 'Every Word Knows Something of a Vicious Circle', trans. by Philip Boehm <https://www.nobelprize.org/uploads/2018/06/muller-lecture_en.pdf> [accessed 20 February 2023]

—— 'Gelber Mais und keine Zeit', in *Immer derselbe Schnee*, pp. 125–45

—— *Heimat ist das, was gesprochen wird. Rede an die Abiturienten des Jahrgangs 2001* (Blieskastel: Gollenstein, 2001)

—— *Immer derselbe Schnee und immer derselbe Onkel* (Munich: Hanser, 2011)

—— 'Immer derselbe Schnee und immer derselbe Onkel', in *Immer derselbe Schnee*, pp. 96–109

—— *In der Falle* (Göttingen: Wallstein, 1996)

—— 'In jeder Sprache sitzen andere Augen', in *Der König verneigt sich und tötet* (Munich: Hanser, 2003), pp. 7–39

—— 'Jedes Wort weiß etwas vom Teufelskreis', in *Immer derselbe Schnee und immer derselbe Onkel*, pp. 7–21

—— 'Jedes Wort weiß etwas vom Teufelskreis', Nobel Lecture, online video recording, NobelPrize.org, 7 December 2009 <https://www.nobelprize.org/prizes/literature/2009/muller/lecture/> [accessed 10 February 2021]

—— *Lebensangst und Worthunger: im Gespräch mit Michael Lentz: Leipziger Poetikvorlesung 2009* (Berlin: Suhrkamp, 2010)

—— *Mein Vaterland war ein Apfelkern. Ein Gespräch mit Angelika Klammer* (Munich: Hanser, 2014)

—— *Der Mensch ist ein großer Fasan auf der Welt* (Frankfurt a.M.: Fischer Verlag, 2009)

—— 'So ein großer Körper und so ein kleiner Motor', in *Immer derselbe Schnee*, pp. 84–95

—— *Der Teufel sitzt im Spiegel* (Berlin: Rotbuch, 1991)

—— 'Wie Erfundenes sich im Rückblick wahrnimmt', in *Der Teufel sitzt im Spiegel*, pp. 33–56

—— 'Wie Wahrnehmung sich erfindet', in *Der Teufel sitzt im Spiegel*, pp. 9–32

Nabokov, Vladimir, *Speak, Memory: An Autobiography Revisited* (New York: Putnam's, 1966)

Neher, André, *The Exile of the Word: From the Silence of the Bible to the Silence of Auschwitz* (Philadelphia, PA: Jewish Publishing Society, 1980)

Netzer, Katinka, 'Die Brüder Grimm und die ersten Germanistenversammlungen', in *Die Grimms – Kultur und Politik*, ed. by Bernd Heidenreich and Ewald Grothe (Frankfurt: Societätsverlag, 2008), pp. 290–326

Newmark, Peter, *A Textbook of Translation* (New York: Prentice Hall, 1988)

Nipperdey, Thomas, *Deutsche Geschichte 1800–1866: Bürgerwelt und starker Staat* (Munich: Beck, 1983) <https://doi.org/10.17104/9783406704635>

The Nobel Foundation, *Les Prix Nobel: 2009* (Stockholm: The Nobel Foundation, 2010)

Nobel Prize Outreach AB 2021, 'Herta Müller — Facts' <https://www.nobelprize.org/prizes/literature/2009/muller/facts/> [accessed 10 February 2021]

North, Paul, *The Yield: Kafka's Atheological Reformation* (Stanford, CA: Stanford University Press, 2015)

Nunberg, Geoffrey, Ivan A. Sag, and Thomas Wasow, 'Idioms', *Language*, 3 (1994), pp. 491–538

Occlestone, N. L., and others, 'The Discovery and Development of New Therapeutic Treatments for the Improvement of Scarring', in *Advanced Wound Repair Therapies*, ed. by David Farrar (Oxford: Woodhead Publishing, 2011), pp. 112–29 <https://doi.org/10.1533/9780857093301.1.112>

OED Online (Oxford: Oxford University Press, 2020) <https://www.oed.com/>

Ovid, *Tristia*, ed. by John Barrie Hall (Stuttgart: Teubner, 1995)

Pagis, Dan, *Chidush u-Masoret be-Shirat ha-Chol ha-'Ivrit* (Jerusalem: Keter, 1976)

Parker, Andrew, *The Theorist's Mother* (Durham, NC: Duke University Press, 2012)

Pelli, Moshe, 'On the Role of *Melitzah* in the Literature of Hebrew Enlightenment', in *Hebrew in Ashkenaz: A Language in Exile*, ed. by Lewis Glinert (Oxford: Oxford University Press, 1993), pp. 99–110

Pisano, Libera, 'Misunderstanding Metaphors: Linguistic Scepticism in Mauthner's Philosophy', in *Yearbook of the Maimonides Centre for Advanced Studies 2016*, ed. by Giuseppe Veltri and Bill Rebiger (Berlin: De Gruyter, 2016), pp. 95–122 <https://doi.org/10.1515/9783110501728-007>

—— 'Silence, Translation and Grammatical Therapy: Some Features of Linguistic Scepticism in the Thought of Rosenzweig and Wittgenstein', in *Yearbook of the Maimonides Centre for Advanced Studies 2017*, ed. by Giuseppe Veltri and Bill Rebiger (Berlin: De Gruyter, 2017), pp. 121–43 <https://doi.org/10.1515/9783110527971-008>

Plato, *Phaedrus*, in Plato, *Lysis. Symposium. Phaedrus*, ed. and trans. by Chris Emlyn-Jones and William Preddy (Cambridge, MA: Harvard University Press, 2022), pp. 344–531

—— *Republic*, trans. by C. D. C. Reeve (Indianapolis, IN: Hackett, 2004)
Pourciau, Sarah, *The Writing of Spirit: Soul, System, and the Roots of Language Science* (New York: Fordham University Press, 2017) <https://doi.org/10.5422/fordham/9780823275625.001.0001>
Prinz, Joachim, 'Amerika — hast Du es besser? Notizen von einer Reise', *Der Morgen. Monatsschrift der Juden in Deutschland*, 13.3 (1937/38), pp. 104–11
Prudente, Teresa, 'From "The Aloe" to "Prelude" and from *The Moths* to *The Waves*: Drafts, Revisions and the Process of "Becoming-Imperceptible" in Virginia Woolf and Katherine Mansfield', *Textus: English Studies in Italy*, 27.3 (2015), pp. 95–118
—— *A Specially Tender Piece of Eternity: Virginia Woolf and the Experience of Time* (Lanham, MD: Lexington Books, 2009)
Putzi, Jennifer, *Identifying Marks: Race, Gender, and the Marked Body in Nineteenth Century America* (Athens: University of Georgia Press, 2006), pp. 102–09 <https://doi.org/10.1353/book14696>
Rella, Franco, *Il silenzio e le parole* (Milan: Feltrinelli, 1984)
Restuccia, Frances L., '"Untying the Mother Tongue": Female Difference in Virginia Woolf's *A Room's of One's Own*', *Tulsa Studies in Women's Literature*, 4 (1985), pp. 253–64
Robinson, Hilary, *Reading Art, Reading Irigaray: The Politics of Art by Women* (London: I.B. Tauris, 2006)
Ronell, Avital, *Dictations: On Haunted Writing* (Champaign: University of Illinois Press, 2006)
—— *The Telephone Book: Technology, Schizophrenia, Electric Speech* (Lincoln: University of Nebraska Press, 1989)
Rose, Jacqueline, 'Of Knowledge and Mothers: On the Work of Christopher Bollas', in *On Not Being Able to Sleep: Psychoanalysis and the Modern World* (London: Vintage, 2004), pp. 149–66 <https://doi.org/10.1515/9780691225654-013>
Rosenthal, Gilbert S., 'Tikkun ha-Olam: The Metamorphosis of a Concept', *The Journal of Religion*, 85.2 (2004), pp. 214–40
Rosenzweig, Franz, *The Star of Redemption*, trans. by Barbara E. Galli (Madison: Wisconsin Press, 2005)
Ross, Alison, *The Aesthetic Paths of Philosophy: Presentation in Kant, Heidegger, Lacoue-Labarthe, and Nancy* (Stanford, CA: Stanford University Press, 2007) <https://doi.org/10.1515/9781503626188>
Rosten, Leo, *The New Joys of Yiddish: Completely Updated* (New York: Three Rivers Press, 2010)
Roure, Pascale, 'La métaphore de la langue maternelle. Nationalisme linguistique et apories identitaires selon Fritz Mauthner', *Trajectoires*, 3 (2009) <https://doi.org/10.4000/trajectoires.245>
Rousseau, Jean-Jacques, *Discours sur l'origine et les fondements de l'inégalité parmi les hommes*, in *Œuvres complètes*, III (1964), pp. 111–223

—— 'Essai sur l'origine des langues', in *Œuvres complètes*, v (1995), pp. 371–429

—— *Œuvres complètes*, 5 vols (Paris: Gallimard, 1959–95)

Sand, Shlomo, *The Invention of the Land of Israel: From Holy Land to Homeland* (New York: Verso Books, 2012)

Sartre, Jean-Paul, *Anti-Semite and Jew: An Exploration of the Etiology of Hate*, trans. by George J. Becker (New York: Schocken, 1995 [1948])

—— *Réflexions sur la question juive* (Paris: Gallimard, 1954)

Scalia, Gianni, *Fuori e dentro la letteratura: stranieri e italiani* (Bologna: Pendragon, 2004)

Schapkow, Carsten, 'German Jews and the Great War: Gustav Landauer's and Fritz Mauthner's Friendship during Times of War', *Quest: Issues in Contemporary Jewish History* 9 (October 2016), pp. 1–17 <https://www.doi.org/10.48248/issn.2037-741X/806>

—— '"Ohne Sprache und ohne Religion?" Fritz Mauthners Sprachkritik und die zeitgenössischen Debatten über Deutschtum und Judentum', in *An den Grenzen der Sprachkritik. Fritz Mauthners Beiträge zur Sprach- und Kulturkritik*, ed. by Gerald Hartung (Würzburg: Königshausen & Neumann, 2013), pp. 19–49

Schlegel, Friedrich, 'On Incomprehensibility', in *Friedrich Schlegel's 'Lucinde' and the Fragments*, trans. and intro. by Peter Firchow (Minneapolis: University of Minnesota Press, 1971), pp. 259–71

Schleunes, Karl, *Schooling and Society: The Politics of Education in Prussia and Bavaria 1750–1900* (Oxford: Berg, 1989)

Scholem, Gershom, 'On Lament and Lamentation', trans. by Lina Barouch and Paula Schwebel, *Jewish Studies Quarterly*, 21 (2014), pp. 1–12

Scott, James, *Seeing Like a State: How Certain Schemes to Improve the Human Condition Have Failed* (New Haven, CT: Yale University Press, 1998)

Semprún, Jorge, *Literature or Life*, trans. by Linda Coverdale (London: Viking, 1997)

Shillony, Helena, *Edmond Jabès: Une rhétorique de la subversion* (Paris: Lettres modernes, 1991)

Sly and the Family Stone, *Stand* (Epic/Sony, 1969)

Smith, Adam, 'Consideration Concerning the First Formation of Languages', in *Works*, 5 vols (London: Cadell & Davies, 1811), v, pp. 3–48

Sokel, Walter Herbert, *The Myth of the Power and the Self: Essays on Franz Kafka* (Detroit, MI: Wayne State University Press, 2002)

Solomon, Petre, *Paul Celan: The Romanian Dimension* (Syracuse, NY: Syracuse University Press, 2019) <https://doi.org/10.2307/j.ctv14h530>

Spitzer, Leo, 'Muttersprache und Muttererziehung', in *Essays in Historical Semantics* (New York: Russell & Russell, 1948)

Spivak, Gayatri Chakravorty, 'Echo', in *The Spivak Reader*, ed. by Donna Landry and Gerald MacLean (New York: Routledge, 1996), pp. 175–202

—— *Nationalism and the Imagination* (London: Seagull Books, 2010)

Steig, Reinhold, *Clemens Brentano und die Brüder Grimm* (Bern: Lang, 1969)

Steinthal, Heymann, 'Von der Liebe zur Muttersprache', in *Gesammelte kleine Schriften*, 2 vols (Berlin: Dümmlers, 1880), I, pp. 97–107

Stevens, Gillian, 'Nativity, Intermarriage, and Mother-Tongue Shift', *American Sociological Review*, 50.1 (February 1985), pp. 74–83 (p. 74) <https://doi.org/10.2307/2095341>

Stewart, Susan, *Crimes of Writing: Problems in the Containment of Representation* (Durham, NC: Duke University Press, 1994)

Stollznow, Karen, *On the Offensive: Prejudice in Language Past and Present* (Cambridge: Cambridge University Press, 2020) <https://doi.org/10.1017/9781108866637>

Swoyer, Chris, 'The Linguistic Relativity Hypothesis: Supplement to "Relativism"', *Stanford Encyclopedia of Philosophy* (Spring 2003) <https://stanford.library.sydney.edu.au/archives/spr2015/entries/relativism/supplement2.html> [accessed 17 July 2020]

Tsvetaeva, Marina, *Poema Kantza* (Moskow: Directmedia, 2012)

Turner, Terence T., 'The Social Skin', in *Not Work Alone: A Cross-Cultural View of Activities Superfluous to Survival*, ed. by Jeremy Cherfas and Roger Lewin (Beverly Hills, CA: Sage, 1980), pp. 112–40

'Untying the Mother Tongue: On Language, Affect, and the Unconscious', conference programme, ICI Berlin, 11–12 May 2016 <https://doi.org/10.25620/e160511>

Verzeichniss der Abhandlungen der Königlich Preussischen Akademie der Wissenschaften von 1710–1870 in alphabetischer Folge der Verfasser (Berlin: Dümmler, 1871)

Veteranyi, Aglaja, *Warum das Kind in der Polenta kocht* (Stuttgart: Deutsche Verlags-Anstalt, 1999)

—— *Why the Child Is Cooking in the Polenta*, trans. by Vincent Kling (Champaign, IL: Dalkey Archive Press, 2012)

Vico, Giambattista, *The New Science*, trans. from the 3rd edn by Thomas Goddard Bergin and Max Harold Fisch (Ithaca, NY: Cornell University Press, 1948)

—— *Principi di scienza nuova*, 3rd edn, 2 vols (Naples: Stamperia Muziana, 1744)

Wehler, Hans-Ulrich, *Deutsche Gesellschaftsgeschichte 1700–1815* (Munich: Beck, 1987)

Weiler, Gershon, *Mauthner's Critique of Language* (Cambridge: Cambridge University Press, 1970)

—— 'On Fritz Mauthner's Critique of Language', *Mind*, 67 (1958), pp. 80–87

Weinbaum, Alys Eve, 'Nation', in *Keywords for American Cultural Studies*, ed. by Bruce Burgett and Glenn Hendler (New York: New York University Press, 2007), pp. 164–70

Wiedemann, Barbara, *Antschel Paul — Paul Celan. Studien zum Frühwerk* (Tübingen: Niemeyer, 1985)

Wimmer, Andreas, *Waves of War: Nationalism, State Formation, and Ethnic Exclusion in the Modern World* (Cambridge: Cambridge University Press, 2013) <https://doi.org/10.1017/CBO9781139198318>

Wittgenstein, Ludwig, 'A Lecture on Ethics', in Wittgenstein, *Philosophical Occasions: 1912–1951*, ed. by James Klagge and Alfred Normann (Cambridge: Hackett, 1992), pp. 37–44

—— *Philosophical Investigations*, trans. by G. E. M. Anscome, P. M. S. Hacker, and Joachim Schulte, ed. by Hacker and Schulte (Oxford: Wiley-Blackwell, 2009)

—— *Tractatus Logico-Philosophicus*, trans. by F. P. Ramsey and C. K. Ogden, intro. by Bertrand Russell (London: Kegan Paul, 1922)

Woolf, Virgina, *Collected Essays*, 4 vols (London: Hogarth, 1966–67)

—— 'Craftsmanship', in *The Crowded Dance of Modern Life: Selected Essays*, 2 vols (London: Penguin, 1993), II, pp. 137–43

—— *Granite & Rainbow* (London: Hogarth, 1960)

—— 'The Man at the Gate', in *The Death of the Moth and Other Essays* (New York: Harcourt, 1974), pp. 104–10

—— 'On Not Knowing Greek', in *Collected Essays*, I (1966), pp. 1–13

—— *Orlando* (London: Vintage, 1992)

—— *A Room of One's Own* (London: Hogarth, 1935)

—— 'The Russian Point of View', in *Collected Essays*, I (1966), pp. 238–46

—— 'A Sketch of the Past', in Woolf, *Moments of Being*, ed. by Jeanne Schulkind (New York: Harcourt Brace, 1985), pp. 61–160

—— *To the Lighthouse* (London: Penguin, 1996)

—— *The Waves* (Oxford: Oxford University Press, 2014)

Wordsworth, William, 'Preface (to the Second Edition)', in William Wordsworth and Samuel T. Coleridge, *Lyrical Ballads: 1798 and 1802*, ed. by Fiona Stafford (Oxford: Oxford University Press, 2013), pp. 95–116 <https://doi.org/10.4324/9780203823613>

Yildiz, Yasemin, *Beyond the Mother Tongue: The Postmonolingual Condition* (New York: Fordham University Press, 2013)

Zalman, Chabad Rabbi Shneur, of Liadi, *Tanya*, Part I, *Likkutey Amarim*, Chapter 48 <https://www.sefaria.org/Tanya%2C_Part_I%3B_Likkutei_Amarim.48?lang=bi> [accessed 12 February 2023]

Notes on the Contributors

Deborah Achtenberg is Professor Emeritus of Philosophy and Emeritus Faculty Associate in Gender, Race, Identity at the University of Nevada, Reno. She is author of *Cognition of Value in Aristotle's Ethics: Promise of Enrichment, Threat of Destruction* (SUNY Press, 2002) and *Essential Vulnerabilities: Plato and Levinas on Relations to the Other* (Northwestern University Press, 2014). Some other publications include 'Force Inside Identity: Self and Other in Améry's "On the Necessity and Impossibility of Being a Jew"' (Journal of French and Francophone Philosophy, 2016), 'Bearing the Other and Bearing Sexuality: Women and Gender in Levinas's "And God Created Woman"' (Levinas Studies, 2016), and 'The Role of the Ergon Argument in Aristotle's Nicomachean Ethics' (Ancient Philosophy, 1989). She is currently working on an essay about Lev Shestov and Emmanuel Levinas.

Antonio Castore studied at the University of Turin, Italy, where he earned a MA in Modern Literatures (2001) and a PhD in Comparative Literature (2006). He has lectured on Italian poetry and translation studies, with a special focus on the rendering of Shakespeare's dramatic language. He is author of two monographs: *Grottesco e riscrittura* (2012), which explores the relation between the grotesque aesthetics and the concept of 'rewriting', intended in the broad sense of a textual, cultural, and aesthetic reshaping of borders, inclusive of the borders of the body; and *Il dialogo spezzato. Forme dell'incomprensione in letteratura* (*The Broken Dialogue*) (2011), which is devoted to the examination of the concept of misunderstanding or mis-communication with respect to the works of Shakespeare, Levi, Kafka, and Bachmann. He is also editor and translator of Shakespeare's *The Comedy of Errors* (2015) and *Pericles: Prince of Tyre* (2018). He is a former research fellow at the ICI Berlin, as well as at the Folger Shakespeare Library (Washington D.C.). His research interests span a broad range of topics, from literary theory to the interconnections between literature and linguistics, philosophy, and architecture. His has published articles in Italian, German, and English on the rhetoric and philosophy of dialogue, language(s) and translation, and the theory and representation of the city.

Jeffrey Champlin is Academic Director of the Open Learning Initiative Academic Support Programs and Lecturer in the Humanities at Bard College Berlin. His research emphasizes connections between literature and political theory. In terms of administrative and pedagogical development, he has a particular focus on students from areas of crisis and conflict. Jeffrey has previously taught at New York University, Middlebury College, Barenboim-Said Akademie, and Bard's campuses in New York, Berlin, and Palestine. He is the author of *Born Again: Romanticism and Fundamentalism* (University of Toronto Press, 2024) and *The Making of a Terrorist: On Classic German Rogues* (Northwestern University Press, 2015).

Federico Dal Bo was born in 1973 and holds a PhD in Translation Studies from the University of Bologna (2005), as well as a PhD in Jewish Studies from the Free University of Berlin (2009). He worked as a teaching assistant in Theoretical Philosophy at the University of Bologna, as research assistant at the Institute for Jewish Studies at the Free University of Berlin, and as research assistant at the University of Heidelberg working on the project 'Material Text Cultures'. Dal Bo's recent publications include *Massekhet Keritot. Text, Translation, and Commentary: A Feminist Commentary on the Babylonian Talmud* (Mohr Siebeck, 2013), *Emanation and Philosophy of Language: An Introduction to Joseph ben Abraham Giqatilla* (Cherub Press, 2019), *Deconstructing the Talmud: The Absolute Book* (Routledge, 2019), *Qabbala e traduzione. Un saggio su Paul Celan* (Orthotes, 2019), and *The Lexical Field of the Substantives of 'Word' in Ancient Hebrew: From the Bible to the Mishnah* (Harrassowitz, 2021).

Michael Eng is Assistant Professor of Philosophy and faculty affiliate in Gender, Women's, and Sexuality Studies at Appalachian State University in the United States. He specializes in contemporary continental philosophy, aesthetics, and philosophies of race and gender. His book *The Scene of the Voice: Thinking Language after Affect* is forthcoming from SUNY Press as part of the Series in Contemporary Continental Philosophy.

Jakob Norberg is Professor of German at Duke University. He is the author of *The Brothers Grimm and the Making of German Nationalism* (Cambridge University Press, 2022) and numerous articles on German political thought in journals such as *PMLA, Cultural Critique, Textual Practice*, and *New German Critique*.

Libera Pisano is currently Marie Sklodowska-Curie fellow at University Pompeu Fabra in Barcelona. She received her PhD in Theoretical Philosophy from La Sapienza (Rome) in 2014 with a dissertation titled *Lo spirito manifesto. Percorsi linguistici nella filosofia hegeliana* (ETS, 2016). She has been Research Associate at University of Hamburg, and research fellow at the Maimonides Centre for Advanced Studies, at the University of Calabria and at the Humboldt University of Berlin. She is the author of several essays on the role of language and politics in contemporary German and German-Jewish thought.

Juliane Prade-Weiss is Professor of Comparative Literature at Ludwig Maximilian University Munich. She was a European Union Marie-Skłodowska-Curie fellow at Vienna University, and a DFG research fellow at Yale University to complete her habilitation, published as *Language of Ruin and Consumption: On Lamenting and Complaining* (Bloomsbury, 2020). Previously, she was an Assistant Professor of Comparative Literature at Goethe-University Frankfurt, where she earned her Dr. phil. with a thesis on the infantile within the human-animal distinction in philosophical and literary texts from antiquity to modernity, published as *Sprachoffenheit: Mensch, Tier und Kind in der Autobiographie* (Königshausen & Neumann, 2013). She is editor of *(M)Other Tongue: Literary Reflexions on a Difficult Distinction* (Cambridge Scholars, 2013).

Teresa Prudente is Associate Professor of English Literature at the University of Turin, Italy. She has authored a monograph on Virginia Woolf's temporalities titled *A Specially Tender Piece of Eternity: Virginia Woolf and the Experience of Time* (2009) and a book on the relationship between Woolf, James Joyce, and science titled *To Saturate Every Atom: Letteratura e Scienza in Woolf e Joyce* (2012). She also edited and translated into Italian Shakespeare's play *The Two Noble Kinsmen* (2015). Her research focuses on interdisciplinary investigations connecting literature with linguistics, epistemology, and, more recently, the cognitive sciences.

Caroline Sauter teaches Comparative Literature at Goethe University Frankfurt. With a Dr. phil., her work is situated at the intersection of literature and theology, focusing on literary and translation theory, (mostly Jewish) language philosophy, and the poetics of love. She has published numerous scholarly articles in those fields. Sauter is the author of a monograph on Walter Benjamin's translation philosophy titled *Die virtuelle Interlinearversion* (2014) and is the co-editor of several books, most recently, the translator and editor of Jacques Derrida's 'Qu'est-ce qu'une traduction "relevante"?', together with Esther von der Osten. Before joining the faculty in Frankfurt, Sauter was a researcher at ZfL Berlin, and held a Feodor Lynen research fellowship at Harvard University.

Index

Cultural Inquiry

EDITED BY CHRISTOPH F. E. HOLZHEY
AND MANUELE GRAGNOLATI

VOL. 1 TENSION/SPANNUNG
Edited by Christoph F. E. Holzhey

VOL. 2 METAMORPHOSING DANTE
Appropriations, Manipulations, and Rewritings in the Twentieth and Twenty-First Centuries
Edited by Manuele Gragnolati, Fabio Camilletti, and Fabian Lampart

VOL. 3 PHANTASMATA
Techniken des Unheimlichen
Edited by Fabio Camilletti, Martin Doll, and Rupert Gaderer

VOL. 4 Boris Groys / Vittorio Hösle
DIE VERNUNFT AN DIE MACHT
Edited by Luca Di Blasi and Marc Jongen

VOL. 5 Sara Fortuna
WITTGENSTEINS PHILOSOPHIE DES KIPPBILDS
Aspektwechsel, Ethik, Sprache

VOL. 6 THE SCANDAL OF SELF-CONTRADICTION
Pasolini's Multistable Subjectivities, Geographies, Traditions
Edited by Luca Di Blasi, Manuele Gragnolati, and Christoph F. E. Holzhey

VOL. 7 SITUIERTES WISSEN UND REGIONALE EPISTEMOLOGIE
Zur Aktualität Georges Canguilhems und Donna J. Haraways
Edited by Astrid Deuber-Mankowsky and Christoph F. E. Holzhey

VOL. 8 MULTISTABLE FIGURES
On the Critical Potentials of Ir/Reversible Aspect-Seeing
Edited by Christoph F. E. Holzhey

VOL. 9 Wendy Brown / Rainer Forst
THE POWER OF TOLERANCE
Edited by Luca Di Blasi and Christoph F. E. Holzhey

Vol. 10 DENKWEISEN DES SPIELS
Medienphilosophische Annäherungen
Edited by Astrid Deuber-Mankowsky and Reinhold Görling

Vol. 11 DE/CONSTITUTING WHOLES
Towards Partiality Without Parts
Edited by Manuele Gragnolati and Christoph F. E. Holzhey

Vol. 12 CONATUS UND LEBENSNOT
Schlüsselbegriffe der Medienanthropologie
Edited by Astrid Deuber-Mankowsky and Anna Tuschling

Vol. 13 AURA UND EXPERIMENT
Naturwissenschaft und Technik bei Walter Benjamin
Edited by Kyung-Ho Cha

Vol. 14 Luca Di Blasi
DEZENTRIERUNGEN
Beiträge zur Religion der Philosophie im 20. Jahrhundert

Vol. 15 RE-
An Errant Glossary
Edited by Christoph F. E. Holzhey and Arnd Wedemeyer

Vol. 16 Claude Lefort
DANTE'S MODERNITY
An Introduction to the Monarchia
With an Essay by Judith Revel
Translated from the French by Jennifer Rushworth
Edited by Christiane Frey, Manuele Gragnolati,
Christoph F. E. Holzhey, and Arnd Wedemeyer

Vol. 17 WEATHERING
Ecologies of Exposure
Edited by Christoph F. E. Holzhey and Arnd Wedemeyer

Vol. 18 Manuele Gragnolati and Francesca Southerden
POSSIBILITIES OF LYRIC
Reading Petrarch in Dialogue

Vol. 19 THE WORK OF WORLD LITERATURE
Edited by Francesco Giusti and Benjamin Lewis Robinson

Vol. 20 MATERIALISM AND POLITICS
Edited by Bernardo Bianchi, Emilie Filion-Donato,
Marlon Miguel, and Ayşe Yuva

Vol. 21 OVER AND OVER AND OVER AGAIN
Reenactment Strategies in Contemporary Arts and Theory
Edited by Cristina Baldacci, Clio Nicastro, and Arianna Sforzini

Vol. 22 QUEERES KINO / QUEERE ÄSTHETIKEN ALS DOKUMENTATIONEN DES PREKÄREN
Edited by Astrid Deuber-Mankowsky and Philipp Hanke

Vol. 23 OPENNESS IN MEDIEVAL EUROPE
Edited by Manuele Gragnolati and Almut Suerbaum

Vol. 24 ERRANS
Going Astray, Being Adrift, Coming to Nothing
Edited by Christoph F. E. Holzhey and Arnd Wedemeyer

Vol. 25 THE CASE FOR REDUCTION
Edited by Christoph F. E. Holzhey and Jakob Schillinger

Vol. 26 UNTYING THE MOTHER TONGUE
Edited by Antonio Castore and Federico Dal Bo

www.ingramcontent.com/pod-product-compliance
Lightning Source LLC
LaVergne TN
LVHW091404190726
843491LV00006B/1247

* 9 7 8 3 9 6 5 5 8 0 4 9 7 *